TASK	UTILITY	CHAPTER
Add a volume label to a disk	NCD	20
Add conditional branching to a batch file	BE ASK	17
Blank the screen	Diskreet	15
Cache your hard disk	NCACHE-F, NCACHE-S	12
Calculate system benchmarks	System Info	22
Change a volume label	NCD	20
Change the country information	NCC	18
Change the cursor size	NCC	18
Change the file creation date and time	Disk Editor	4
Change the keyboard type rate	NCC	18
Change the mouse response time	NCC	18
Change the screen colors	NCC	18
Change the screen colors from a batch file	BE SA	17
Change the video mode	NCC	18
Change to another directory	NCD	20
Change your hard disk interleave factor	Calibrate	11
Clear the screen from a batch file	BE CLS	17
Compare two files	Disk Editor	4
Configure the Norton Utilities	NORTON	1
Create a rescue disk	Disk Tools	5
Create an Ndisk	Diskreet	15
Decrypt a file	Diskreet	15
Delete a directory	NCD	20
Delete a volume label	NCD	20
Determine if a file will fit on a disk	FileFind	19
Display the current drive letter	Disk Monitor	14
Draw a box from a batch file	BE BOX	17

Mastering the
Norton Utilities 5

Mastering the Norton Utilities™ 5

Peter Dyson

SYBEX®

San Francisco ■ Paris ■ Düsseldorf ■ Soest

Acquisitions Editor: Dianne King
Developmental Editor: Gary Masters
Project Editor: Kathleen Lattinville
Technical Editor: Daniel Tauber
Word Processors: Scott Campbell, Paul Erickson, Winnie Kelly, and Lisa Mitchell
Chapter Art and Layout: Charlotte Carter
Technical Art: Delia Brown
Screen Graphics: Cuong Le
Desktop Publishing Production: Dan Brodnitz, Len Gilbert, Rina Malonzo
Proofreader: Barbara Dahl
Indexer: Nancy Guenther
Cover Designer: Thomas Ingalls + Associates
Cover Photographer: Mark Johann
Screen reproductions produced by XenoFont.
XenoFont is a trademark of XenoSoft.
SYBEX is a registered trademark of SYBEX, Inc.
TRADEMARKS: SYBEX has attempted throughout this book to distinguish proprietary
trademarks from descriptive terms by following the capitalization style used by the
manufacturer.
SYBEX is not affiliated with any manufacturer.
Every effort has been made to supply complete and accurate information. However,
SYBEX assumes no responsibility for its use, nor for any infringement of the intellectual
property rights of third parties which would result from such use.
The text of this book is printed on recycled paper.
Library of Congress Card Number: 90-71164
ISBN: 0-89588-725-8
Manufactured in the United States of America
10 9 8 7 6 5 4 3 2

To Nancy

Everything should be made as simple as possible, but not simpler.

Albert Einstein

ACKNOWLEDGMENTS

A book is never the sole product of the person whose name appears on the cover. Many people have worked on this project, providing technical assistance and advice.

I particularly want to thank Dianne King, acquisitions editor at SYBEX, for all her help and guidance. I would also like to thank Gary Masters for the keen and meticulous eye he applied through all stages of the development, and Kathleen Lattinville for doing another excellent job with this manuscript. Thanks also to Daniel Tauber for his technical edit; Scott Campbell, Paul Erickson, Winnie Kelly, and Lisa Mitchell for word processing; Charlotte Carter for chapter art and layout; Delia Brown for desktop publishing; Cuong Le for screen graphics; Dan Brodnitz, Len Gilbert, and Rina Malonzo for typesetting; Barbara Dahl for proofreading; and Nancy Guenther for the index.

At Peter Norton Computing, Inc, thanks go to Alicia Colin for the prerelease copies of version 4.5 of the Norton Utilities, and to J. J. Schoch of Technical Support for answering my questions. Thanks especially to Kraig Lane for help and technical advice as well as prerelease copies of version 5 of the Norton Utilities.

Finally, on a personal note, thanks to Nancy for all her patience, encouragement, and support; Stephen Wilson for reading and commenting on the early drafts; and Gene Weisskopf for getting me involved with this endeavor in the first place.

Contents at a Glance

Table of Contents

INTRODUCTION

The Norton Utilities are a unique collection of small, efficient programs. Each program performs a series of closely related operations. The Norton Utilities initially became famous for their near-legendary ability to recover erased files, but over time the programs have evolved into a well-rounded package of programs that gives you complete access to every piece of hardware and software on your system.

WHY USE THE NORTON UTILITIES

The Norton Utilities occupy a unique position in the DOS world. They supplement the basic DOS operating system in several important ways: they provide tools for repairing disks and restoring erased files and directories, they provide programs that let you examine and optimize your computer's resources efficiently, they include several powerful security programs, and they extend the capabilities of several DOS commands.

PREVENTING AND RECOVERING FROM DISASTERS

Problems with hard and floppy disks are both common and preventable. The NDD (Norton Disk Doctor) utility provides you with a means of checking your disks for potential problems and fixing them before they cost you any data—and hard work.

Even when your disks are in top condition, you can still lose data by accidentally erasing files or directories that you need. DOS does not offer a viable solution to this problem, but the Norton Utilities provide several.

The UnErase program can rescue files or directories after they have been erased by the DOS ERASE or DELETE commands (if you haven't saved anything else to the disk since erasing them). To aid file recovery, the FileSave program copies deleted files to a reserved area of the disk so that they cannot be overwritten. The Disk Editor lets you examine data at the sector level and can help you with the complex manual recovery of erased files. You can also use the UnFormat program to restore the entire contents of your hard disk if you format it by mistake.

File Fix diagnoses and repairs damaged Lotus 1-2-3, Symphony, and dBASE data files, and the Image program makes a copy of the system area of your hard disk in case you need the information in an emergency.

COMPUTER SECURITY

DOS provides few security features to protect your data. If you keep confidential information on your computer, you can use the Diskreet utility to encrypt or decrypt those files. You can also use Diskreet to create and store your files in a password-protected disk called an Ndisk. The Disk Monitor program prevents the unauthorized writing of data to your disks, as protection against viruses or other surreptitious access. The WipeInfo utility obliterates data from your hard disk so completely that it can never be recovered, not even by the Norton Utilities.

OPTIMIZATION

If you have been using your computer for some time, chances are that at least some of your files have become fragmented, or broken into several smaller pieces. DOS was designed to work this way to cope with files that vary in size as their data changes. The Speed Disk program can test the degree of fragmentation that has taken place on your disk and then perform a recommended optimization to consolidate your files and speed up your disk access.

Another way to speed up disk access is to use one of the disk caching programs provided with the Norton Utilities. These programs act as intermediary data buffers between your hard disk and your application programs.

If the interleave factor on your hard disk is not set to the optimum number, your disk will not perform at peak efficiency. The Calibrate utility can test the disk's interleave factor and change it by performing a low-level nondestructive format that will increase your productivity.

EXTENDING THE CAPABILITIES OF DOS

Because DOS does not perform some operations well, the Norton Utilities includes several programs that extend the scope and capabilities of DOS. For example, the BE (Batch Enhancer) utility supplements the DOS batch-programming language with programs that let you control screen colors and attributes, and provide true conditional branching from inside a batch file. BE also lets you easily write batch files that display windows and boxes on the screen.

Similarly, the NCC (Norton Control Center) utility enables you to configure your system better than DOS does. It gives you more control over the computer's serial communications ports, and you can use it to specify the cursor size, the video mode, the mouse characteristics, the time and date, the country information, and the keyboard type and delay rate. When you install the Norton Utilities you can also choose to replace the DOS FORMAT command with a faster and safer formatting program, Safe Format.

If you work in different directories regularly, you will find that the Norton Utilities NCD (Norton Change Directory) program makes it easier to access or revise them. This utility lets you change directories without specifying the complete path of the new directory. The DOS DIR command is of limited use when you want to find a misplaced file. However, if you can remember part of the contents of the file, you can use FileFind to search for that text and help you locate the file.

With all the programs that the Norton Utilities package now provides, you can more quickly accomplish tasks formerly done with DOS without having to memorize the various syntaxes of the numerous DOS commands.

THE BEGINNINGS OF THE NORTON UTILITIES

In 1982, when the Norton Utilities were first released, they comprised six utilities: UnErase, Hard UnErase, Disk Look, Hard Look, Disk Mod, and Hard Mod. Each program was marketed individually and could only be run on IBM PCs with a 10MB hard-disk system.

The programs quickly caught on, especially the UnErase program. The next release, Version 2.0, came out in 1983 and contained the six original programs and many more utilities, all combined into one package. Some of these utilities provided features that DOS had not yet added. The following year saw another release, a significant one in the program's development. All the utilities were rewritten in C (originally, Peter Norton wrote them in Pascal) for Version 3.0 and were made compatible with all floppy-disk and hard-disk systems, including IBM-compatibles. The Disk Look, Hard Look, Disk Mod, and Hard Mod programs were revamped and grouped together as Disk Information and Explore Disk. At this point the Norton Utilities became firmly entrenched in the DOS market.

In 1985 the Norton Utilities Version 3.1 was released. This upgrade made it possible to recover entire directories at a time, improved NU's Explore Disk and Disk Information features, and presented the new QU (Quick UnErase) utility.

Version 4.0, which was released in 1987, was marketed as two separate versions and became known as the Standard Edition and the Advanced Edition. The Standard Edition presented two new programs: NI (Norton Integrator), which displayed a full-screen menu for running the other Norton Utilities, and NCD (Norton Change Directory). In addition to these new programs, the Norton Utilities Advanced Edition included the new SD (Speed Disk) program, the FR (Format Recover) program, and the capability to edit absolute sectors.

The next release, Version 4.5, continued with the Standard and Advanced Editions. Both editions included the new programs BE (Batch Enhancer), FD (File Date), NCC (Norton

Control Center), and SF, the safe format program. The Advanced Edition added the powerful capabilities of NDD (Norton Disk Doctor) to help with disk-related problems, and the Advanced Edition's byte editors enabled you examine and change file allocation tables, partition tables, or directories and then change them right on the screen.

WHAT'S NEW IN VERSION 5

The current programs were released in the summer of 1990 as the Norton Utilities Version 5. If you have not yet upgraded to this latest version, I urge you to do so, because it contains several major new programs.

With Version 5, the old distinction between the Standard and the Advanced Editions of the utilities has been removed; there is only one release of Version 5.

The Norton Utilities now include a completely redesigned user interface with full mouse support, context-sensitive help, and pull-down menus; they also maintain the traditional command-line arguments for experienced users.

Major new programs include the following:

- Calibrate examines the interleave factor used on your hard disk and can change it to increase the speed of data transfers to and from your hard disk. The program performs a non-destructive low-level format on your hard disk.

- Norton Cache consists of two disk caching programs, NCACHE-F and NCACHE-S.

- NORTON is a new shell program that you can use to launch all the other Norton utilities, and you can use it as a DOS shell to launch your own application programs.

- File Fix repairs damaged Lotus 1-2-3, Symphony, and dBASE files.

- FileSave copies deleted files into a reserved area to prevent them from being overwritten. This makes recovering a deleted file a near certainty.

- Image makes a copy of the system area of your hard disk for use in unformatting your hard disk or in recovering deleted files.

- Diskreet can encrypt and decrypt files, and can hide your confidential files in a new kind of disk called an Ndisk.

- Disk Monitor provides write protection for your files against viruses and also lets you park your hard disk heads.

Many of the existing Norton Utilities have been enhanced and now have additional capabilities.

- Disk Editor lets you examine and edit any part of your disks, including the file allocation tables, the boot record, and the data area.

- Disk Tools can revive a defective diskette, mark bad clusters, make and restore a rescue disk, and make a disk bootable.

- Speed Disk now lets you sort your files by name, size, date, or extension.

- System Info contains many new information screens, including lists of hardware and software interrupts, terminate-and-stay-resident programs, and memory usage.

- FileFind combines the capabilities of several of the older utilities. You can search your files and directories for specific text, manipulate the bits in the file's attribute byte, set the creation date and time on a file, and test to see if a file or files will fit onto a target drive.

- WipeInfo obliterates data from your disk so that it can never be recovered, not even by the Norton Utilities.

REQUIREMENTS FOR RUNNING THE NORTON UTILITIES

To use the Norton Utilities on your computer, you must have at least DOS Version 2.0; however, a few of the utilities require DOS Version 3.0 or later to take full advantage of their features. When I discuss DOS in this book, I assume you are using DOS 3 or later on your system and that you have a hard disk. The Utilities require approximately two and three quarters megabytes of free hard disk space for a complete installation. You will also need at least 512K of conventional memory to run the utilities.

HOW TO USE THIS BOOK

This book is organized into 24 chapters in six parts. Each chapter describes a specific utility and provides examples of how to use the program to get the best out of your system.

Part I, "Introducing the Norton Utilities 5 and Disk Basics," presents essential information about the utilities and your computer; it builds a strong foundation necessary for any level of user. You will learn how to install the utilities on your hard disk and how to use the new interface. Part I also contains a detailed look at disks and their internal organization.

Part II, "Recovery," describes the utilities you use to diagnose and fix problems with files or disks. You will learn how to rescue deleted files, how to make a copy of the vital information contained in the system area of your hard disk, and even how to recover the contents of your hard disk after it has been accidentally formatted.

Part III, "Optimization," concentrates on increasing the efficiency of the resources of your computer system, including how to examine the interleave factor on your hard disk and how to change it (if necessary) to speed up your hard disk operations. You will learn how to install a disk cache program to cache your hard disk reads or writes, and how to look at and eliminate file fragmentation.

Part IV, "Security," covers several important aspects of computer security. This section describes how to stop unauthorized data from being written to your disks, how to encrypt and decrypt important files, and how to password-protect and hide these important files from other people. Part IV ends with a description of how to obliterate files from your hard disk so completely that they can never be recovered, not even by the Norton Utilities.

Part V, "Tools," details the extensive Norton Utilities tool set, including how to extend your batch programming to add color and windows to your screen-handling routines. You will also learn how to control your computer hardware, how to locate lost files, and how to change directories quickly and efficiently. Finally, you will find out how to examine all the dark corners in your computer to reveal both hardware and software information.

Part VI, "Quick Help," tells you how to get even more out of the utilities. It contains a complete reference guide to all the Norton Utilities and explains how to use every command line switch. Part VI also shows you how to use the NORTON program to help you find and fix problems you might have with your system.

The Appendix details the different numbering schemes used in the book and provides a handy ASCII table reference.

The first page of the front endpapers lists all of the Norton Utilities, brief descriptions of them, and the chapters in which you can find more complete information. The next page and the back endpapers reverse this chart and describe the tasks that you can use each utility to perform.

THE MARGIN NOTES

As you read through this book, you will come across notes in the margins that are prefaced with a symbol. Each symbol corresponds to the note's type.

This symbol indicates a general note about the features being discussed. I often use it to refer you to other chapters for more information or to remind you of an important concept learned in previous chapters.

I use this symbol to denote tips or tricks that you may find useful when running the utility being discussed. These can be shortcuts that I have discovered or even important techniques that need to be emphasized.

Pay close attention when you see this symbol in the margin: I use it to alert you to potential troublespots when running a utility and often give you ways of avoiding these problems.

Part I introduces the Norton Utilities and discusses the important—sometimes crucial—operations they can perform for you. Even if you have used an earlier version of the Utilities, you should still read Part I; it will refresh your memory and teach you how to use the new program interface.

Chapter 1 explains how to install or update the Norton Utilities on your hard disk, how to use the Utilities from inside the NORTON shell program, and how to use the keyboard or mouse effectively. Chapter 2 reviews disk and directory structure. This chapter provides the basic information you need to understand later chapters about rescuing erased files, formatting disks, and unfragmenting your hard disk.

PART

Introducing Norton Utilities 5 and Disk Basics

Installing and Using
the Norton Utilities

CHAPTER 1

IN THIS CHAPTER I DESCRIBE HOW TO INSTALL THE Norton Utilities onto your hard disk. An essential preliminary to this installation process is making backup copies of the original program disks; this protects you in case an accident occurs with the original disks. You will also learn the three ways of running the Norton Utilities: from inside the NORTON shell program, from the DOS command prompt in full-screen mode, and from the DOS prompt in command line mode.

THE DISTRIBUTION PACKAGE

The distribution package for the Norton Utilities consists of both 5¼-inch 360K floppy disks and 3½-inch 720K disks, so you can choose the appropriate size for your system. Two manuals are included: the *User's Guide* describes all the utilities except the Disk Editor, and the *Disk Explorer* manual contains the Norton Disk Companion, the user's guide to the Disk Editor, and a troubleshooting section that explains how to fix common problems. The package also includes a pull-out card that describes the installation procedure on one side and a brief description of emergency file and data recovery techniques on the other.

Check to see if there is a READ.ME file on the install disk. The READ.ME file contains the latest information about the package, information that may not be in the program manual. To examine this file before you install the package, use the DOS TYPE command. Because the file is longer than one screen, use the DOS MORE filter to display the contents of the file one screen at a time. With the install disk in drive A, type:

TYPE A:READ.ME | MORE

You can also use the DOS PRINT command to send READ.ME to your printer, or you can load the file into your word processor and print it from there.

THE NORTON UTILITIES IN BRIEF

This section provides a short description of each of the programs in the Norton Utilities. A complete listing of all the command line options for these programs is given in Chapter 23.

BE	The Batch Enhancer extends your capability of making interactive batch files and includes routines to clear the screen and manipulate screen colors and attributes. BE can also draw boxes, open windows, position the cursor at a specific screen location, and write a character at that location.
Calibrate	Calibrate tests the interleave factor on your hard disk and can change it if required by performing a low-level format.
Disk Editor	Disk Editor lets you examine and edit the entire contents of a disk. You can also use it for advanced file recovery techniques.
Disk Monitor	Disk Monitor prevents unauthorized data from being written onto your disk, displays the drive letter of the drive being accessed, and parks disk heads.
Diskreet	Diskreet encrypts and decrypts individual files or creates a password-protected disk, called an Ndisk.

Disk Tools	Disk Tools provides six utilities that let you make a disk bootable, recover from the DOS RECOVER command, revive a floppy disk, and create or restore a rescue disk.
FileFind	FileFind locates lost files and lets you change the file's attributes.
File Fix	File Fix repairs damaged data files created by Lotus 1-2-3, Symphony, dBASE, and other programs that generate compatible files.
FileSave	FileSave prevents deleted files from being overwritten for a specified time. This increases your chances of successfully recovering the file.
Image	Image makes a copy of the system area of a disk that can be used to help recover the disk after an accidental format.
NORTON	The NORTON program is a shell program that lets you run any of the Norton Utilities from a full-screen menu. It displays help screens for the utilities and offers an extensive troubleshooting and help system. You can also add your own programs to the NORTON menu.
Norton Cache	Two Norton Cache programs are provided to speed hard disk access.
NCC	Norton Control Center lets you control many of your computer's hardware functions, including the video mode, screen colors, and keyboard rate.

NCD	Norton Change Directory lets you change to any directory on the disk without having to specify the entire DOS path name. NCD can make, remove, and rename directories, and also display a graphic representation of a disk's entire directory structure.
NDD	Norton Disk Doctor II finds and fixes logical or physical problems on floppy or hard disks.
Safe Format	Safe Format is a quick, data-saving alternative to the **DOS FORMAT** command.
Speed Disk	Speed Disk examines disk files and reorganizes them to eliminate file fragmentation. Several levels of optimization are provided, ranging from simple directory relocation to the complete unfragmentation of all the files on your disk.
System Info	System Information gives a detailed report on the hardware and system software installed in your computer and calculates three performance indicators.
UnErase	UnErase searches for and unerases deleted files automatically. It also provides a powerful manual unerase mode.
UnFormat	UnFormat lets you recover data on a hard disk after the disk has been accidentally reformatted with the DOS FORMAT command.
WipeInfo	WipeInfo erases the contents of a disk. Contents erased with WipeInfo cannot be unerased, not even by the Norton Utilities.

The UnFormat utility does not work with floppy disks that have been formatted with the DOS FORMAT command.

There is no equivalent of the version 4.5 Line Print utility in version 5.

If you are upgrading from version 4.5 of the Norton Utilities, you will notice that the functions of many of the older utilities are incorporated into this latest release. Table 1.1 shows how the program functions from version 4.5 were incorporated into the 5 release.

Table 1.1: Version 5 of the Norton Utilities Includes All the Capabilities of Version 4.5, and More

VERSION 5 UTILITY NAME	VERSION 4.5 UTILITY NAME
BE	BE
Calibrate	New Program
	Disk Test
Disk Editor	Norton Utility
Disk Monitor	New Program
Diskreet	New Program
Disk Tools	Norton Disk Doctor
FileFind	File Date
	File Attribute
	File Find
	File Size
	Text Search
	List Directory
File Fix	New Program
FileSave	New Program
Image	New Program
Norton	Norton Utility
Norton Cache	New Program
Norton Change Directory	Norton Change Directory
	Volume Label
Norton Control Center	Norton Control Center
	Time Mark

Table 1.1: Version 5 of the Norton Utilities Includes All the Capabilities of Version 4.5, and More (continued)

VERSION 5 UTILITY NAME	VERSION 4.5 UTILITY NAME
Norton Disk Doctor II	Norton Disk Doctor
	Disk Test
Safe Format	Safe Format
Speed Disk	Speed Disk
	Directory Sort
System Info	System Info
	Disk Info
UnErase	Quick UnErase
UnFormat	Format Recover
WipeInfo	Wipe Disk
	Wipe File

MAKING FLOPPY-DISK BACKUPS

As with any software you buy, the first thing you should do after taking it out of the box is back it up. You should do this even if you plan to install the software on your hard disk. In the event that the original disks are damaged or destroyed, the backup copies ensure that the software is still available.

To make a floppy-disk copy of the distribution package, place the first distribution disk in drive A and a formatted blank disk in drive B, and then enter the following command at the DOS prompt:

DISKCOPY A: B:

If you just have a single floppy disk drive, type:

DISKCOPY A: A:

Repeat this procedure with each of the other distribution disks in the package. Store the original disks in a safe place and work with the copies rather than the original disks. After you finish copying the original distribution disks, you are ready to install the package on your hard disk.

INSTALLING THE NORTON UTILITIES ON YOUR HARD DISK

Do not install the Norton Utilities on a hard disk that contains lost files or directories.

If you bought the Norton Utilities because you currently need to perform a recovery operation such as restoring a directory or unerasing a file, do not install the programs on your hard disk yet. Instead, use the Norton Utilities from your floppy disk drive to recover the file (or directory). After the recovery is complete, you can continue with the installation procedure. If you install the Norton Utilities without first recovering the file, the installation program might overwrite the area of the disk occupied by the erased file, making its recovery impossible. The following Norton Utilities can be run directly from the distribution disks in the case of an emergency: Calibrate, Disk Editor, Disk Tools, Norton Disk Doctor II, UnErase, and UnFormat. The other utilities are in compressed form on the distribution disks and must be decompressed by the INSTALL program before you can use them.

USING THE NORTON UTILITIES' INSTALL PROGRAM

The Norton Utilities provide an installation program that guides you through the installation procedure step by step, explaining the choices available at each stage. Be sure you have more than two and a half megabytes of free space on your hard disk if you plan to do a complete installation of all the utility programs. To use the INSTALL program, insert the Install disk into drive A and type:

A:INSTALL

The first screen lets you choose the correct monitor characteristics. Select Black & White if you have a monochrome monitor or if you are using a laptop computer. Choose Color if you have a color monitor or a monitor capable of resolving color information into different shades. Next, the INSTALL program looks for an earlier installation of the Norton Utilities. A warning screen then appears to remind you not to install the utilities on your hard disk if you want to recover an erased file. At this point, you have the choice of continuing the installation or returning to DOS.

If you continue, the INSTALL program will copy the files from the distribution disks, uncompressing any files that are compressed, into the directory you specify. INSTALL can also add the appropriate commands into your AUTOEXEC.BAT or CONFIG.SYS files so that your computer loads and configures some utilities automatically. Finally, the install program personalizes your copy of the utilities.

The next window contains three choices: New Install, Reconfigure, and Return to DOS. Choose New Install to install the Norton Utilities on your hard disk for the first time, or choose Reconfigure if you want to change an installation you made previously. I describe how to reconfigure an installation later in this chapter. To abandon the installation, choose Return to DOS.

Choose New Install, and the next window offers the choice of making a full installation or a partial installation. Choose Full Install to load all the Norton Utility programs onto your hard disk. Next, select the floppy disk drive you will be using to make the installation from. In the next window, the installation program assumes that you want to install the programs in a directory on the C drive called NORTON. Although you can change this directory name if you want, it makes good sense to keep all the utilities together and not mix them up with any other files, and the name NORTON will remind you what the directory contains. Throughout this book I will use examples that assume the utilities are installed in a directory called NORTON. Many of the program files in this version of the Norton Utilities are distributed as compressed files to conserve space on the disks. This

Help is not available inside the INSTALL program.

means that you must use the INSTALL program to uncompress them, rather than directly copying the files to the disk yourself.

As the programs are copied to the hard disk, a horizontal display at the bottom of the screen shows the progress being made by moving from the left (no files copied) to the right (all files copied). After all the files on a floppy disk have been copied, IN-STALL prompts you to insert the next disk. INSTALL checks the number of each disk to verify that you insert the disks in order.

If you have used an earlier version of the Norton Utilities you will remember that the programs all had easy-to-remember two-letter names. If you want to continue that tradition, the IN-STALL program will rename five of the most popular utilities to their short names. Table 1.2 lists both the long and short names of these programs.

The next step in the installation process renames any files in your path called FORMAT with the name XXFORMAT, and then renames the Norton Utilities Safe Format program to FORMAT. This substitutes Safe Format for the DOS version of FORMAT so that whenever you type FORMAT, Safe Format runs instead. Safe Format has many more safety features built into it than does the DOS FORMAT command, and it is also quicker and easier to use. However, if you are using DOS 4, renaming FORMAT to XXFORMAT will cause problems with the BACKUP command. BACKUP looks for the FORMAT command during execution. Consider renaming XXFORMAT back

Table 1.2: The Install Program Can Rename these Utilities to Their Short File Names

PROGRAM NAME	LONG FILE NAME	SHORT FILE NAME
Disk Editor	DISKEDIT.EXE	DE.EXE
FileFind	FILEFIND.EXE	FF.EXE
Safe Format	SFORMAT.EXE	SF.EXE
Speed Disk	SPEEDISK.EXE	SD.EXE
System Info	SYSINFO.EXE	SI.EXE

to FORMAT when you use BACKUP. See Chapter 21 for more details about Safe Format.

The next step in the installation lets you configure the Norton Utilities using the window shown in Figure 1.1. This window offers the following five selections:

- **Password.** You can password-protect as many as 11 of the Norton Utilities programs so that they cannot be used by anyone who does not know the password. Press the spacebar or click the mouse to toggle the checkmark in each box. You can password protect Calibrate, Disk Editor, Disk Monitor, Disk Tools, File Fix, Norton Disk Doctor II, Safe Format, Speed Disk, UnErase, UnFormat, and WipeInfo. If you choose to add password protection, the INSTALL program makes you type the password twice, stores the password on disk, and then returns you to the Configuration window.

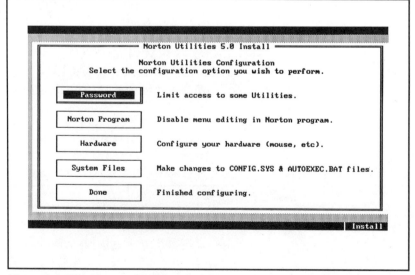

Figure 1.1: The Norton Utilities Configuration window lets you set passwords and make changes to AUTOEXEC.BAT and CONFIG.SYS

- **Norton Program.** Use this selection to disable or enable menu editing in the NORTON shell program. (I will discuss menu editing later in this chapter.)

- **Hardware.** You can configure several aspects of your computer hardware, including video and mouse options. Choose one screen color from the list at the left of the window, and choose one of the Graphics Options from the list at the right. **Standard** displays a solid square mouse cursor and uses parentheses and square brackets to define checkboxes and radio buttons. **Graphical Controls** displays round radio buttons and square checkboxes with a square mouse cursor; and **Graphical Controls** and **Mouse Pointer** displays graphics characters for the checkboxes and an arrow character for the mouse cursor. Choose this last option if you have an EGA or VGA adapter. Screen Options lets you choose between zooming or pop-up windows, and between a solid or a patterned screen background. The Mouse Options let you choose between a right-handed or left-handed mouse, and choose **Fast Mouse Reset** if you have a serial, IBM PS/2, or Compaq mouse port.

- **System Files.** Use **System Files** if you want the INSTALL program to make changes to your AUTOEXEC.BAT or CONFIG.SYS files. You can also do this yourself when the installation is complete by using a text editor. **System Files** adds the name of the directory in which you installed the utilities into the PATH statement of your AUTOEXEC.BAT file and lets you add Disk Monitor, FileSave, Image, or the Norton Disk Doctor into AUTOEXEC.BAT. You can also add one of the Norton Cache programs or the file encryption program driver DISKREET.SYS into your CONFIG.SYS file. When you have made the appropriate additions, select **Save** to record the changes.

- **Done.** Select this option when you have finished configuring the utilities.

Finally, a window opens to let you enter your name and company name so that you can personalize your copy of the Norton Utilities. You must enter your name, the company information is optional. The information you enter here is shown briefly each time you start the NORTON shell program.

If you made any changes to either AUTOEXEC.BAT or CONFIG.SYS, choose Reboot so that the changes are loaded. Otherwise, select Go to Utilities or Return to DOS to complete the installation.

MAKING A PARTIAL INSTALLATION

If you don't want to install all the utilities, choose Partial Install instead of Full Install, and you will see the window shown in Figure 1.2.

Use the arrow keys or the mouse to move from utility to utility. Press the spacebar to toggle the checkmark on or off, or click on the box with the mouse. The default setting installs all the utilities, which occupy approximately two and a half megabytes

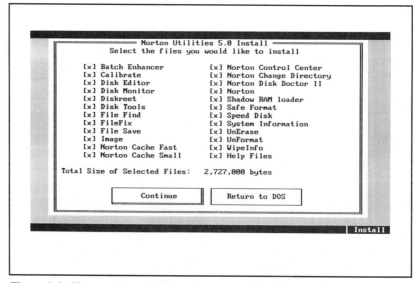

Figure 1.2: Choose the utilities you want to install from the list shown in this window

of disk space. As you deselect each utility in this window, its file size is subtracted from the total at the bottom of the window; thus, you can see exactly how much space the chosen utilities will occupy on your disk. After you have completed your selection, move the highlight to the Continue box, or click on it with the mouse, to select the floppy drive you want to use for the installation.

CHANGING YOUR NORTON UTILITIES CONFIGURATION

You can use the DOS COPY command to copy INSTALL.EXE onto your hard disk.

If you want to change the configuration of the Norton Utilities any time after you have installed them, simply run the INSTALL program again. Because the INSTALL program is not copied onto your hard disk with the utilities, you have to access it from the Install disk. Follow the same steps described in the "Using the Norton Utilities' INSTALL Program" section until you see the window that asks you to choose between New Install and Reconfigure. Choose Reconfigure, modify the appropriate settings, and then continue with the installation as described.

INSTALLING VERSION 5 OVER AN EARLIER VERSION OF THE NORTON UTILITIES

If you have a previous version of the Norton Utilities installed on your hard disk and you are upgrading to version 5, the INSTALL program will find this earlier version, and ask if you want to place the upgrade in the same directory. If you want to install the utilities in the same directory, a window opens and offers you three choices:

- Back Up Files. This selection copies the program files from the earlier version into a new subdirectory called NORTON.BAK. Several program files from the 4.5 version will not be backed up; instead, they will remain in the NORTON directory. These utilities are listed in Table 1.3.

- Overwrite Files. Choose this selection if you want to overwrite the old files with the new ones. Again, certain files will not be overwritten, as shown in Table 1.3.

- Return to DOS. Choose this selection to return to DOS.

These programs are kept in the NORTON directory in case you have batch files that require them there. Also, some users may find these programs easier or faster to use than the new programs. The 4.5 version of the FileFind utility is renamed from FF.EXE to FL.EXE to avoid confusion with the version 5 utility.

Table 1.3: These Version 4.5 Programs Are Retained in the NORTON Directory After the Installation of Version 5

VERSION 4.5 PROGRAM NAME	VERSION 4.5 FILE NAME
Directory Sort	DS.EXE
File Attribute	FA.EXE
File Date/Time	FD.EXE
File Find	FF.EXE *
File Size	FS.EXE
Line Print	LP.EXE
Text Search	TS.EXE

* Note: FF.EXE is renamed to FL.EXE so it does not conflict with FileFind in version 5.

RUNNING THE NORTON UTILITIES

The Norton Utilities can be run from the DOS command prompt or from within the NORTON shell program. Many of

When you are first learning how to use the Norton Utilities, it's a good idea to run them from the NORTON shell program (see the "Using the Norton Shell Program" section later in this chapter).

the utilities can also be run in their own interactive, full-screen modes. Table 1.4 lists the names of all the utilities and their corresponding DOS file names.

Table 1.4: To Run the Program Listed on the Left, Type the File Name Listed on the Right

UTILITY NAME	FILE NAME
BE	BE
Calibrate	CALIBRAT
Disk Editor	DISKEDIT
Disk Monitor	DISKMON
Diskreet	DISKREET
Disk Tools	DISKTOOL
FileFind	FILEFIND
File Fix	FILEFIX
FileSave	FILESAVE
Image	IMAGE
Norton	NORTON
Norton Cache	NCACHE-F
	NCACHE-S
Norton Change Directory	NCD
Norton Control Center	NCC
Norton Disk Doctor II	NDD
Safe Format	SFORMAT
Speed Disk	SPEEDISK
System Info	SYSINFO
UnErase	UNERASE
UnFormat	UNFORMAT
WipeInfo	WIPEINFO

Chapter 23 contains a complete listing of the parameters for all the utilities. I use *parameters* to describe any information that you can specify with a command to determine how and on what the command operates. *Switches* are special parameters that are preceded by a slash. The effects of switches vary when used with different commands.

USING THE UTILITIES FROM THE COMMAND PROMPT

You can run the Norton Utilities programs from the DOS command prompt, exactly as you would any other program or DOS command.

Most of the Norton Utilities commands require the general format:

utility parameters

in which *parameters* represents one or more of the optional parameters associated with the utility.

For example, to make the Norton Disk Doctor perform a short test on your hard disk, you would type:

NDD /QUICK

or, if you want the System Info utility to cycle through the benchmark tests automatically, you would type:

SYSINFO /DEMO

USING THE UTILITIES IN FULL - SCREEN MODE

Almost all of the utilities offer a full-screen mode that replaces the stark DOS prompt with well-designed windows, easy-to-use menus, and a variety of helpful information. The exceptions to this rule are the terminate-and-stay-resident utilities like the Norton disk cache programs, and the batch enhancer, BE.

To enter the full-screen mode of one of the other utilities, simply type its name and press Enter. The program names and the name you must type from the DOS command line are listed in Table 1.4.

THE NORTON UTILITIES SCREEN LAYOUT

All the Norton Utilities that use a full-screen display share a common user interface designed to make it easy for you to move from one program to another. I'll use the UnErase display to illustrate this user interface. Figure 1.3 shows the UnErase main screen.

UnErase uses a system of windows and pull-down menus to make choosing a command quick and easy. This system also enables the program to display several different screen elements at the same time—menus, help screens, windows, dialog boxes, lists, and so on.

The UnErase screen shown in Figure 1.3 has the following components:

- The horizontal *menu bar* runs across the top of the screen and contains the names of the pull-down menus. In UnErase, this menu bar contains the entries File, Search, Options, and Quit. You can select any of these menu items by clicking on them with the mouse; or if you prefer to use the keyboard, press F10 to turn on all the menu items or press the Alt key along with the first letter of the menu selection you want to use. Pressing F1 accesses the Norton Utilities help system, which

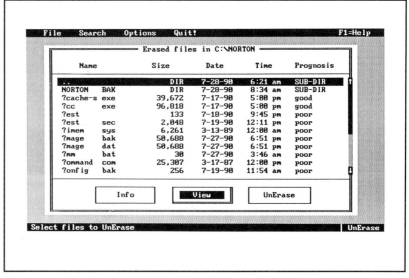

Figure 1.3: The UnErase main screen

I will describe later in the section "How to Get Help."

- The center of the screen lists the deleted files in the current directory and shows the name, size, date, time, and recovery prognosis of each file. This list can range from just one entry to more files than can be displayed in one window. Notice that the first entry in the list is highlighted; move this highlight to select the item you want to work with.

- Near the bottom of the window, the program displays three boxes that offer you additional choices and options.

- The last line of the screen displays help text that reminds you of the operation in progress; the right side of this line shows the current program name.

USING THE KEYBOARD   To select a pull-down menu, hold down the Alt key and type the menu's initial letter. For example, to see the File menu, hold down the Alt key and type **F**; to see the Search menu, hold down the Alt key and type **S**. You can also press F10 to turn on all the pull-down menus.

Similarly, to select an item from the menu, type the highlighted letter. For example, in the File menu, type **C** to choose View the Current Directory, or type **A** to choose View All Directories. Because each letter can represent only one option in each menu, sometimes the choices are less than intuitive. You can also move the highlight with the up and down arrow keys and then press Enter. To close a menu, press Esc.

After you display a pull-down menu, you can use the left or right arrow keys to display the next menu to the left or right.

Some of the most frequently used menu selections have keyboard shortcuts. For example, to choose View the Current Directory, hold down the Alt key and press **C**; to choose View All Directories, hold down the Alt key and press **A**.

To move through the list of files in the main window, use the up or down arrow keys to move one line at a time, or use the PgUp or

PgDn keys to move an entire window at a time. The Home key moves to the start of the file list displayed in the window; the End key moves to the end of the list.

Use the Tab key to move from the main window to the three boxes at the bottom of the screen, and then use the left or right arrow keys to choose the correct box. Press Enter to confirm your choice. To close a window, press Esc.

If a window contains radio buttons or checkboxes, press the spacebar or the **X** key to toggle the button or checkmark on and off.

USING THE MOUSE The programs in version 5 of the Norton Utilities are optimized for the mouse user, and navigating your way through the pull-down menus with a mouse is fast and easy. To select a pull-down menu, click on the name in the menu bar at the top of the screen. To select an option from the menu, simply move the mouse pointer and click on the item you want. To remove a pull-down menu from the screen, click the mouse in the display area outside the pull-down menu.

To scroll through the list of files shown on the screen, hold down the right mouse button and drag the mouse. As the mouse moves, the highlighted bar moves. You can also move through a list by using the scroll bars at the right side of the window. Clicking on the scroll arrow moves the highlight in the direction of the arrow. Click on the scroll bar and hold down the mouse button to scroll continuously.

You can also use the scroll bar to move to a specific point in the display. For example, if you move the scroll box to the middle of the scroll bar, the screen displays data from the middle of the list.

Move the mouse pointer from the main window to the boxes at the bottom of the screen, and then simply click on the appropriate box to select it. To select a radio button or checkbox, click the mouse on that field to toggle the bullet or checkmark on and off.

Press both mouse buttons at the same time to close a window or a pull-down menu.

HOW TO GET HELP   At the DOS prompt, you can get helpful information about any of the utilities by typing the utility program's file name followed by a question mark. For example, to display help text about Disk Editor, type:

DISKEDIT ?

The BE program is slightly different because it has two levels of help. If you type:

BE ?

you will see general information about the BE program. However, if you type:

BE BEEP ?

help about the specific BE BEEP subcommand is displayed (see Figure 1.4). Thus, to display help about any subcommand, merely type BE followed by the subcommand and a question mark.

```
C:\NORTON>BE BEEP ?
Batch Enhancer, Norton Utilities 5.0, Copyright 1990 by Peter Norton

    BEEP  [switches]
 or
    BEEP  [filespec]

Switches
    /Dn   Duration of the tone in n/18 seconds
    /Fn   Sound a tone of frequency n
    /Rn   Repeat the tone n times
    /Wn   Wait between tones n/18 seconds
    /E    Echo text in quotes following notes

C:\NORTON>
```

Figure 1.4: Getting help for the BE BEEP program

If you are using the utilities in full-screen mode, press F1 to open a help window at any time, or if you are using a mouse, click on the F1=Help entry in the menu bar at the top of the display. The help window that opens displays the context-sensitive help text. Use the up and down arrows, PgUp and PgDn, or Home and End to move through the help text. With the mouse, click on the scroll bars to move through the help text. In the Norton Utilities, help is arranged under a series of headings or topics. You can either access a specific part of the program and ask for help about it, or you can choose help directly from a general list of program topics. The bottom of each help screen usually lists four selections:

- Next displays the first help screen of the next help topic.

- Previous displays the first help screen of the previous help topic.

- Topics displays the list of help topics for this particular program. Use the mouse or arrow keys to select a topic and display its help screen.

- Cancel ends the help module and returns control to the utility program.

As you make choices from the pull-down menus throughout the windowed utilities, the message bar across the bottom of the screen usually contains brief information about using that menu selection.

USING THE NORTON SHELL PROGRAM

The NORTON shell program can run all the other utilities, presenting them in an integrated main menu. The shell displays much information that is of considerable benefit to new users. Experienced users will also find the NORTON program helpful for running infrequently used utilities. You should start running the Norton Utilities from the shell until you become

If you have used previous versions of the Norton Utilities, you will see that the NORTON program bears a strong resemblance to the old Norton Integrator; however, you will find that NORTON is much more powerful.

BE, the Batch Enhancer, is the only utility that you cannot run in this way. You should use BE inside a batch file. See Chapter 17 for details.

familiar enough with their operation to run them from the DOS command prompt.

To start the NORTON shell program, simply type:

NORTON

at the DOS prompt. Figure 1.5 shows the initial NORTON program screen.

The left side of the screen lists the names of the utilities. The right side of the screen displays a help screen entitled Description. As you move the highlighted selection bar down the list of programs, the help screen changes to display a description for the currently highlighted utility. The command line at the bottom of the listing also changes to indicate the currently highlighted program. After you highlight the appropriate utility, type in any parameters you want to use, and press the Enter key to run the utility. When you finish with the program, control returns to the NORTON main menu screen.

The Home key moves the highlight to the top of the list of programs in the Commands menu, the PgUp and PgDn keys

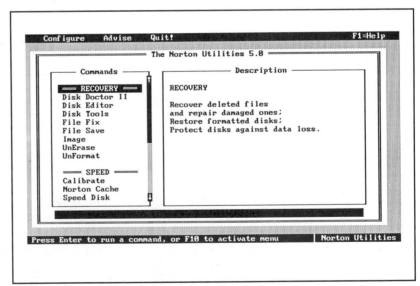

Figure 1.5: The initial NORTON shell program screen

move it up and down the list, the End key moves the highlight directly to the last entry in the list, and the up and down arrow keys move the selection bar up or down the list one entry at a time.

With the mouse, merely move the pointer to the utility you want to work with, click the mouse button once to highlight the utility and display the short help screen at the right side of the window, and then click on it twice to actually run the utility program.

If you press the F1 key at the main menu, the NORTON help screen is displayed (see Figure 1.6). This screen explains how to operate the shell program itself, telling you which keys you can press at the main NORTON screen. Press Esc to cancel the help screen, or click both mouse buttons together.

The menu bar across the top of the screen contains three pull-down menu selections:

The selections under the Advise pull-down menu are described in Chapter 23.

- Configure lets you customize the shell program and also lets you add your own applications programs to the NORTON menu.

- Advise contains three modules that you should refer to if you are having problems with your computer or if DOS reports errors. The selections contained in the Advise pull-down menu are described in detail in Chapter 23.

- Quit! returns you to DOS when you have finished using the Norton Utilities.

The next sections describe how to configure the NORTON program and explain how you can add a backup menu item to the main menu.

CONFIGURING THE NORTON PROGRAM

When you first install the Norton Utilities, they are arranged inside the shell program under four headings: Recovery, Speed,

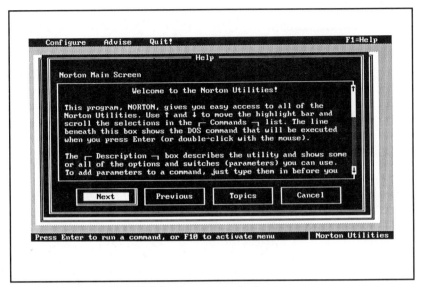

Figure 1.6: The NORTON shell program help screen

Security, and Tools. If you want to list the utilities in alphabetical order, choose the Sort by Name selection from the Configure pull-down menu, or hold down the Alt key and press **N**. The utilities are now shown in a single list without headings. To redisplay the original list, select Sort by Topic from the Configure pull-down menu, or hold down the Alt key and press **T**.

Use Video and Mouse Options from the Configure pull-down menu if you want to alter the settings you chose during the initial installation of the utilities. If you have a color monitor, select the **Alternate Color** radio button to see what happens. To restore the utilities to their original color configuration, return to this window, and select the **Color** radio button.

To exit the NORTON program and return to DOS, choose the Quit selection, press Esc, or click both mouse buttons at the same time.

ADDING YOUR OWN PROGRAMS TO THE NORTON SHELL PROGRAM

The following three selections in the Configure pull-down menu let you add new entries or modify existing entries in the NORTON main menu:

- Add Menu Item lets you add a new topic or command to the list. It also lets you type new text that will be shown in the Description box at the right side of the NORTON main screen whenever your new entry is highlighted.

- Edit Menu Item lets you change any of the details of your entry or any of the other entries in the menu.

- Delete Menu Item lets you remove the item from the list when you no longer need it. You cannot delete a topic if there is still a command associated with it; like files and directories, you must remove all the commands before you can delete the topic.

If you are a programmer or you are used to setting up batch files, note that all the entries in the Norton main menu are kept in a file called NORTON.CMD. If you want to, you can modify this file using a text editor, rather than using the items in the Configure pull-down menu.

ADDING YOUR OWN BACKUP UTILITY

You can add a fast and convenient backup capability to the NORTON program by including the DOS BACKUP command in the main menu Commands list. Before I show you how to do this, let me stress the importance of backing up files.

Throughout this book I'll remind you to make a backup copy of your entire system as a preliminary step for some operations. For example, before running the Speed Disk utility for the first time, you should back up your hard disk. A *backup* is an up-to-date copy of all your files that you can use to reload your system in the event of an accident. This is purely insurance that protects the hundreds or possibly thousands of files on your hard disk against potential disasters. If the unthinkable did occur—you lost all of your system's data and didn't have backup copies of it—it could take you weeks or even months to recreate your system, if indeed it could be recreated.

WHEN SHOULD I BACKUP MY FILES?   You should get into the habit of backing up your system regularly so that you never have to completely redo your work as a result of damaged or missing files. How often you make a backup varies according to how much work you do on the computer. For example, computer programmers create and modify many files during a week and stand to lose a lot of work in the event of an accident. Because of this, they probably should back up files on a daily basis, perhaps even twice a day. A person running what-if financial analyses might back up files only every two or three days because the amount of data generated in three days could be easily recreated if necessary. A person who uses programs that generate few data files can probably get by with backing up files once a week. Think of it this way:

> You should make a backup copy of your files at that point when recreating that data will cost you a considerable amount of extra work.

There are several other occasions when you should back up your entire system. If you are going to move your computer, you should first make a complete backup of the hard disk. You should do this even if you are only moving to the office next door; hard disks are notoriously sensitive and yours might not survive the trip. Similarly, if you are sending your computer in for any kind of service work, including work on the disk drives, verify that you have a complete system backup first.

If you must remove any directories and their files because you are running out of space on your hard disk, you should back up the disk completely. Make a backup before making the deletions and carefully note the date you made it. You might need those files again. Similarly, if someone leaves your company after using a computer, a complete backup is a good way to preserve that person's work and also free the hard disk for use by the replacement person.

ADDING THE DOS BACKUP COMMAND TO THE NORTON PROGRAM   Choose Add Menu Item from the Configure pull-down menu, and select Topic from the Add Menu Item window. The name you specify can be as many as 14 characters long. Type BACKUP into the highlighted box, and use the up and down arrow keys or the mouse to position the BACKUP entry at the right place in the list of topics, as shown in Figure 1.7.

Use the Tab key to move the cursor to the Description box and press Enter, or click on the box with the mouse, and then type the text you want the program to display whenever this topic is selected. A small editor window opens to accept your text. Note that you can press the F2 key to cycle through four different text attributes: Normal, Reverse, Bold, and Underline. Select the

You can only add new topics when the NORTON main menu is sorted by topic; you can add a command at any time.

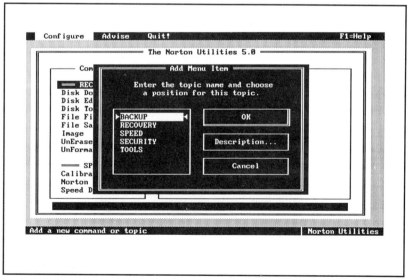

Figure 1.7: Place the new topic BACKUP at the top of the list

text attribute before you type your text. For example, if you want the Description area on the main screen to read:

This uses the DOS BACKUP command to backup files to drive A

and you want the word BACKUP in reverse (black text on a white background, type:

This uses the DOS F2BACKUPF2F2F2 command to backup files to drive A

When you press the F2 function key before you type the word BACKUP, you turn on "reverse video" mode; the three F2 keypresses at the end of the word cycle the text attribute through Bold, Underline, and back to Normal mode again. Now the rest of your text will be displayed in Normal mode.

To enter your text, use the Tab key to move the cursor to the OK box and press Enter, or click on the box with the mouse. This returns you to the Add Menu Item window; choose OK again to return to the main NORTON screen. You can see that the BACKUP topic is now at the top of the main menu list and that there are no entries under it yet. The word BACKUP is centered in the column and is enclosed by the same double-line characters as the other topics on the screen. To add the actual DOS BACKUP command into the list, choose Add Menu Item and then select the Command box. Figure 1.8 shows the next step. Type the name (as many as 16 characters) you want to display in the main menu into the Name in Menu box; in this example, we'll use DOS Backup. Next, type the actual DOS command for the BACKUP program into the DOS Command box. This command sequence can be as many as 128 characters long, even though the box in the window is much smaller than this. If you want your DOS command to back up all files from drive C to the floppy disk in drive A, type:

BACKUP C:*.* A: /S

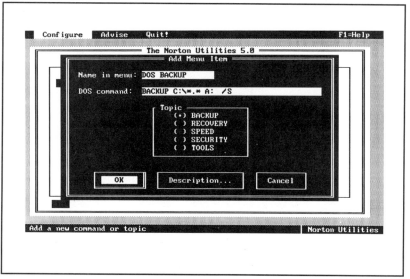

Figure 1.8: Enter the name that will appear in the main menu and then the actual DOS command

as shown in Figure 1.8. Note that you can use the DOS wildcard characters ? and *. You can also use the radio buttons to assign the new command to a different topic heading. When you've finished, move the cursor to the Description box and press Enter, or click on the box with the mouse. Now you can type the help text that the program will display in the Description section of the main NORTON screen when you highlight this new entry. Enter a list of the BACKUP command switches as a quick reminder, as shown in Table 1.5. When you have completed your entry, select OK to return to the Add Menu Item window, and select OK again to return to the main NORTON screen. Your new DOS Backup entry will now appear on the main screen as shown in Figure 1.9.

The next time you want to back up your files to a floppy disk, simply run the NORTON program, and select DOS Backup. Insert a blank floppy disk into drive A, and use the command line at the bottom of the window to add any additional switches for

Do not activate the DOS commands SUBST, JOIN, APPEND, or ASSIGN before you use BACKUP; otherwise, you might not be able to restore the files properly.

Table 1.5: BACKUP's Switches

SWITCH	FUNCTION
/A	Adds files to a backup disk.
/D:*date*	Backs up files by date.
/F	Formats the destination disk if required.
/L	Creates a log file.
/M	Backs up modified files.
/S	Backs up subdirectories.
/T:*time*	Backs up files by time on date specified by /D. Specify a for a.m. or p for p.m.

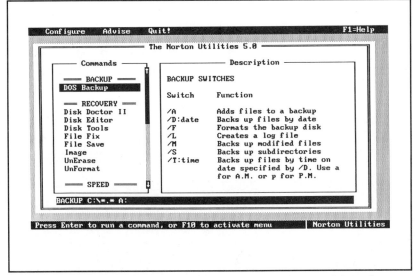

Figure 1.9: When all the entries are complete, your new DOS Backup command is listed in the NORTON main menu

To differentiate your sets of backup files easily, label them with their disk number and creation date, storing each set separately.

If you want to restore the Norton menu to its original state, rerun the INSTALL program, choose the Partial Install option, and simply reload the NORTON program from your distribution disk.

the BACKUP command. To start the procedure, press Enter or click on the DOS Backup menu item with the mouse. As the backup progresses, DOS prompts you to insert new disks as necessary; when the operation is complete, control returns to the NORTON program again.

ADDING YOUR OWN APPLICATIONS PROGRAMS

By following the previous process, you can also add entries for your favorite applications programs into the NORTON main menu. The menu can list only 256 commands, but it is not likely that you will ever need that many.

Create a topic called **APPLICATIONS**, and then create commands under this topic for your word processor, spreadsheet, or database. Remember to include the complete path name in the **DOS Command** box if the directories containing these applications programs are not included in your path statement. Figure 1.10 shows an example of how this might look on the main NORTON screen.

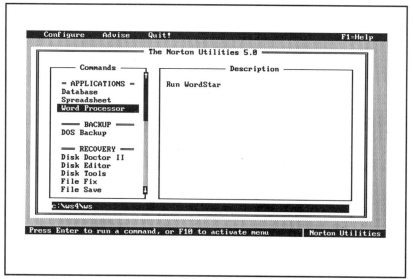

Figure 1.10: Create an APPLICATIONS topic and include your word processor, spreadsheet, and database under it

USING THE NORTON UTILITIES WITH MICROSOFT WINDOWS OR WITH DESQVIEW

Microsoft Windows and Desqview both bring multitasking capabilities to DOS. Multitasking means you can run several different applications programs at once, and switch from one to another without quitting any of them. You may run into problems if you try to run some of the Norton Utilities in either of these environments. Because the Norton Utilities run as DOS tasks, not as Windows or Desqview applications, they do not observe all the protocols required for successful data exchange and multitasking operation. The Norton Utilities contain extensive error-checking routines to avoid anything unpleasant happening if you do attempt to run them in either of these environments. In general, those utility programs that can modify the File Allocation Table are potential problems. The following Norton Utilities will refuse to run in a multitasking setting: Calibrate, Disk Editor, Disk Tools, File Fix, Safe Format, Speed Disk, the Norton Disk Doctor, UnErase, and UnFormat. If you try to start one of these utilities, you will see a screen similar to the one shown in Figure 1.11 for Speed Disk.

If you run the CPU benchmark test in System Info in a multitasking environment, your system will be slower than if you run System Info under DOS. This is due to all the extra work the processor is doing to keep track of all the concurrent activities. All the other utilities will work as you would expect.

USING THE NORTON UTILITIES ON A NETWORK

You can use the Norton Utilities from a networked drive, and you can actually use many of the more important utilities on the file server itself. However, as with the multitasking environments described in the previous paragraph, those utilities that

Figure 1.11: You will see this error window if you try to run Speed Disk under Microsoft Windows

are capable of modifying the File Allocation Table should not be run on the file server.

The Norton Utilities save their configuration information in files with the extension INI. Because each user on the network may have different hardware, the NU environment variable should point to a directory on the local disk. For example, if you have a directory called SETUP, add the following line into your AUTOEXEC.BAT file:

SET NU = C:\SETUP

to tell the utilities to keep all the configuration settings in that directory.

If you want the benefits that FileSave or Norton Change Directory offers, ask your network supervisor to install them. When FileSave is run for the first time, it creates an invisible directory from the root called TRASHCAN, and everyone on the net should have "All Rights" (except "Search") to this directory.

Norton Change Directory (NCD) makes similar demands; it creates a directory from the root called NCDTREE, and it stores all the directory structure information in this directory. Networks do not usually give users any rights to the root directory, so again your network supervisor will have to create this directory and grant users "All Rights" so that the NCD file can be updated properly.

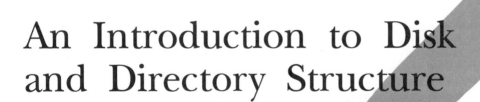

An Introduction to Disk
and Directory Structure

CHAPTER *2*

BEFORE YOU CAN RECOVER FROM A DISASTER ON YOUR system or even manage the Norton Utilities on your hard disk, you need to understand the basic concepts of disk organization. In this chapter I describe floppy disks and hard disks and how they work in DOS. After you have become familiar with these concepts, you will explore your own system in later chapters using several of the Utilities, including Disk Edit and Calibrate.

DISK STRUCTURE

The better you understand how the underlying hardware works, the easier you will find it to understand what happens when you add or delete a file in DOS, and the procedures you must follow if you have to recover the deleted file.

SIDES

In early versions of DOS, single-sided disks were common; that is, only one side of the disk could store data.

The most fundamental characteristic of a floppy disk is that it has two sides. Data can be written to or read from either side. The system identifies the sides with a numbering system. The first side is considered to be side 0, and the second side is side 1.

Hard disks, on the other hand, have several recording surfaces, which are called *platters*. Platters are mounted on the same spindle inside the hard disk's sealed enclosure, and each has two sides. The numbering scheme is the same as that used for floppy disks: the first side is 0, the next 1, the first side of the second platter 2, and so on. Each side of a floppy disk and each side of a hard disk's platter can be write protected independently.

TRACKS

Each disk or platter side is divided into concentric circles known as *tracks*. The outermost track on the top of the disk is numbered track 0, side 0, and the first track on the other side of the disk is numbered track 0, side 1. Track numbering increases inwards toward the center of the disk (or platter).

The number of tracks on a disk varies with the media type. 360K floppy disks have 40 tracks per side, 1.2MB floppy disks have 80 tracks per side, and hard disks can have from 300 to 600 tracks per platter side. On a floppy disk, the tracks cover only a small area of the disk, about three-quarters of an inch. A 360K floppy disk is recorded with 48 tracks per inch, a 1.2MB floppy disk is recorded with 96 tracks per inch, and a 3½" floppy disk is recorded with 135 tracks per inch. You will often find tracks per inch abbreviated TPI.

CYLINDERS

Tracks that are at the same concentric position on a disk (or on platters) are referred to collectively as a *cylinder*. On a floppy disk a cylinder contains two tracks (for example, track 0, side 0 and track 0, side 1); on a hard disk with four platters, a cylinder comprises eight tracks. Figure 2.1 shows cylinders on such a hard disk.

SECTORS AND ABSOLUTE SECTORS

When DOS reads or writes data, it must read or write at least one complete sector.

Each of the tracks on a disk are in turn divided into the same number of *sectors,* which are areas of equal size. In all DOS versions a sector consists of 512 bytes, and each sector is separated from the next by an inter-sector gap. The number of sectors contained in each track on the disk (as well as the total number of sectors) varies according to the media type. Most 360K and 720K floppy disks have 9 sectors per track, a 1.2MB floppy disk has 15, a 1.4MB floppy has 18, and most hard disks have 17. Figure 2.2 shows the relationship between tracks and sectors.

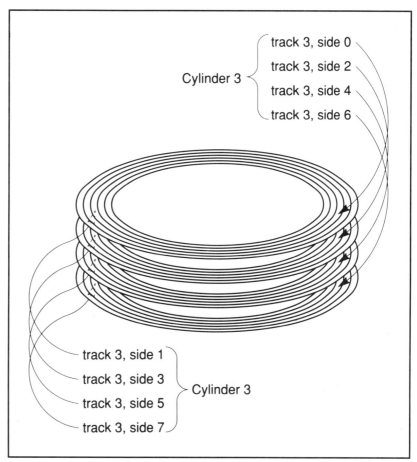

Figure 2.1: Cylinders on a hard disk with four platters

In the absolute-sector numbering scheme, the first sector on a disk is identified as side 0, cylinder 0, sector 1.

DOS identifies all the sectors on a disk by numbering them sequentially. On a 360K floppy, for example, the sectors are numbered 0–719, and a specific sector might be identified as, say, sector 317. Another way to reference a given sector is to identify it according to its disk side and cylinder and then specify its position in that cylinder. In this case, you might specify a sector's location as side 0, cylinder 25, sector 7. When you use the latter method, you are referring to *absolute sectors.*

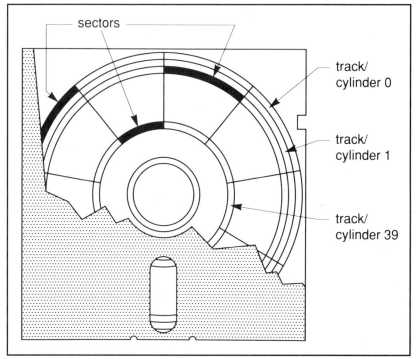

Figure 2.2: A 360K floppy disk has 40 tracks, numbered from 0 to 39, and 9 sectors in each track

THE INTERLEAVE FACTOR

For several reasons, the sectors on a disk are not always numbered sequentially. First, a floppy disk rotates at about 200 RPM inside the disk drive, and a hard disk rotates at about 3600 RPM, or one-sixtieth of a second per rotation. DOS reads and writes data in single sectors, but by the time a sector's worth of data is read and stored in memory, the head might have already passed over the next sector. The PC must now wait through a complete disk rotation before it can read the next sector. To minimize this delay, an *interleave factor* is introduced. Interleaving requires that logically sequential sectors are not physically adjacent to each other on the disk but are separated by some number of sectors. Now DOS can read a sector and store the data in memory as the head passes over and ignores the next physical sector. By the time

DOS is ready to read the disk again, the next logical sector is available. In this way, the performance of the disk and the layout of the sectors on the disk can be optimized. When numerically sequential sectors are one sector apart on the disk, the interleave factor is said to be 2:1; when they are two sectors apart, the interleave is 3:1. Chapter 11 describes how you can use Calibrate to look at and optimize your interleave factor.

CLUSTERS

The number of sectors per cluster varies according to the disk media and the DOS version. 360K and 720K floppy disks have 2 sectors per cluster, while 1.2MB and 1.4MB floppy disks have clusters of a single 512-byte sector. Hard disks have clusters of 4, 8, or 16 sectors.

Although DOS is capable of writing and reading a single sector, it allocates disk space for files in *clusters*, which consist of one or more sectors. So, no matter how small a file is, it will always occupy at least one cluster on the disk. A one-byte file will occupy one cluster, and a 511-byte file on a 1.2MB disk will also occupy one cluster. Figure 2.3 shows an example of this with a file of 1025 bytes and a cluster size of 1024 bytes, or two sectors. The file data occupies all of one cluster and only one byte of a second cluster, yet the area of the second cluster not filled with data is not available for another file. This unused area is called *slack*. The next file must start at the next available cluster. If the first file increases in length, it will occupy more of the second cluster. If the cluster is filled up and more space is needed, the file will continue in the next available cluster—in this case, the fourth cluster.

Clusters are called *logical* units. Tracks and sectors are *physical* units.

DOS identifies clusters by numbering them sequentially, with the first cluster labeled cluster 2. Cluster numbering begins in the data area of the disk, so the first cluster on a disk (cluster 2) is actually the first cluster in the data area. This is less confusing when you understand that, unlike tracks and sectors, clusters are not physically demarcated on the disk. DOS merely "decides" to view groups of sectors as clusters for its own convenience.

Remember that the absolute-sector method of referencing sectors locates them according to their physical position on the disk. Because clusters have no physical manifestation, there is no comparable, or "absolute," method of referencing them.

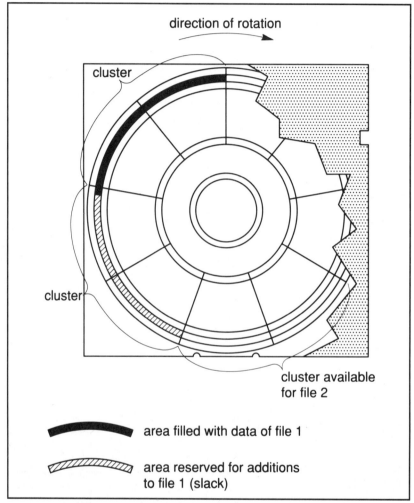

Figure 2.3: Assuming there are two sectors per cluster, a file that needs
1025 bytes of disk space is 1 byte bigger than one cluster and
will occupy two complete clusters

EXAMINING THE SYSTEM AREA

When you format a floppy disk, DOS reserves the outermost
track on side 0 for its own use. This area is called the system area

You can reference sectors in the system area with the DOS numbering system or the absolute-sector method. You cannot reference clusters in the system area because cluster numbering begins in the data area.

and is subdivided into three parts: the boot record, the *file allocation table*, or FAT, and the root directory. On a hard disk the boot record is part of a larger area called the *partition table*. The remaining space on the disk after the system area is called the data area. This is the part of the disk where application programs and data are located. The data area is far larger than the system area.

THE BOOT RECORD

The boot record, which is on all formatted disks, contains the BIOS parameter block (BPB). This block holds information about the disk's physical characteristics, which is needed by device drivers. The information contained in the BPB is shown in Table 2.1.

Table 2.1: Information Contained in the BIOS Parameter Block (in the boot record)

INFORMATION STORED	NUMBER OF BYTES USED	ADDITIONAL INFORMATION
Version of DOS used to format the disk	8	
Number of bytes per sector	2	
Number of sectors per cluster, per track, and per disk (or hard-disk partition)	1	
Number of reserved sectors used by the system area	2	
Number of FAT copies and sectors used	1	

Table 2.1: Information Contained in the BIOS Parameter Block (in the boot record) (continued)

INFORMATION STORED	NUMBER OF BYTES USED	ADDITIONAL INFORMATION
Number of root directory entries	2	112 entries on 360K floppy or 1024 entries on hard disk
Number of sectors on disk	2	720 sectors for 360K floppy, thousands for hard disk
Media descriptor	1	Indicates the type of disk
Number of sectors per FAT	2	Sectors per FAT vary according to on disk's capacity (FAT references every cluster)
Number of sectors per track	2	360K floppy has 9 sectors per track, 1.2MB floppy has 15, hard disk usually has 17
Number of heads	2, 4	Floppy-disk drive uses 2 bytes; hard disk uses 4 bytes
Number of hidden sectors	2	Hidden sectors are the system area

Note that the disk space occupied by the boot record is one sector, which includes the BPB, boot program, and slack.

The boot record also contains the boot program used to start the computer after a system reset or after power is applied. When you turn on the computer, it runs a set of diagnostic routines to ensure the hardware is in good order before proceeding. If you have a hard disk or have loaded a floppy disk, the ROM bootstrap program next loads the boot record from the disk into the computer's memory and turns control over to the bootstrap program.

The bootstrap program then checks the disk for the DOS system files (IO.SYS and MSDOS.SYS or IBMBIO.COM and IBMDOS.COM). If the files are there, it loads them into the computer and passes complete system control to DOS's COMMAND.COM. During this process, the CONFIG.SYS and AUTOEXEC.BAT files are loaded, as are any installable device drivers that a mouse or a RAM disk may need (for example, the device driver VDISK.SYS). After everything has been loaded and you see the DOS prompt, your computer is ready for use.

However, when the computer can't find the DOS system files, it displays the error message:

Non-System disk or disk error
Replace and strike any key when ready

on the screen and waits for you to either remove the non-system disk from the floppy-disk drive so it can use the hard disk, or place a system disk in your floppy-disk drive.

THE PARTITION TABLE

The partition table, present on all hard disks, lets you divide a hard disk into areas (called *partitions*) that appear to DOS as separate disks and to reserve disk space for other operating systems (which you can then install and use to create their own partitions). A DOS disk can contain as many as four partitions, although only one of these may be active at a time. The partition table begins with a code called the *master boot record*. This code contains a record of which partition was the active partition— the one used to boot the system. The master boot record also contains the locations of the boot records for the operating system of the active partition (and any other operating system installed on the disk). When the computer is restarted, it uses this information to boot the active partition's operating system.

If you have a hard disk but accidentally place or leave a non-system floppy disk in drive A and attempt to boot, your computer won't find your DOS files because it will try to use the floppy disk and will ignore the hard disk's presence. Just remove the floppy and reboot.

Floppy disks do not have partition tables and cannot be partitioned.

The DOS command FDISK creates the partition table. You can use it to re-partition a disk and select the active partition.

THE FILE ALLOCATION TABLE

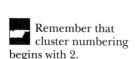
On a 360K floppy disk, the area occupied by both copies of the FAT (plus slack) is four sectors.

The next part of a disk's system area is occupied by the file allocation table (FAT), which is also created by the FORMAT command. The FAT is part of the system that DOS uses to keep track of where files are stored on a disk. The FAT is so important that DOS actually creates two copies of it. If the first copy becomes corrupted, DOS uses the second copy. Think of the FAT as a two-column table. In one column is a sequential list of numbers that, from DOS's point of view, are the "addresses" of each of the clusters in the disk's data area. In the other column is a sequential list of numbers that give specific information about each corresponding cluster. If a cluster is being used to store file data, the second column contains the "address" of the next cluster in that file. (Remember that the data in a file is not necessarily stored in consecutive clusters.) Otherwise, the second column contains a special code that indicates one of the following:

- the cluster is available for storing data

- the cluster is bad and will not be used for storing data

- the cluster is reserved and will not be used for storing data

- the cluster is the last cluster in a file

Remember that cluster numbering begins with 2.

Figure 2.4 illustrates how FAT entries are chained together. File A starts in cluster 2 and then continues in cluster 8. The entry for cluster 8 points to cluster 11. Cluster 11 in turn points to cluster 12, where the file ends. Thus, File A is split up into four clusters, three of which are not in sequence. File B is less fragmented. It occupies clusters 3, 4, 5, 6, 7, 9, and 10. The entry for cluster 7 points to cluster 9, where the file continues. Cluster 9 points to 10, which contains the end-of-file value.

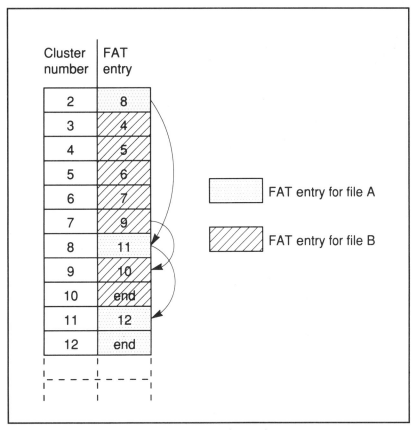

Figure 2.4: How FAT entries are chained together.

THE ROOT DIRECTORY

On a 360K floppy disk, the root directory takes up seven sectors of disk space.

Directly following the FAT sectors is the root directory, which is the third part of the system area found on a formatted disk. The root directory's size cannot be changed, but it is proportional to the media type. For example, a 360K floppy has space for 112 entries in the root, while a hard disk has space for 512 or 1024 entries.

IBMBIO.COM and IBMDOS.COM are *hidden* files, which means their names do not appear in a directory listing and you can't use them in a command at the DOS prompt.

If the disk is a system disk, the first two files in the root directory are always the files containing the DOS BIOS interface and the DOS kernel. The disk's bootstrap program loads these files into memory when it starts up DOS.

Each directory entry is 32 bytes long and may contain information about a file or a subdirectory. The format of an entry is as follows:

Base name	8 bytes
Extension	3 bytes
Attribute	1 byte, each bit represents an attribute
	bit 0, file is read-only
	bit 1, file is hidden
	bit 2, file is a system file
	bit 3, entry is a volume label
	bit 4, entry is a subdirectory
	bit 5, archive bit
	bit 6, unused
	bit 7, unused
Reserved	10 bytes, reserved for future use
Time of creation	2 bytes
Date of creation	2 bytes
Starting FAT entry	2 bytes
File size	4 bytes

You can use letters, numbers, and any character except . " / \ [ ] | < > + : * ? , = ; and a space in your files and directory base names and extensions.

The file name is an 11-byte entry, divided into an 8-byte base name and a 3-byte extension, which are separated by a period.

The period is not stored as a byte but you must type it if you want to use a file extension.

The attribute byte can have one or more of the attribute bits set at the same time. For example, a system file can also be hidden. An attribute is said to be *set* if the appropriate attribute bit has a value of 1. If the attribute byte has no bits set, or a value of 0, the file is a normal data or program file that can be written to or erased. This probably applies to the majority of your files.

See Chapter 19 for information about viewing and changing file attributes.

- *Read-only files* can be used, but you can't change their contents.

- *Hidden files* do not appear in directory listings made by DIR. You can't duplicate them with the COPY command or delete them. However, you can copy them by using the DISKCOPY command; this makes a sector-by-sector duplicate of the original disk.

- *System files* are read-only files.

- The *volume label* is a short piece of text used to identify the disk. You can specify as many as 11 characters for it when you label your disk. The label's directory entry resembles that of an empty file.

- *Subdirectory* names have the same format as file names.

- The *archive bit* is used by the DOS BACKUP and XCOPY programs. If a new file is written to disk or an existing file is modified, this bit is set (changed to 1). After the BACKUP program has copied the file, it resets the bit to 0. This way, BACKUP knows which files have changed and therefore need to be copied.

If the first byte of a directory entry has a value of 0, the entry is unused and indicates the end of the active directory entries. If the first byte of a file name is a period (that is, the . and .. files), the file is reserved by DOS.

EXAMINING THE DATA AREA

The rest of the DOS partition on a hard disk or the remaining space on a floppy disk is the data area that stores files and sub-directories. This is the largest part of a disk and is where all your programs—spreadsheets, word processors, program language compilers, data files, and so on—are found.

Subdirectories differ from the root directory in that they do not have fixed locations on the disk and can be created and deleted.

Figures 2.5 and 2.6 illustrate disk structure in different ways and draw together the concepts presented in this chapter. Both figures show the structure of a 360K floppy disk.

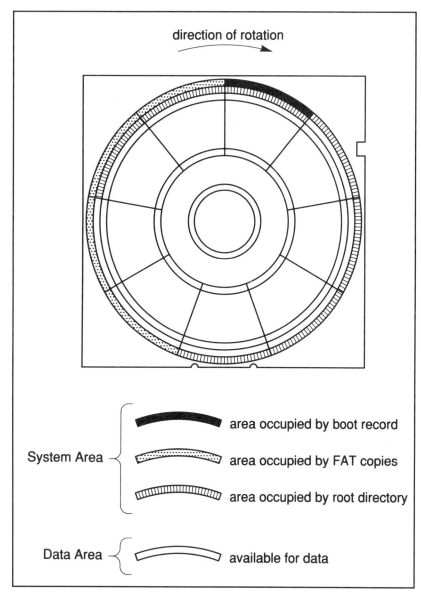

Figure 2.5: Locations of system area and data area on a 360K floppy disk

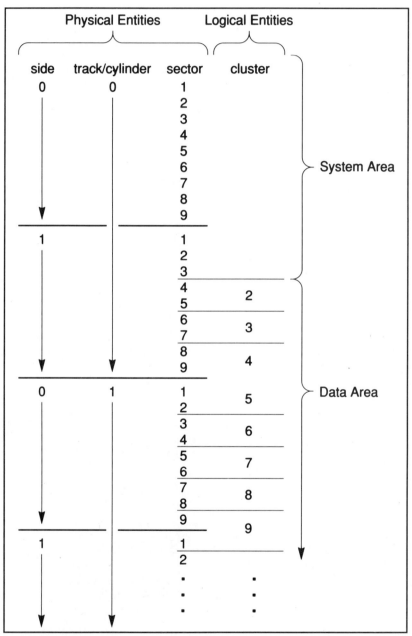

Figure 2.6: Relationships between elements of disk structure on a 360K floppy disk

Part II shows you how to use the Norton Utilities to help protect your data, including how to recover erased or damaged files and how to restore a hard disk that has accidentally been formatted.

Chapter 3 discusses diagnosing and fixing disk problems with the Norton Disk Doctor. In Chapter 4 you learn how to use the Disk Editor to examine and edit all of a floppy or hard disk. Chapter 5 shows you how to use six crucial Disk Tools, and Chapter 6 focuses on repairing damaged Lotus 1-2-3, Symphony, and dBASE data files, even if the dBASE file has been zapped. In Chapter 7, you learn how to use FileSave to protect deleted files from being overwritten immediately, and Chapter 8 explains how Image makes a copy of the vital system area of your hard disk. Chapter 9 is an complete description of how to use UnErase to recover deleted files, partial files, and deleted directories. Finally, Chapter 10 describes how to use UnFormat to restore the contents of your hard disk after an accidental format.

PART

Recovery

Norton Disk Doctor II (NDD)

Detecting and Correcting Disk Errors

CHAPTER 3

WHAT DO YOU DO IF YOUR DISK CONTAINS FILES THAT you cannot read? You can use the Norton Disk Doctor II to diagnose and fix the unreadable files.

DOS provides the CHKDSK command for finding and fixing FAT errors and the RECOVER command for accessing files that contain bad sectors. However, DOS does not include programs that can find or fix physical errors on a floppy or hard disk. The diagnostics program disk supplied with some computers may be able to locate errors, but it usually can't fix them. Fortunately, Norton Disk Doctor II finds and fixes any logical or high-level physical errors on your floppy or hard disk.

The Norton Disk Doctor finds and fixes most of the disk-related problems you are likely to encounter. It fixes bad or corrupted partition tables, bad or missing boot records, and a corrupted BPB (BIOS Parameter Block). In the area of file structure problems, Norton Disk Doctor can repair bad or corrupted FATs, reconstruct cross-linked files, and fix physical problems that prevent you from reading directories or files. Finally, this new version of the program can also reverse any changes that were made during the repair process and return the disk to it's original state.

I do not go into great depth about the cause and nature of disk errors in this chapter. Suffice it to say, you should run NDD after DOS reports a disk error.

You can run Norton Disk Doctor from the DOS prompt or by selecting it from within the NORTON shell program. To run Norton Disk Doctor from the DOS prompt, type:

NDD

with no parameters or switches. The opening screen is shown in Figure 3.1.

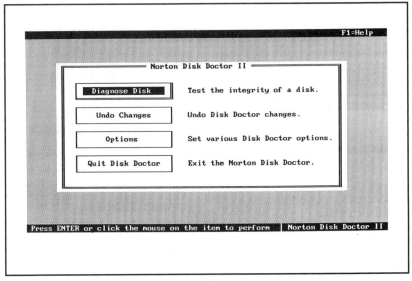

Figure 3.1: The Norton Disk Doctor II opening screen

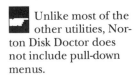
Unlike most of the other utilities, Norton Disk Doctor does not include pull-down menus.

You can select four options from the main Norton Disk Doctor screen: Diagnose Disk, Undo Changes, Options, and Exit Disk Doctor.

FINDING DISK PROBLEMS WITH DIAGNOSE DISK

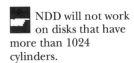
NDD will not work on disks that have more than 1024 cylinders.

Diagnose Disk is the most important part of the Norton Disk Doctor. After choosing this selection, you are asked to select a disk drive from the list of active drives, as shown in Figure 3.2.

To check only one disk drive in NDD, simply highlight it and press Enter.

Use the arrow keys to move the highlight and press the spacebar to select the drives you want to check, or click on the appropriate drive with the mouse. This inserts a small check-mark next to the drive letter. Press Enter to start the analysis.

NDD recognizes partitions made by most software, including DOS 3.31, DOS 4.0, Disk Manager, and SpeedStor.

Norton Disk Doctor analyzes the following areas of your disks:

- Partition Table. If the disk you specified is a hard disk, Norton Disk Doctor checks the partition table.

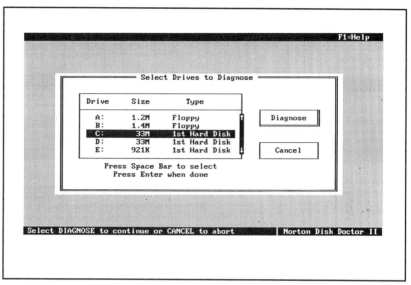

Figure 3.2: Norton Disk Doctor's Select Drives to Diagnose screen

- DOS Boot Record. NDD examines the boot record to ensure that it is not damaged. The BIOS Parameter Block is also checked to verify that the media descriptor byte is correct for the type of disk being checked.

- File Allocation Tables. The File Allocation Table (FAT) is a list of the addresses of all the files and directories on a disk. Because this is the index into all your program and data files, DOS keeps two copies of the FAT on each disk. Norton Disk Doctor checks for read errors in both of the copies of the FAT. If it finds a read error, NDD copies the good FAT over the FAT containing the read error. Next, both tables are checked to see that they are identical and that they only contain legal DOS entries.

- Directory Structure. Norton Disk Doctor reads every directory on the disk, searching for illegal file names and file sizes, FAT errors, and cross-linked files.

- File Structure. NDD also checks the file structure in the same way as it checks the directories.

- Lost Clusters. These disk clusters are marked as "in use" by the FAT, but they are not actually allocated to a file anywhere. Norton Disk Doctor converts lost clusters into files and writes them into the root directory.

If it finds an error, Norton Disk Doctor describes the problem and asks whether you want to fix it. Figure 3.3 shows the screen NDD displays when it finds an error in the FAT.

When NDD asks if you want to correct the problem, select **Yes** to fix the problem or **No** to move to the next set of tests. Choose **Cancel** to return to the main Norton Disk Doctor menu.

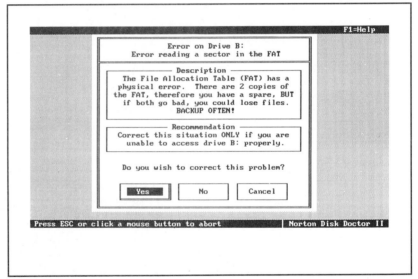

Figure 3.3: FAT Error found by Norton Disk Doctor

SURFACE TEST

Next, you have the option of running a complete sector-by-sector test of the entire disk. If you have a large hard disk, this test can take some time to run. Disk Doctor can check a 65MB hard disk in less than 10 minutes if it doesn't find any bad clusters. It will take longer if it finds errors.

Disk errors can take a variety of forms, and Norton Disk Doctor is especially helpful for isolating, and in some cases curing, problems associated with *read errors*. Because Norton Disk Doctor actually reads or attempts to read the data from each cluster on the disk, it differs from the DOS CHKDSK command, which tests only for logical errors in the data contained in the FAT and the directories.

When a disk-read error occurs, DOS responds with a variety of messages. The typical DOS prompt following such a device error is likely to be "Abort, Retry, Ignore, Fail?"; however, the actual selections in this sequence vary according to which version of DOS you are using and the nature of the error. In any case, this prompt is DOS's way of giving you the choice of how to deal with the error. If you choose "Abort," DOS stops executing the program that initially performed the read. "Retry" tells DOS to try the operation again. Choosing "Fail" causes DOS to return control to the original application with an error code indicating failure. Selecting "Ignore" causes DOS to return control to the application without such a code, presenting the illusion that the operation has already been performed. Disk errors occur for a variety of reasons, usually at the most inconvenient moment; Surface Test is a good way to find and isolate them. The Surface Test selection screen is shown in Figure 3.4. Set up the appropriate Surface Test parameters by making selections from this screen.

The test criteria you can specify from the Surface Test screen include the following:

- Test. Choose from Disk Test or File Test.

  - Disk Test. This test reads every part of the disk, including the system area and the data area. Because it is so thorough and it checks the entire disk, the disk-read test can take a long time to run.

  - File Test. This checks all current data and program files and directories for errors. However, it does not check the erased file space, the unused file

A cluster already marked as bad is not usually an indication of a deteriorating disk; most hard disks have a small number of clusters containing sectors that are marked as bad by the low-level formatting program.

space, or the system area, which is why it usually takes less time to run than Disk Test.

- **Passes.** Enter the number of times you want the test repeated, from 1 to 999 times.

- **Test Type.** Choose the type of test you want to run.

  - **Daily.** This runs a fast check of the disk.

  - **Weekly.** Weekly runs a comprehensive disk test that takes at least twice as long to run as the daily selection. It also detects errors that the daily test might miss.

  - **Auto Weekly.** The default setting for Norton Disk Doctor, this test is a combination of daily and weekly tests.

- **Repair Setting.** This option lets you choose how you want NDD to respond when it finds an error.

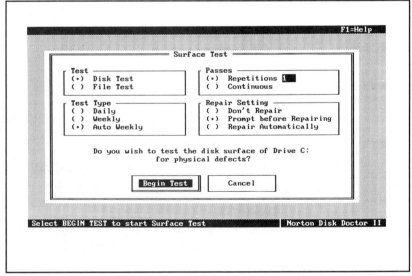

Figure 3.4: Norton Disk Doctor lets you select the test criteria to use for the surface test

- **Don't Repair.** This setting tells NDD to ignore any read errors. You are not likely to use this setting.

- **Prompt Before Repairing.** When NDD finds an error, the program informs you of the error and then asks you if you want to move the file to a safe area on the disk. This is the setting you will use most often.

- **Repair Automatically.** This selection makes the repair process as automatic as possible. Bad sectors are moved without delay.

The actual test screen is shown in Figure 3.5. Sectors in use by files are shown as a light box with a dark center, and unused sectors are shown as darker boxes. Bad sectors are marked with a **B**, and the actual area under test is shown by the "snowflake" character.

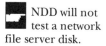 NDD will not test a network file server disk.

While the disk test is being made, an analog display shows the progress of the test (as percentage completed) at the bottom left of the screen (see Figure 3.5). The program updates this dis-

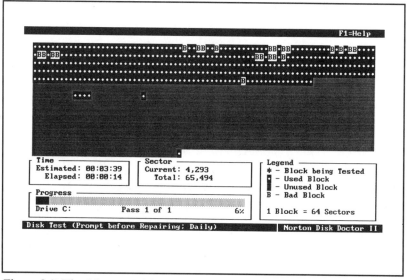

Figure 3.5: The Norton Disk Doctor display while running Disk Test

being tested and the total number of sectors on the disk are shown on the screen. The estimated and elapsed time are also shown to give you an idea of how long this test will take. The disk test first checks the system area of the disk; then it checks the data area. Any errors encountered are displayed on the screen.

As the file test proceeds, the names of the directory and file being tested are displayed in the File box; NDD changes the names as they are checked. The names of any files that contain unreadable clusters are displayed on the screen with an error message.

If a data sector is found to be bad, but is not in use by a file, NDD marks it as bad so that it will not be available for use in the future. If a data sector is bad and is being used by a file, the program copies the file to a safe location on the disk, and the sector is marked as bad. Norton Disk Doctor displays the names of any files that it moves. You must check the list afterward to ensure that all your files are safe.

When the test is done, NDD lists the areas of the disk that were tested, along with the status of the test. The test status codes include the following:

- OK. No problems were found.

- Fixed. A problem was found and fixed.

- Not Fixed. A problem was found, but it was not fixed.

- Skipped. The test was not performed.

- Canceled. The test was interrupted and did not run to completion.

An example of this screen is shown in Figure 3.6.

NDD also generates a tabulated report suitable for printing or capturing as a file, as shown in Figure 3.7. You can examine the report on the screen: merely use the Page Up or Page Down keys to move through the report, or click on the scroll bars with the mouse. To print the report select the Print box. If you don't have time to look at the report now, select the Save As box to save the report in a file. When the Save Report window opens,

Don't save the report on the disk you are testing, because if the disk is in poor condition you may never be able to load the report to read it.

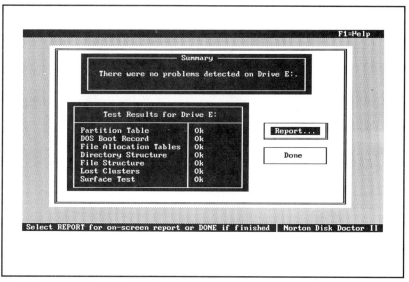

Figure 3.6: The Norton Disk Doctor screen at the end of the test run
for drive E

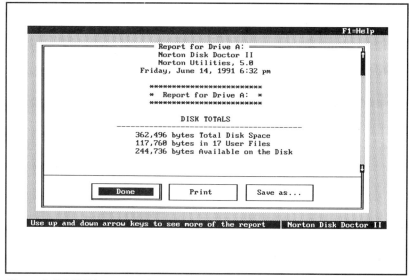

Figure 3.7: NDD's report for a 360K floppy disk

enter the name you want to use for the report file. After the file is saved, another window opens to confirm that the report was written to the specified file name.

UNDO CHANGES

This version of Norton Disk Doctor contains a major advance in disk testing capability. Unlike other disk repair programs, Norton Disk Doctor can actually reverse the repair process and remove the changes made during the repair cycle. Details of any changes made to a disk by NDD are saved in a file called NDDUNDO.DAT located in the root directory. To restore a disk to its original condition, select Undo Changes from the main menu. When the disk selection window appears, choose the drive letter of the disk that contains NDDUNDO.DAT. Norton Disk Doctor uses its information to reverse the changes and return the disk to its original condition.

OPTIONS

You can use the Options selection from the main Norton Disk Doctor menu to configure the program to your own requirements. The Disk Doctor Options screen is shown in Figure 3.8. Three selections are available: Surface Test, Custom Message, and Tests to Skip.

SURFACE TEST

Select this option to enter your choices for the Surface Test. This screen is exactly the same as the screen shown in Figure 3.4. Make your selections from Test, Test Type, Passes, and Repair Settings.

Figure 3.8: Disk Doctor Options selection screen

CUSTOM MESSAGE

If you are a network manager or are in charge of several computers in a department, you will find the Custom Message selection very useful. You can enter a message here that Norton Disk Doctor will display if the program finds an error in the system area of a disk. Because this is the most important part of a disk, you might not want your users to proceed with repairs on their own. You can enter a message including your name, department name, and extension number, as shown in Figure 3.9. After you have entered the text, use the F2 function key to set the display attribute of your message. Choose from Normal, Reverse, Bold, or Underline. This will add even more impact to your message. Don't forget to check the Prompt with Custom Message box, and then save this message by choosing or clicking on the Save Settings box.

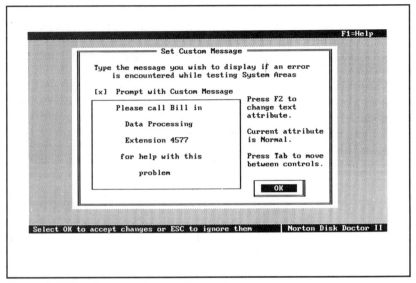

Figure 3.9: Use Custom Message if you are system manager for a group
of computers

When NDD encounters an error in the system area of the disk,
the user's only option is to choose the **Cancel Test** box at the bottom of the screen. They cannot continue with the NDD tests.

TESTS TO SKIP

The Tests to Skip selection provides more configuration choices so that you can customize the program even further. This is
particularly useful if your computer is not a true IBM compatible.
There are four options in Tests to Skip, as Figure 3.10 shows.

- **Skip Partition Tests.** If you use nonstandard hard disk
  partition software, Norton Disk Doctor might not
  recognize your partitions. Check this selection to turn
  off the partition table tests.

- **Skip CMOS Tests.** If your CMOS settings are nonstandard, check this selection to turn off the CMOS tests.
  (See Chapter 21 for details about CMOS.)

- **Skip Surface Tests.** If you never intend to use the Norton Disk Doctor Surface Test, select this option. I recommend you do not check this box; the Surface Test is one of the program's most useful features, and you should not forget about it.

- **Only 1 Hard Disk.** Check this box if your computer consistently reports that you have two hard disks when you know you only have one. For example, if you use an AT&T 6300, NDD finds two hard disks even when the computer only contains one. This is a problem with the computer, not a problem with Norton Disk Doctor.

When you have finished making your selections, you can save them by highlighting the **Save Settings** box and pressing Enter or by clicking on the box with the mouse. The next time you run Norton Disk Doctor, the selections you just saved will be loaded into the program automatically. This way you don't have to reconfigure the program each time you run it.

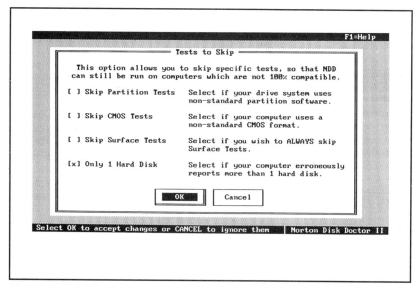

Figure 3.10: The Tests to Skip screen lets you configure NDD to your particular computer hardware

QUIT DISK DOCTOR

The final Norton Disk Doctor menu selection is Quit Disk Doctor. Use this selection to return to the NORTON shell or, if you started NDD from the command line, to return to DOS.

UNDERSTANDING DISK ERRORS

If Norton Disk Doctor discovers an increasing number of errors, you should replace or repair your hard disk as soon as possible. How critical an error is depends on where the bad sector is on your disk. If the error is in the system area of the disk, in the boot record, in the FAT, or in the root directory, you may lose all the data on the disk. In the case of a hard disk, this can represent a great deal of data. (This is another reason to be sure that your floppy-disk or tape backups are always up to date.) If the bad sector contains the boot record, the hard disk may refuse to boot. If NDD reports errors on a floppy disk, try cleaning the disk heads. Then reformat the disk and run NDD on it again to see if the problems have cleared up. If that does not work, throw the disk away. Never use a dubious disk as a backup disk for archive storage. Make your backups on error free disks. When you need to reload your system from your backup disks, you can't afford to have any errors.

RUNNING NORTON DISK DOCTOR FROM THE COMMAND LINE

You can also run the Norton Disk Doctor from the DOS prompt with one of two switches: /COMPLETE tests every sector on the disk, and /QUICK tests only the system area of the disk. To run NDD on drive C without the data sector tests, type:

NDD C: /QUICK

To run NDD on drive C and test all of the data area, type:

NDD C: /COMPLETE

You can use NDD on your hard disk every time you start your computer if you include the following line in your AUTOEXEC.BAT file:

NDD C: /QUICK

This will perform a brief analysis of your hard disk every time you boot up your computer.

Disk Editor
(DISKEDIT)

Viewing and Editing the Contents of a Disk

CHAPTER *4*

Disk Editor is based on the old NU program, but it has greatly expanded capabilities.

THE DISK EDITOR LETS YOU EXAMINE AND EDIT ANY part of a floppy or hard disk, sometimes even if DOS refuses to recognize the disk. As you would expect, you can work with directories and files; however, you can also use Disk Editor to look at the boot record, the partition table, and the File Allocation Tables.

Disk Editor also lets you view disk information in its native format. For example, the partition table information is presented in a format that is tailored to that specific data, the boot record uses an entirely new format for its different type of data, and so on. This makes Disk Editor easier to use, because you don't need to make complex offset calculations to determine how a specific piece of information should be stored. Disk Editor performs these calculations for you.

Disk Editor enables you to peer into the dark corners of your disks and review information that is not normally accessible without a great deal of complex programming. You can also use the program to evaluate and fix disk problems. The Norton Disk Doctor II, described in Chapter 3, can find and fix almost all common disk problems, but if you decide that you want to be in complete control of the repair operation, you can make the repair yourself with the Disk Editor.

From inside the NORTON program, choose Disk Editor from the main menu. To start the program, position the highlight on the Disk Editor selection and press Enter, or click on the entry with the mouse. To start the program directly from the DOS command line, type:

DISKEDIT

If you configure Disk Editor in Write mode, the screen in Figure 4.1 is not displayed.

and press Enter. The preliminary Disk Editor screen is shown in Figure 4.1.

Then Disk Editor read the directory structure of the disk and displays the current directory.

Figure 4.1: The opening Disk Editor screen reminds you that the program is configured in read-only mode

CONFIGURING DISK EDITOR

When you use Disk Editor for the first time, the program is configured to work in read-only, or display, mode. You can use the program to look at your disk, but you cannot use it to make changes to your disk. Disk Editor is a powerful program, and it can damage your programs or data if you use it incorrectly or carelessly. If you want to use the program to write changes to the disk, you have to change the configuration.

To view or change the Disk Editor configuration, select the Configuration option from the Tools pull-down menu. This displays the Configuration window shown in Figure 4.2.

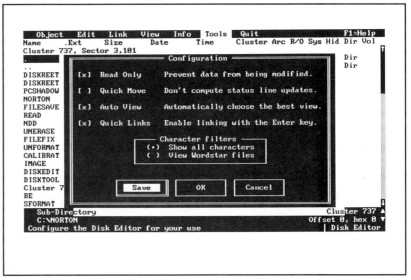

Figure 4.2: The Configuration window enables you to select several Disk Editor options

You can make several selections from this window:

- **Read Only.** If there is a check mark next to this selection, you can use the Disk Editor to examine your disk, but you cannot write changes to the disk. When the program is in read-only mode, all selections in the main Edit menu are disabled with the exception of Mark. As a safety net, you should leave the program in this configuration until you have to write to the disk; then, change this setting. Press the spacebar or the **X** key to set or cancel this selection. You can also click on the box with the mouse.

- **Quick Move.** Disk Editor usually displays the name of the file you are working with on the status line. When you turn on this selection, the file name is not written on the status line, and the program works slightly faster.

- **Auto View.** When this selection is on, Disk Editor automatically chooses the right display format for the item you want to examine, whether it be the boot record or the root directory. When **Auto View** is off, Disk Editor always uses the Hex Viewer.

- **Quick Links.** When **Quick Links** is on, you can move from one object to a related object, without going through the main menu selection process. For example, if you are looking at a FAT entry, you can go directly to the file itself. By default, the **Quick Links** selection is turned on, so by pressing Enter or double clicking with the mouse, you can quickly access the related item.

The Appendix contains a complete list of all the ASCII characters.

The settings in the Character Filters option determine how information is displayed in Disk Editor. The standard ASCII characters use seven of the eight bits in a byte. The extended ASCII character set uses all eight bits to display graphics characters. Some programs, such as WordStar also use use the high-order bit in a byte, but they use it to generate formatting information. The Character Filters option let you choose how this data is displayed.

- **Show All Characters.** This is the default mode; it displays all the bits in a byte, including extended ASCII graphics characters.

- **View WordStar Files.** If you want to look at WordStar files, use this selection. In this mode, Disk Editor ignores the high-order bits and displays WordStar files correctly. It also inhibits the display of graphical characters in other file types. Feel free to switch back and forth with **Show All Characters** when you are viewing files.

When you have completed your selections from this window, highlight the Save box and press Enter, or click on the box with the mouse, to save the settings. This configuration information is saved in a file called NU.INI. To use these settings for only the current Disk Editor session, choose OK; to abandon the changes, select Cancel.

CHOOSING AN OBJECT

Disk Editor can access disk information in several different ways. When you work with a file, you can choose to access the file, the clusters that make up the file, or the sectors that make up those clusters. The main difference between these objects is the way you use Disk Editor to access them—files are usually described by name, but clusters and sectors are accessed by number or by a range of numbers. The next step in using Disk Editor is specifying an object to work with.

DRIVE

To choose a drive to work with, select Drive from the Object pull-down menu, or press Alt-D from the main Disk Editor screen. Note that you must select a drive before you can choose the file or clusters you want to edit. The drive selection window is shown in Figure 4.3.

Table 4.1 at the end of this chapter summarizes all of the shortcut keys you can use with Disk Editor.

Use the up and down arrow keys to highlight the disk you want to edit; then press the Tab key to move to the OK box and press Enter, or click on OK with the mouse.

Normally you will be working with Logical Disks; however, if your disk is badly damaged, choose Physical Disks so that Disk Editor can access the disk without regard to its formatting or its partitioning. If you want to access a partitioned hard disk as a single object, even though it has been divided into several smaller logical drives, choose Physical Disks.

DIRECTORY

Next, you should choose the appropriate directory by selecting Directory from the Objects pull-down menu, or by pressing

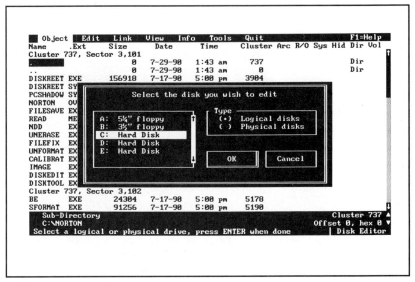

Figure 4.3: The Drive Selection window lets you choose the disk you
want to edit

Alt-R from the main Disk Editor display. This displays the Change
Directory window, as shown in Figure 4.4. The left side of the
window shows a graphical display of your directory structure;
the right side contains the **Speed Search** box. You can use the
up and down arrow keys to move to the appropriate directory
on the graphical display, or you can enter the directory name
into the **Speed Search** box. You don't have to enter the complete directory name; merely type in enough characters to make
the name unique. As you type letters, Disk Editor moves the
highlight to the matching directory name. If you have two directories with similar names **Speed Search** will find the first one;
you can then press the Control key and Enter to move to the
next directory. Note that the Control (Ctrl) key is represented
by the ^ character on the Change Directory window. Disk Editor
will not display a character if it does not appear in a directory
name. If Disk Editor refuses to accept a character, you know that
there is no such directory on that disk.

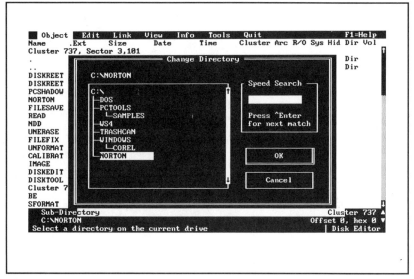

Figure 4.4: The Change Directory window lets you select a directory to work with

FILE

To choose a file, select File from the Object pull-down menu, or press Alt-F from the main Disk Editor display. The Select File window opens, as shown in Figure 4.5. To select a different drive, directory, or file, highlight the new name (object) and press Enter, or double click on the object with the mouse.

CLUSTER

To work directly with clusters, choose Cluster from the Object pull-down menu, or press Alt-C. The Select Cluster Range window opens, as shown in Figure 4.6. This window displays the range of valid cluster numbers; in Figure 4.6 the range is from cluster 2 through cluster 16,334. To look at a group of clusters enter the first number in the Starting Cluster box and the last number in the Ending Cluster box. If you want to look at a single cluster, enter the same number into both boxes. Finally, if you specify a Starting Cluster number but no Ending Cluster number,

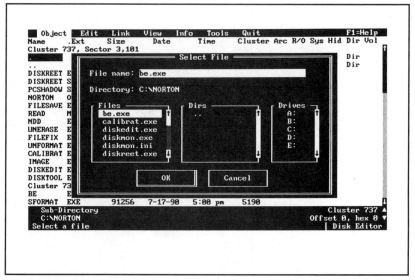

Figure 4.5: The Select File window lets you select a file, directory, and disk drive

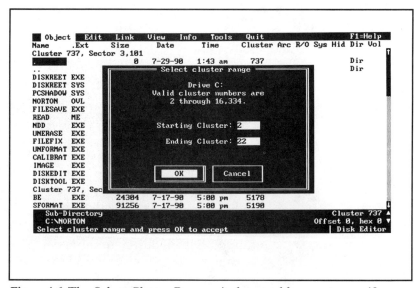

Figure 4.6: The Select Cluster Range window enables you to specify a range of clusters

you will select all the clusters on the disk, beginning with the number of the Starting Cluster.

SECTORS

Some application programs report disk errors in terms of physical, or absolute, sectors rather than logical sectors. Using Disk Editor you can work with either.

As with clusters, you can specify a range of sectors to work with. Choose Sector from the Objects pull-down menu, or type Alt-S, to display the Select Sector Range window shown in Figure 4.7.

In Figure 4.7, the valid range of sectors is from 0 through 65,492. Certain areas on the disk are reserved for particular functions. Sector 0 is used as the boot record, sectors 1 through 64 are the first copy of the FAT, sectors 65 through 128 are the second copy of the FAT, sectors 129 through 160 are used as the root directory, and the remaining sectors, 161 through 65,492 define the data area of the disk where files are kept.

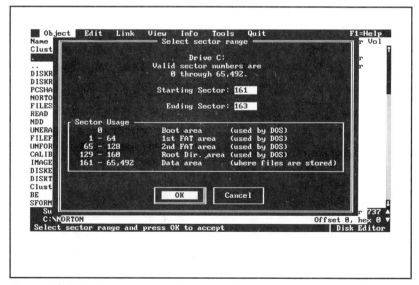

Figure 4.7: The Select Sector Range window enables you to specify a range of sectors

When you use this numbering scheme to refer to sectors, you are said to be using *logical sectors*.

PHYSICAL SECTORS

Choose Physical Sector from the Objects pull-down menu to work directly with physical sectors. You can also press Alt-P from the main Disk Editor screen. The Select Physical Sector Range window is shown in Figure 4.8. To display sectors from this screen, you must specify the cylinder number, the disk platter side number, the sector number, and the number of sectors you want to examine. The right side of the window shows the legal ranges of these values.

PARTITION TABLE

To work with the partition table on your disk, choose Partition Table from the Objects pull-down menu, or press Alt-A

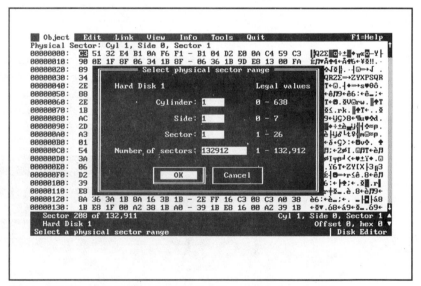

Figure 4.8: The Select Physical Sector Range window enables you to choose sectors based on their position on the disk

from the main screen. The partition table display is shown in Figure 4.9.

In Figure 4.9, the four lines in the display represent the four possible partitions. If DOS-12 appears at the beginning of the line, the DOS partition has a 12-bit FAT; DOS-16 indicates a 16-bit FAT. Additional information includes the starting and ending side, cylinder, and sector, along with the total number of sectors in each partition. The partition labeled "Yes" in the Boot column is the partition that actually loads when you boot up the computer.

I strongly advise against editing the partition table unless you know exactly what you are doing. You can make a disk completely unbootable if you make a mistake here. The best way to change partition table information is to use the DOS command specifically designed for that purpose—FDISK.

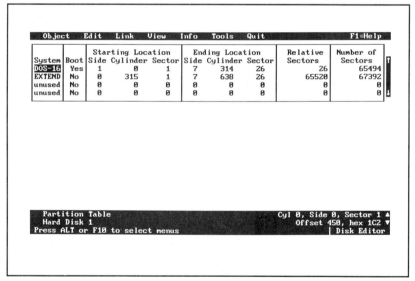

Figure 4.9: Partition Table display gives complete details of your partition table

BOOT RECORD

To examine the information contained in the boot track of your disks, select Boot Record from the Object pull-down menu, or press Alt-B from the Disk Editor main screen. The boot record information will be displayed in the format shown in Figure 4.10.

Figure 4.10 lists the boot record of a 65MB hard disk formatted under PC DOS 3.3. This information includes the name stored in the OEM (Original Equipment Manufacturer) field, a great deal of data describing the hard disk's characteristics, including the number of bytes per sector and sectors per cluster, the number of reserved sectors, and the number of copies of the FAT on the disk. Listed next are the maximum number of entries that the root directory can hold and the number of sectors on this logical disk. This information is followed by the media descriptor byte, the number of sectors per FAT, sectors per track, and the number of sides, or disk heads, that this disk has. The next item shown in Figure 4.10 represents the number of hidden sectors on the disk.

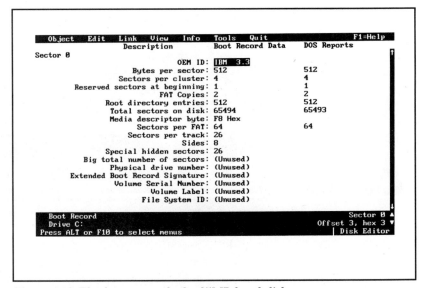

Figure 4.10: The boot record of a 65MB hard disk

The final six entries are shown as unused in Figure 4.10, but these fields will contain data when you view disks formatted by DOS 4.0 or later.

FILE ALLOCATION TABLES

There are two copies of the FAT stored on each hard and floppy disk, and one copy on a RAM disk. To examine the first copy of the FAT, select 1st Copy of the FAT from the Object pull-down menu, or press Alt-F1. To look at the other copy select 2nd Copy of the FAT, or press Alt-F2. Figure 4.11 shows the beginning of the first FAT copy on a 65MB disk.

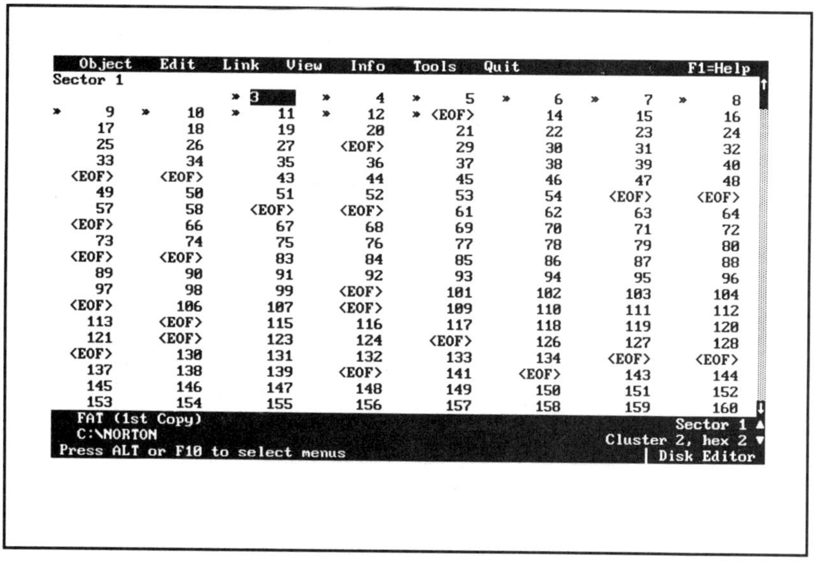

```
    Object   Edit   Link   View   Info   Tools   Quit              F1=Help
  Sector 1                                                                 ↑
                    »  3        »    4      »   5      »   6    »   7   »   8
      »   9  »   10  »   11   »   12   » <EOF>      14      15      16
         17      18      19      20      21      22      23      24
         25      26      27   <EOF>      29      30      31      32
         33      34      35      36      37      38      39      40
      <EOF>   <EOF>      43      44      45      46      47      48
         49      50      51      52      53      54   <EOF>   <EOF>
         57      58   <EOF>   <EOF>      61      62      63      64
      <EOF>      66      67      68      69      70      71      72
         73      74      75      76      77      78      79      80
      <EOF>   <EOF>      83      84      85      86      87      88
         89      90      91      92      93      94      95      96
         97      98      99   <EOF>     101     102     103     104
      <EOF>     106     107   <EOF>     109     110     111     112
        113   <EOF>     115     116     117     118     119     120
        121   <EOF>     123     124   <EOF>     126     127     128
      <EOF>     130     131     132     133     134   <EOF>   <EOF>
        137     138     139   <EOF>     141   <EOF>     143     144
        145     146     147     148     149     150     151     152
        153     154     155     156     157     158     159     160
   FAT (1st Copy)                                          Sector 1  ▲
   C:\NORTON                                           Cluster 2, hex 2 ▼
   Press ALT or F10 to select menus                        Disk Editor
```

Figure 4.11: Information from the first FAT displayed in FAT format

See Chapter 2 for a detailed description of how the FAT works.

The first two entries in the FAT are reserved for special DOS information; therefore, they do not appear in this display. Each file entry in a directory contains the first cluster number allocated to the file, and that number is used as the entry point into the FAT. From that point forward, every location in the FAT contains the number of the next cluster in the file, until the last cluster, or end-of-file, mark (EOF) is found. Valid FAT entries are:

0000H	Available cluster
FF0–FF6H	Reserved cluster
FF7H	Bad cluster
FF8–FFFH	Last cluster
number	Next cluster in the file

In Figure 4.11, related clusters that belong to the same current file (indicated by the cursor) are shown in a highlighted color. The full path name of that file is shown at the lower left of the screen.

USING THE INFO MENU

Before you start an editing session, it is useful to examine the object you have selected in more detail. The selections in the Info pull-down menu help you to do this.

Choose Object Info to display more information about the object you have chosen to work with. The information shown in this screen varies according to the current object. If you are working with a file, Object Info displays information about the file, including the full path name, a list of attributes, the creation date and time, starting cluster and sector number, size in bytes, and the number of fragments the file is divided into. Alternatively, if you are working with one of the copies of the FAT, Object Info shows you information unique to the FAT.

If you are working with a file, you can display a map of the file by selecting Map of Object from the Info pull-down menu. The map shows all the clusters in the data area on the disk, and it highlights the clusters occupied by the current file. The display lets you see how the file is fragmented and graphically depicts how much free space remains on the disk. Note that you cannot use Map Of Object if you are working with sectors.

To display information about the current drive, choose Drive Info from the Info pull-down menu. The screen reports the disk drive name and size, as well as logical information such as the number of bytes per sector and sectors per cluster, the total number of clusters, and the FAT type. The listed physical information includes the drive number, number of heads, number of tracks, and the number of sectors per track.

CHOOSING A VIEW

You can choose several different ways to display this disk information, but if Auto View (in the Configuration option of the Tools menu) is turned on, Disk Editor automatically selects the best view for the object you are working with. If you turn off Auto View, Disk Editor always uses the Hex Viewer.

However, if you want to see what an object looks like using another view, you can select another viewer from the View pulldown menu. Note that all the viewers have shortcut keystrokes. For example to switch to the Hex Viewer, press F2. You can edit the information shown on the screen in all the viewers except the Text Viewer. To edit in text mode, change to the Hex Viewer, and edit in the text portion of the display at the right side of the screen.

HEX VIEWER

Select As Hex from the View pull-down menu to use the Hex Viewer, or press F2 from the main Disk Editor screen. You can use the Hex Viewer to look at many different kinds of files, including EXE files, files made by your word processor, or files made by your spreadsheet. Figure 4.12 shows a portion of the Norton Utilities READ.ME file displayed in the Hex Viewer. The leftmost column of figures on the screen shows the locations of the data in terms of a byte count offset (in hexadecimal) from the beginning of the file. The central area of the display shows the data in the file as two-digit hex numbers. Each line displays 16 bytes of information. On the right side of the display, these same 16 bytes are shown in ASCII form.

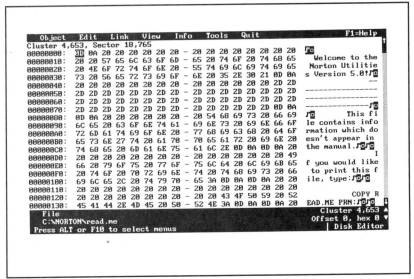

Figure 4.12: The READ.ME file from the Norton Utilities displayed in the Hex Vewer

From the display of the READ.ME text file it is easy to see the correspondence between the hex part and the ASCII part of the display. For example, 20H is a space character, 4EH is *N*, 6FH is *o*, 72H is *r*, 74H is *t*, 6FH again is *o*, and 6EH is a lowercase *n*: all of which spells *Norton*. This correspondence is not as obvious when you examine an EXE file in the Hex Viewer; in fact, some of the data in the file will be completely unreadable. This is because a program file is a *binary file,* not ASCII (text), and contains statements that were never intended to be read as text. These nondisplayable characters are shown in the text portion of this screen as dots. Cluster and sector boundaries are represented by a line that contains only the cluster and sector numbers. The byte offset of the cursor is shown in both decimal and hex at the bottom right of the display.

Use the following keys to move through the display: the up and down arrow keys move a line at a time; the PgUp and PgDn keys move a screenful at a time; Ctrl-PgUp moves to the previous sector; Ctrl-PgDn moves to the next sector; the Home key places the cursor directly at the beginning of the file; and the End key moves the cursor to the end of the last cluster.

With a mouse, moving through the file is even easier. Simply click on the scroll bar with the mouse at the place in the file you want to jump to, and click at the location on the screen that you want to edit.

Both the hex and text parts of this display have their own cursor; you can tell the active cursor because it blinks. Each cursor edits inside its own part of the display. Press the Tab key or click the mouse to change to the other cursor. When the active cursor is in the hex part of the display, you can edit the file by entering hexadecimal values. In the text part of the display, you merely type a character from the keyboard. To enter special characters, hold down the Alt key and enter the corresponding ASCII decimal code using the numeric keypad.

When you make changes to the file, the other half of the display is updated automatically. Any changes you make in the hex portion of the screen are automatically displayed in the text area, and vice versa. Any changes you make are highlighted in both the hex and the text parts of the screen. To cancel a change, press the Backspace key, or select Undo from the Edit pull-down menu. Undo, or Ctrl-U, restores the file to its original condition one byte at a time. In order to restore the file to its original condition in one key-stroke, choose Discard Changes from the Edit pull-down menu. A window opens and gives you the choice of either Discarding or Reviewing your changes. If you select Discard, your changes are removed; if you select Review, you can reexamine your changes before you decide their fate.

The cursor only blinks if you are using Disk Editor in write mode; both cursors are solid in read-only mode.

Remember, you must change the configuration of Disk Editor from Read-only mode to Write-mode before you can make changes.

TEXT VIEWER

Select As Text from the View pull-down menu, or press F3, to look at straightforward ASCII files such as batch files, the CONFIG.SYS, file or the Microsoft Windows configuration file, WIN.INI. Figure 4.13 shows the READ.ME file of the Norton Utilities as displayed in the Text Viewer.

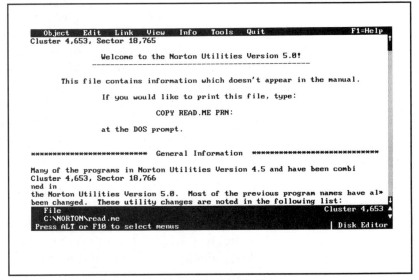

Figure 4.13: The Norton Utilities READ.ME file

You can only look at a file with the Text Viewer; to edit a text file, use the text part of the Hex Viewer.

The text in the file is shown on the screen, and the cluster and sector boundaries are highlighted.

DIRECTORY VIEWER

Use the Directory Viewer to examine directories. Select As Directory from the View pull-down menu, or press F4 from the main Disk Editor screen. Figure 4.14 shows the Norton Utilities directory on my hard disk.

Each line on the screen displays information for one entry, either a file or a subdirectory, including name and extension, size in bytes, file creation date and time, starting cluster number, and attributes. Cluster and sector boundaries are highlighted and displayed on a separate line.

Unused entries are labeled *Unused Directory Entry,* and deleted entries all begin with the Greek lowercase sigma character, E5H. If you look at an object other than a directory with the Directory Viewer, you may see entries described as *Invalid Directory Entries.* This might happen, for example, if you look at a boot record with the Directory Viewer.

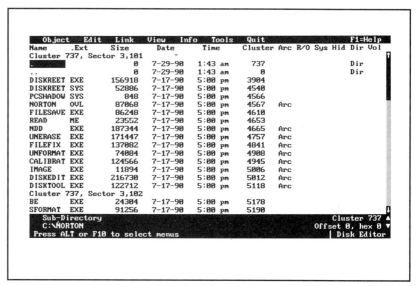

Figure 4.14: The Norton Utilities directory displayed in the Directory Viewer

With the mouse you can click on the entry you want to change, and then use the scroll bars to move through the directory listing.

From the keyboard, press the Tab key to move from field to field, the left and right arrow keys to move inside the field, and the up and down arrow keys to move between lines. The Home key moves to the first entry, and the End key moves to the last entry in the current cluster. Pg Up and Pg Dn keys move one screenful at a time, and the + and − keys on the numeric keypad move one sector at a time. Cluster and sector boundaries are clearly marked as highlighted characters.

You can edit the directory data in this viewer, but your changes cannot exceed the DOS limits for entries; file names, for example, cannot exceed 8 characters with a 3-character extension. The DISKEDIT program checks most of the entries on the Directory Viewer screen for validity. This means you cannot enter an invalid character into a file name or create an illegal date or time.

To work with the attribute fields, move the cursor to the appropriate column and toggle the entry on or off by pressing the spacebar. To change settings for a *group* of files, it is much more efficient to use the Set Attributes or Set Date/Time options from the Tools pull-down menu. This is described in the section "Using the Tools Menu."

Be careful when you edit directory entries: If you make a mistake, DOS might not be able to access the file correctly, and you will lose the file. Always make a backup before you edit a directory entry. Then you can restore the directory entry if your editing does not produce the expected results.

FAT VIEWER

Select As FAT from the View pull-down menu to examine an object with the FAT Viewer, or press F5 from the main Disk Editor screen. Figure 4.15 shows the first copy of the FAT from a 65MB hard disk displayed in the FAT Viewer.

```
 Object   Edit   Link   View   Info   Tools   Quit                  F1=Help
Sector 1
                     »  3        »   4   »    5   »    6   »    7   »    8
  »    9   »   18   »   11   »   12   » <EOF>     14       15       16
      17       18       19       28       21       22       23       24
      25       26       27    <EOF>       29       38       31       32
      33       34       35       36       37       38       39       48
   <EOF>    <EOF>       43       44       45       46       47       48
      49       58       51       52       53       54    <EOF>    <EOF>
      57       58    <EOF>    <EOF>       61       62       63       64
   <EOF>       66       67       68       69       78       71       72
      73       74       75       76       77       78       79       88
   <EOF>    <EOF>       83       84       85       86       87       88
      89       98       91       92       93       94       95       96
      97       98       99    <EOF>      101      102      103      104
   <EOF>      186      107    <EOF>      109      110      111      112
     113    <EOF>      115      116      117      118      119      128
     121    <EOF>      123      124    <EOF>      126      127      128
   <EOF>      130      131      132      133      134    <EOF>    <EOF>
     137      138      139    <EOF>      141    <EOF>      143      144
     145      146      147      148      149      158      151      152
     153      154      155      156      157      158      159      168
 FAT (1st Copy)                                               Sector 1 ▲
 C:\NORTON                                              Cluster 2, hex 2 ▼
 Press ALT or F18 to select menus                         | Disk Editor
```

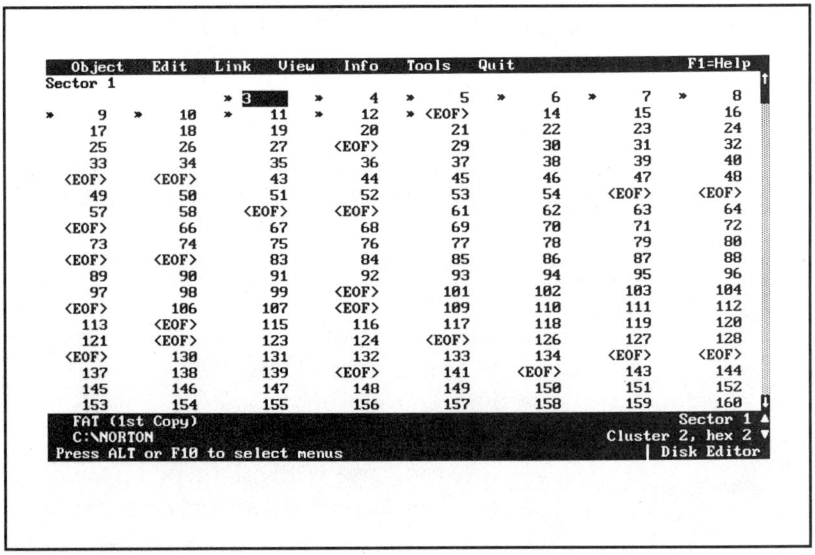

Figure 4.15: The first copy of the FAT from a large hard disk displayed in the FAT Viewer

Each entry on the screen represents one FAT entry and contains one of the following:

0	Unused cluster
number	Next cluster in the file chain
<BAD>	Bad cluster
<EOF>	End of file or last cluster in the file chain

If the Quick Move configuration option (in the Tools menu) is off, all the clusters in the current file chain (the file the cursor is now on) are shown as highlighted numbers. The status line at the bottom of the screen shows which copy of the FAT you are viewing, the full path name of the current cluster chain, the sector number (as a decimal number), and the cluster number (in both decimal and hex).

You can edit in this viewer by overtyping the entry at the highlighted cursor. Type an E to enter <EOF>, and type B to enter <BAD>.

Never try to edit the FAT unless you are confident that you know what you are doing. If you make a mistake, DOS might not be able to access any of your files—ever again. If you are not careful, you can create cross-linked clusters in which the same cluster appears in the cluster chains of two separate files; this might result in your losing the data contained in the original file.

PARTITION TABLE VIEWER

Select As Partition Table from the View pull-down menu, or press F6, to view an object as a partition table. Figure 4.16 shows a partition table from a large hard disk. Each line represents one of the four possible partition tables on a hard disk.

The System entry describes the operating system that owns the partition. Common entries for this column are:

Floppy disks do not have partition tables because they cannot be partitioned between different operating systems.

DOS-12   DOS with a 12-bit FAT

DOS-16	DOS with a 16-bit FAT
EXTEND	Extended DOS partition
BIGDOS	A partition larger than 32MB. DOS 4.0 and Compaq DOS both support disks larger than 32MB
HPFS	OS/2 High Performance File System
NOVELL	A Novell network partition
Unused	An unused entry in the partition table
?	An unrecognized entry in the partition table

Other, less common entries might include XENIX, PC/IX, 386-ix, or BBT from the various versions of UNIX that run on the PC, DM for a Disk Manager partition, or SPEED for a Speed-Stor partition.

The **Boot** column describes which of the several partitions is the bootable partition. Only one should contain the word

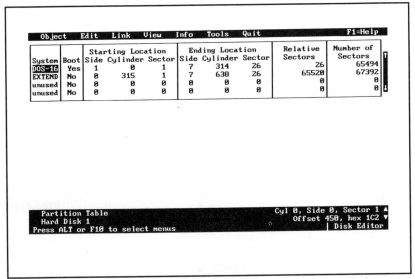

Figure 4.16: A Partition Table displayed in the Partition Table Viewer

BOOT. The Starting Location and Ending Location columns show the physical dimensions of each of the partitions on the disk. The Relative Sectors column shows the starting sector number for each of the partitions, and the last column, Number of Sectors, shows the total number of sectors in each of the partitions.

Once again, do not edit the partition table unless you are certain that you know what you are doing. You could make your hard disk completely inaccessible. The best way to change data in the partition table is to use the DOS command designed for this purpose—FDISK.

BOOT RECORD VIEWER

Choose As Boot Record from the View pull-down menu, or press F7 in the main Disk Editor screen to examine an object with the Boot Record Viewer. Figure 4.17 shows the boot record display for a hard disk.

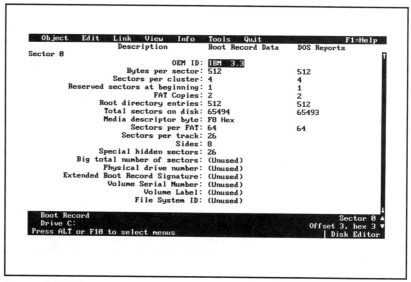

Figure 4.17: The boot record of a hard disk displayed in the Boot Record Viewer

Note in Figure 4.17 that Disk Editor shows data from the boot record in a format that is easy to understand. The contents of the boot record have changed as DOS has changed, so you might see some of the entries in the viewer labeled as *(Unused)*. In Figure 4.17, the hard disk was formatted with DOS 3.3; because the last 6 entries were added when DOS 4 was released, these entries are shown as unused for this disk.

Be careful when you are editing the boot record. If you make a mistake, you may make it impossible for DOS to boot your disk.

WORKING WITH DISK EDITOR WINDOWS

If you can't make sense of a display and you don't know what kind of object you are looking at, try changing to a different viewer. Viewing the data in its proper format will make the information easier to understand.

After you have chosen Split Window, the menu displays the Unsplit Window option in its place.

Until now you have been working with only one Disk Editor window. Disk Editor lets you open a second window if you select Split Window from the View pull-down menu. When you choose this option, the screen displays two copies of the same object, but only one of the windows is active. You can switch between windows easily by selecting Switch Windows from the View pull-down menu, or by pressing Shift-F8. If you are using a mouse, merely click on a window to make it active. Figure 4.18 shows the FAT Viewer displaying two FATs on the screen at the same time.

The Grow Window (Shift-F6) and Shrink Window (Shift-F7) options from the View pull-down menu let you change the sizes of the two windows, one line at a time. With the mouse, changing window size is even easier: Simply drag the top status bar to the new position, and release the mouse button. The windows are rearranged on the screen immediately.

If you want to view one object and edit another, or edit both, you can load a different object into the second window. Simply select the active window, and use the selections in the Object pull-down menu to choose another object.

You can also compare the data contained in two windows by using the Compare Windows selection from the Tools pull-down menu. For example, to compare the two copies of the FAT to see if they are identical, load the 1st Copy of the FAT into the top window and the 2nd copy of the FAT into the bottom window.

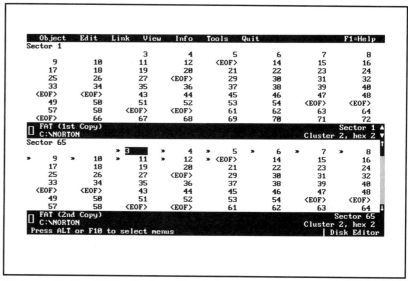

Figure 4.18: Two FATs displayed in different windows using the FAT
Viewer

Position the cursor at the byte where you want the comparison
to start, and select Compare Windows from the Tools pull-down
menu. If the comparison stops with a cluster highlighted, the
two copies of the FAT do not match beyond that point.

To return to a single window display, select Unsplit Window
from the View pull-down menu, or press Shift-F5 from the main
screen.

LINKING TO RELATED OBJECTS

Disk Editor lets you take advantage of what it calls *links* to
change to a related object very quickly. The current object
determines which links are available:

- File. If the current object is a file, you can link to the
current FAT entry or directory entry.

- Directory. If the current (highlighted) object is a directory, you can link to the current FAT entry or to the
current file.

- Cluster Chain. If the current object is a cluster chain, you can link to the first copy of the FAT. The FAT entry (or entries) related to the current cluster chain is highlighted in another color.

- Partition. If the current object is a partition table, you can link to the related boot record.

Using the Window option from the Link pull-down menu is much more powerful than the simple links described above. To activate the option, you must use two windows, one of which must be displaying a FAT or directory. Window establishes a dynamic link between the two windows, so that if you move the cursor in the window that contains a directory or FAT, the re-lated file appears in the other window. As you move the cursor in one window, the information shown in the other window changes accordingly.

USING THE TOOLS MENU

Disk Editor contains a powerful set of tools to help you work with your chosen objects. You can search for text, recalculate partition information, convert between decimal and hexa-decimal, and use the ASCII look-up table.

USING FIND

To find text in a file, first choose an object, and then select Find from the Tools pull-down menu, or press Ctrl-S. For ex-ample, use the Directory and File selections in the Object pull-down menu to specify the NORTON.EXE file as the object. Now, select Find from the Tools pull-down menu to display the Enter Search Text window shown in Figure 4.19.

For this example, enter:

Norton

into the upper ASCII box. As you enter the search string, the characters are converted to hexadecimal values and displayed in the lower box. Move the cursor to the Find box and press Enter, or click on the box with the mouse. When the search text is located it is highlighted in the Hex Viewer. The highlight shows both the hex and text versions of the search string. To see if there are other occurrences of this text in the file, press Ctrl-G, or select Find Again from the Tools pull-down menu. Each occurrence of the search string is highlighted until the program can no longer find a match. A window then appears in the center of the screen with the message *No More Matches Found*.

USING WRITE TO

You can use the Write To option to make a backup copy of an object onto a floppy disk before you start editing. If you make a mistake, you can reload this copy.

Sometimes you need to write the object you have been editing to a new location on the disk, rather than writing it back into its original location. Select Write To from the Tools pull-down

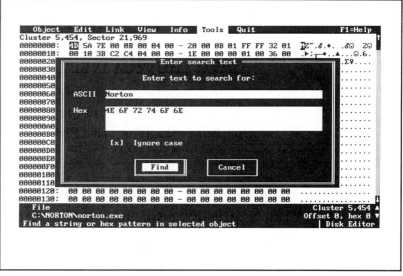

Figure 4.19: Enter the text you want to search for in the Enter Search Text window

menu, and you will see the Write window shown in Figure 4.20. The window lets you write the current object to a file, to specific clusters, to specific logical sectors, or to a set of physical sectors. After you make your choice from this list, Disk Editor asks for a path and file name, or the starting cluster number, sector, or physical sector number. If you choose sectors, another window will display the sector usage on the target drive so that you can see the main elements of the disk system. Then the file is written to the disk.

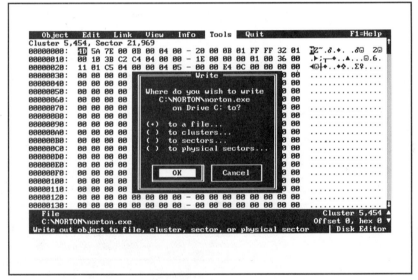

Figure 4.20: The Write window lets you specify where you want to write the current object

RECALCULATE PARTITION

If you are working with a partition table, you can use Recalculate Partition from the Tools pull-down menu to change it. Enter a new Starting Location and Ending Location, and Recalculate Partition will determine the values for Relative Sectors and Number of Sectors. Remember to zero out the Relative Sectors and the Number of Sectors before you start; if you forget, a window will open to prompt you to do so.

CONVERTING FROM DECIMAL TO HEX

Disk Editor contains a small hexadecimal to decimal converter. Select Hex Converter from the Tools pull-down menu to display the Converter window shown in Figure 4.21.

You can make conversions in three different ways. You can enter the hex number into the Hex box; you can move the cursor to the Decimal box, and enter your number in decimal; or you can move to the Character box, and enter the character directly. As you enter your number, the converted result also appears in the other boxes. For example, move the cursor to the Decimal box and enter:

69

The Hex display immediately changes to 45, and the letter E appears in the Character box. Alternatively, enter a character in the Character box, and watch the corresponding numbers appear in the other boxes. To enter a character from the Extended

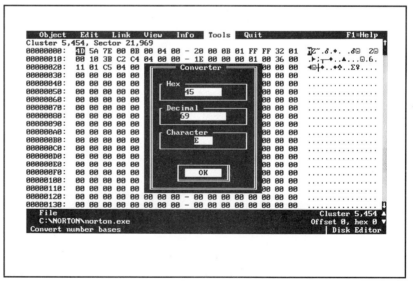

Figure 4.21: The Hex Converter converts values from hexadecimal to decimal, and vice versa

ASCII set, hold down the Alt key and use the numeric keypad to enter the ASCII decimal equivalent of the character. For example, if you hold down the Alt key and type:

254

you will see FE in the Hex box, 254 in the Decimal box, and the small square character in the Character box.

USING THE ASCII TABLE

To find the ASCII decimal equivalent of the Extended ASCII characters, select the ASCII Table option from the Tools pulldown menu. This displays the screen shown in Figure 4.22.

To find the value of a character, simply type it from the keyboard. Press f and the cursor will move to the line showing decimal 102, hex 66, and the f character. If you next press uppercase F, the decimal equivalent is 70, and the hex number is 46.

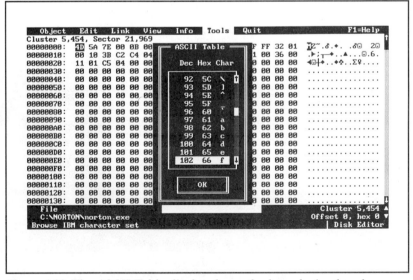

Figure 4.22: The ASCII Table display shows the hexadecimal and decimal equivalents of all the printable characters

USING THE CLIPBOARD TO MAKE CHANGES

Disk Editor contains a 4K Clipboard that you can use with commands from the Edit pull-down menu. If Disk Editor is configured as Read-Only, Mark is the only option available from the Edit pull-down menu.

Use the Mark option from the Edit pull-down menu to select a block of information to work with. For example, you might mark part of a file to copy it to the Clipboard, or mark a set of files in a directory listing so you can change their file attributes and their creation date and time.

For example, to change the file attributes of a group of files, first select the Norton directory from the Objects pull-down menu, and then select Mark from the Edit menu. Use the up and down arrow keys to highlight the block of files you want to work with, and then select Set Attributes from the Tools pull-down menu. The Change Attributes window opens so that you can set or clear the appropriate file attributes. When you have made your choices, select (or click on) the OK box. Next, choose Set Date/Time from the Tools pull-down menu. The Set Date/Time window opens showing the current date and time. Choose the current time, or move the highlight to the time box and enter your own time. Select the file date in the same way. Select OK when you have finished.

Marking with the mouse is even easier. Position the mouse cursor at the beginning of the section you want to mark, hold down the mouse button, and drag the mouse to the end of the section. The marked section is highlighted as you move the mouse.

You can also use Mark in the opposite sense—to unmark a previously marked block.

After you have marked a section of a file, use the Copy option (Ctrl-C) to copy the marked block onto the Clipboard. Remember that the Clipboard can hold only one block of text at at time—the contents of the Clipboard are overwritten each time you copy new text to the Clipboard.

After you have copied something onto the Clipboard, you can select the Clipboard as an Object using the Object pull- down menu. Using this option, you can edit the text in the Clipboard buffer as though it were a file.

The Paste Over option (Ctrl-V) writes the contents of the clipboard at the current cursor location. This information from the Clipboard overwrites all data in the original locations, and any changed bytes are highlighted.

Undo (Ctrl-U) restores the file to its original state *before* the Paste Over command was used.

The Fill option writes a specific character over a marked block of any size. When you select Fill from the Edit pull-down menu, a window opens and lets you choose the fill character. You can specify the fill character in decimal or hex, or as a character.

When all your editing changes are complete, select Write Changes (Ctrl-W) from the Edit pull-down menu to write your changes to the disk. Be sure your work is correct—after you use Write Changes, all the original text and values disappear, and changes cannot be undone. Write Changes is final.

If you are unsure about the changes you have made, review them carefully. If you have any doubts at all, use Discard Changes from the Edit menu to return the object to its original state.

USING THE DOS SHELL

If you need to use a DOS command, you can choose the Shell to DOS option from the Quit pull-down menu to invoke a second command processor from within Disk Editor. Do not load any terminate-and-stay-resident programs from this shell, however, or you might not be able to return to the Disk Editor. When you have finished using DOS, type:

EXIT

to return to the Disk Editor.

LEAVING DISK EDITOR

To leave the Disk Editor, select Quit Disk Editor from the Quit pull-down menu, or type Ctrl-Q. You can also use the Esc key to exit from most windows and options in Disk Editor. Note that the Disk Editor will not let you exit if you still have some unfinished editing. If you have not saved all your changes, you will see a message warning you of that fact. You must save or discard your changes before you can exit the Disk Editor.

USING DISK EDITOR FROM THE DOS COMMAND LINE

You can also use Disk Editor directly from the DOS command line. To run the program in maintenance mode, in other words, to bypass DOS and look at drive C directly, type:

DISKEDIT C: /M

If you use Zenith DOS, your computer may list drive information in the BIOS for drives that are not present on your computer. Start Disk Editor with the /X switch to exclude these disks from processing. For example, to exclude drive E, type:

DISKEDIT /X:E

Table 4.1 contains a list of all the shortcut keys and key combinations that you can use with Disk Editor. They are arranged according to the entries in each pull-down menu.

Table 4.1: Summary of All the Shortcut Keys Used in Disk Editor

KEY	FUNCTION
OBJECT PULL-DOWN MENU	
Alt-O	Select Object menu
Alt-D	Select a drive
Alt-R	Select a directory
Alt-F	Select a file
Alt-C	Select a cluster
Alt-S	Select a sector by number
Alt-P	Select a physical sector
Alt-A	Select the partition table
Alt-B	Select the boot record
Alt-F1	Select the first copy of the FAT
Alt-F2	Select the second copy of the FAT
EDIT PULL-DOWN MENU	
Alt-E	Select Edit menu
Ctrl-U	Undo changes
Ctrl-B	Mark a block
Ctrl-C	Copy to the Clipboard
Ctrl-V	Paste from the Clipboard
Ctrl-W	Write changes to disk
LINK PULL-DOWN MENU	
Alt-L	Select Link menu
Ctrl-F	Link to related file data
Ctrl-D	Link to related directory entry
Ctrl-T	Link to related FAT chain

Table 4.1: Summary of All the Shortcut Keys Used in Disk Editor (continued)

KEY	FUNCTION
VIEW PULL-DOWN MENU	
Alt-V	Select View menu
F2	Select Hex viewer
F3	Select Text viewer
F4	Select Directory viewer
F5	Select FAT viewer
F6	Select Partition Table viewer
F7	Select Boot Record viewer
Shift-F5	Split window
Shift-F6	Grow window
Shift-F7	Shrink window
Shift-F8	Switch windows
INFO PULL-DOWN MENU	
Alt-I	Select Info menu
Alt-T	Select Tools menu
Ctrl-S	Search for text or data
Ctrl-G	Find again
QUIT PULL-DOWN MENU	
Alt-Q	Select Quit menu
Ctrl-Q	Quit Disk Editor

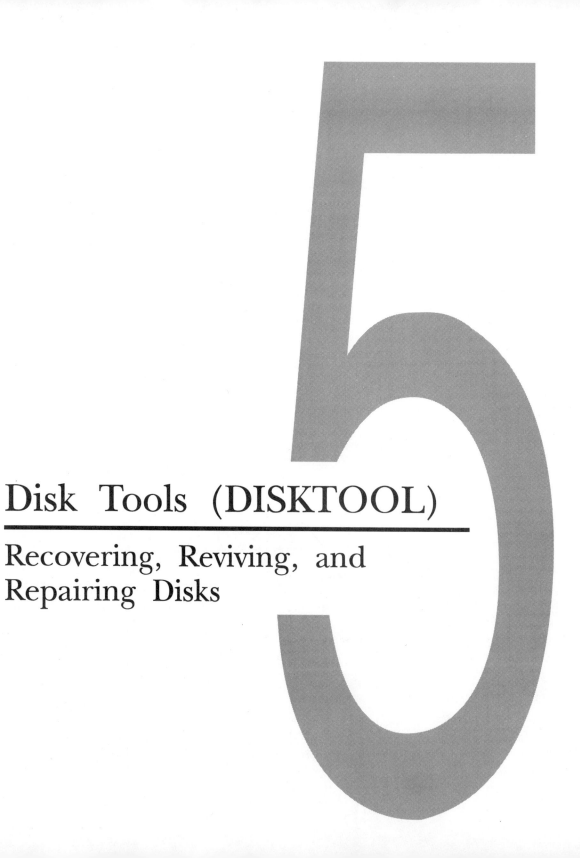

Disk Tools (DISKTOOL)

Recovering, Reviving, and Repairing Disks

CHAPTER **5**

DISK TOOLS IS A SET OF SIX SMALL UTILITY PROGRAMS that facilitate the recovery of data from disks. This program performs the following operations:

- Make a Disk Bootable
- Recover from DOS's RECOVER Command
- Revive a Defective Diskette
- Mark a Cluster
- Create a Rescue Disk
- Restore a Rescue Disk

All of these selections are available from the main Disk Tools screen. To run the program, select Disk Tools from main menu in the NORTON program, or type:

DISKTOOL

from the DOS command line. The Disk Tools main menu is shown in Figure 5.1. Use the arrow keys to make your choice and press Enter, or click on **Proceed** to run the program.

MAKING A DISK BOOTABLE

This selection does whatever is needed to make a disk bootable, including modifying the partition table if necessary—so use it with care.

First, select the disk you want to make bootable from the list of available disks. If the disk is a floppy disk, insert the disk into the drive. Disk Tools then copies the system files from your hard

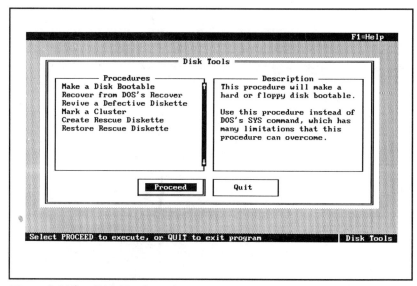

Figure 5.1: The Disk Tools main menu screen

disk onto the floppy disk. When this process is complete, a window opens to tell you that the specified disk is now bootable.

RECOVERING FROM THE DOS RECOVER COMMAND

You can use the DOS RECOVER command to try to recover data from a file after DOS reports a "bad sector" error message. Although you might recover some information from the file, the data contained in the bad sectors will be lost. If you use RECOVER on a disk that has bad sectors in the directory, the program gives each recovered file the following name:

FILE*nnnn*.REC

in which *nnnn* represents the order in which the files were recovered. You will then have to rename each generic FILE*nnnn*.REC file on the disk by looking at the contents of each file and specifying a more meaningful name. You will also have to recreate the disk's directory structure. Note that RECOVER does not restore deleted files. Disk Tools lets you restore your disk to the state it was in before you ran RECOVER. You can also use this option instead of the DOS RECOVER command.

After you select the disk you want to work with, a warning screen appears to remind you that you should only use this procedure if:

- You have already run the DOS RECOVER command

  or

- Your root directory has been destroyed

A final warning screen reminds you that all files on the drive will be lost and asks if you still want to continue. Select **Yes** to continue. The program displays a disk map that shows you the progress made in the recovery, as shown in Figure 5.2.

At the end of this process, Disk Tools checks for cross-linked files on the disk. Directories are renamed DIR0000, DIR0001,

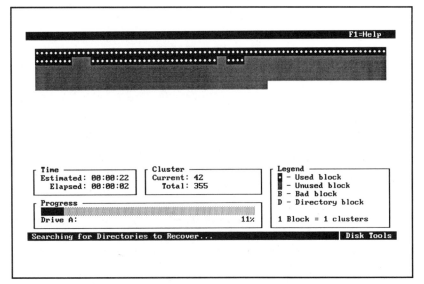

Figure 5.2: The progress screen from the Disk Tool option: Recover
from DOS's RECOVER

and so on, and files in the root directory are renamed
FILE0000, FILE0001, and so on. To rename your directories use
the Norton Change Directory program described in Chapter 20.
You can use the DOS RENAME command to rename your files.

REVIVING A DEFECTIVE DISKETTE

This option revives a floppy disk by reformatting it. The
original data will not be lost during this reformat—it will remain
on the disk.

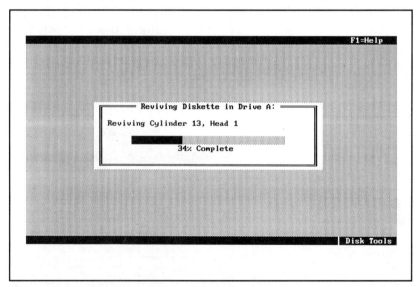

As a precaution,
run the Norton
Disk Doctor on any
floppy disk you must
revive—just to be sure
the disk is not damaged.

After you choose the floppy disk you want to revive, the program displays the screen shown in Figure 5.3. This screen shows
the progress being made as an analog display; it also shows the
percentage of the task completed.

Figure 5.3: The Reviving a Floppy Diskette display shows the progress of
the operation

MARKING A CLUSTER

If you find a bad cluster that should not be used for a file or a directory, you can mark it as bad with the Mark a Cluster option. You can also reverse the process and mark a bad cluster as good. First, select the disk that you want to work with. The Mark Cluster display lists the valid cluster numbers for the disk you have chosen and refuses to accept cluster numbers outside this range. Enter the cluster number, and then choose between **Good** and **Bad**. Choose **Good** only if the cluster was previously marked as bad, but now you want to make the cluster available for use by DOS. Choose **Bad** if the cluster is displayed as good, but now you want to prevent DOS from using it.

CREATING A RESCUE DISKETTE

Creating a "rescue disk" lets you store vital information from your hard disk on a floppy disk that you can keep in a safe place in the event of an accident. The information stored on a rescue diskette includes:

- Partition table information
- Boot record information
- CMOS configuration information

Store the rescue information on a floppy disk, not on a hard disk.

The Create Rescue Diskette screen is shown in Figure 5.4. From the list of available floppy disks, choose the disk to which you want to write the rescue information. After Disk Tools writes all the information to the disk, remove the disk and store it in a safe place. This information is stored in three files— PARTINFO.DAT, BOOTINFO.DAT, and CMOSINFO.DAT. If you change your setup information by adding an additional floppy disk, or if you upgrade to a new version of DOS, remember

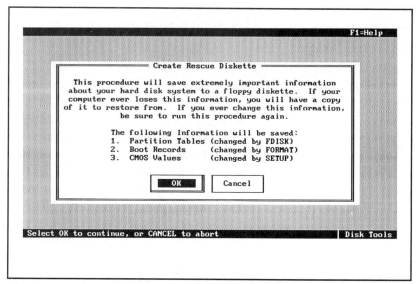

Figure 5.4: The Create Rescue Diskette screen

to run Create Rescue Diskette again to keep your vital information current.

RESTORING A RESCUE DISKETTE

This selection lets you reload vital configuration information from the rescue floppy disk in the event that your hard disk drive is damaged. It is the reverse process of creating a rescue diskette. The Restore System from Rescue Diskette screen is shown in Figure 5.5. Select or click on Yes to restore the CMOS, Partition Table, and Boot Record information onto your hard disk system.

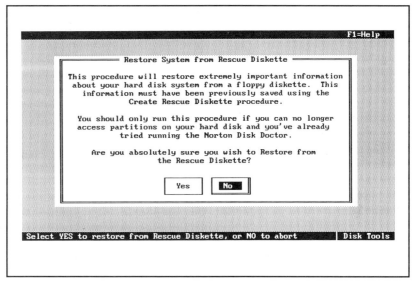

Figure 5.5: The Restore System from Rescue Diskette screen

File Fix (FILEFIX)

Repairing 1-2-3, Symphony,
and dBASE Files

CHAPTER *6*

THE FILE FIX PROGRAM FINDS AND FIXES PROBLEMS IN Lotus 1-2-3, Symphony, and dBASE data files, recovering as much data as possible from the damaged file. File Fix writes this information into a new file. The original damaged file is always left intact so that you can run File Fix again using different settings. File Fix can often repair data files automatically, although occasionally the program may need your help with complex recovery operations involving dBASE file headers. File Fix can also reconstruct data files that have been collapsed or zapped by the dBASE ZAP command.

> File Fix does not include pull-down menus.

To run the program from the NORTON program main menu, select File Fix; from the DOS command line, type:

FILEFIX

The opening screen is shown in Figure 6.1. Select the type of file you want to repair from the three options on the screen.

> Use the UnErase program first if you want to recover erased files; then run File Fix as the second stage of the recovery process. See Chapter 9 for details about UnErase.

You can choose from the following selections:

- 1-2-3. Choose 1-2-3 if you use Lotus 1-2-3 (Version 1, 1A, or 2), Twin, or another program that creates Lotus-compatible files.

- Symphony. Choose Symphony if you use Lotus Symphony (Version 1.0 or 1.1).

- dBASE. Choose dBASE if you use dBASE (III, III+, or IV), FoxBase, Clipper, or any other program that creates dBASE-compatible files.

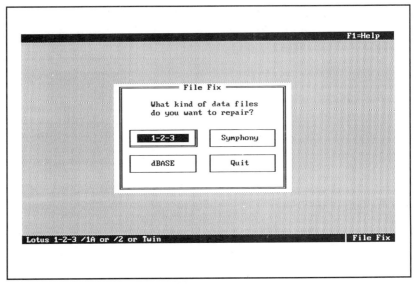

Figure 6.1: The opening File Fix screen lets you choose the file type to
work with

REPAIRING SPREADSHEET FILES

Select 1-2-3 or Symphony if you want to repair a spreadsheet
file. In the following example, we will use a Lotus 1-2-3 file called
GWSCREEN.WK1.

Select the 1-2-3 box and press Enter, or click on the box with
the mouse. Next, you will see the Choose File to Repair screen
as shown in Figure 6.2.

Use the Tab key to move the cursor around the display; if
necessary, choose a different drive or directory. File Fix finds
the files it can repair by searching for the appropriate file name
extension. Enter a file name or select one from the list in the
File list. Figure 6.3 shows the Repair Lotus 1-2-3 File screen.
After you choose the repair mode from this screen, File Fix will

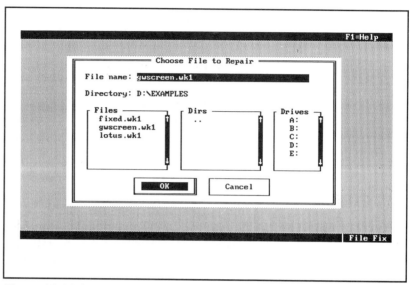

Figure 6.2: Make your selection in the Choose File to Repair screen

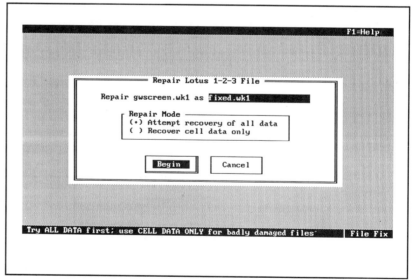

Figure 6.3: The Repair Lotus 1-2-3 File screen

repair GWSCREEN.WK1 and write the recovered information into a file called FIXED.WK1. Select one of the following modes:

- **Attempt Recovery of All Data.** Always try this selection first. It usually recovers the largest amount of data, including information about the spreadsheet cell ranges, column widths, and headers and footers.

- **Recover Cell Data Only.** Use this mode if the **Attempt Recovery of All Data** operation fails; you can usually recover the cell data from the spreadsheet.

The program first checks the file; then it opens a window that reports the percentage of the file that has been corrected. Finally, File Fix displays a window showing the repair statistics. Figure 6.4 shows this screen for the GWSCREEN.WK1 file. The display in Figure 6.4 shows that 5,551 bytes were recovered and that 0 bytes were discarded. This means that the GWSCREEN.WK1 file

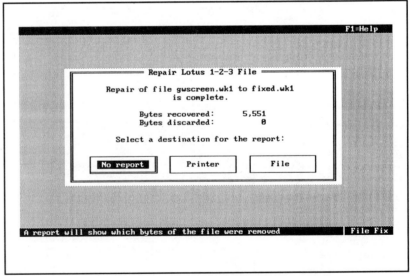

Figure 6.4: The Repair Lotus 1-2-3 display shows the number of bytes recovered

has been completely recovered. Check the repaired file yourself by trying to load the file into the appropriate application program—Lotus 1-2-3 or Symphony.

If you want to see the report on the recovery operation, select **Printer** or **File**. By default, **File** stores the report in a file called FIXED.RPT; however, you can enter another file name if you want. The report contains the details of the recovery operation, as well as a list of all the cells and cell types in the spreadsheet. Figure 6.5 shows the beginning of the report about the GWSCREEN.WK1 file after it was recovered. Choose **No Report** if you don't want to see a report, or if there were no errors.

If the attempt to recover all the data was unsuccessful, select the second mode on the Repair Lotus File screen, **Recover Cell Data Only**. This time, enter a different file name for the repaired file. Even if both rescue operations are not completely successful, you might be able to combine the results and reconstruct the data by hand.

```
                    File Fix Lotus 1-2-3 Repair
                           Norton Utilities
                    Friday, June 14, 1991 11:57 pm

        ************************************************
        *   Report for File D:\EXAMPLES\gwscreen.wk1   *
        ************************************************

                       Repair mode: All data
                       Corrected file: fixed.wk1


            Numeric cells recovered:          18
              Label cells recovered:          34
            Formula cells recovered:          62
              Blank cells recovered:           0
                                        -----------
                 Total cells recovered:       114


                    Recovered bytes:       5,551
                  Unrecovered bytes:           0
               Unrecovered sections:           0
```

Figure 6.5: Part of the FIXED.RPT report on the GWSCREEN.WK1 file after its recovery

REPAIRING DBASE FILES

To repair a dBASE file, select dBASE from the main File Fix menu. Then select the file you want to work with from the selections on the Choose File to Repair screen, as shown in Figure 6.6.

File Fix can recover files that have been deleted by the dBASE ZAP command. ZAP permanently removes all the records from an active database, but it leaves the database structure intact. It has the same effect as the dBASE commands DELETE ALL followed by PACK, but it is much faster. ZAP removes records whether they were previously marked for deletion or not.

To recover a dBASE file, you have a choice of the following three Repair Modes:

- **Fully Automatic.** If your files are not badly corrupted, this option is probably all you need to use. It is a completely hands-off repair operation: File Fix examines the file, extracts all the valid data, and writes that data to the fixed file.

If you turn on SET SAFETY, dBASE asks for permission before zapping all the records in a database.

You cannot recover a zapped file on a network, or on a drive set up by the DOS SUBST or ASSIGN command.

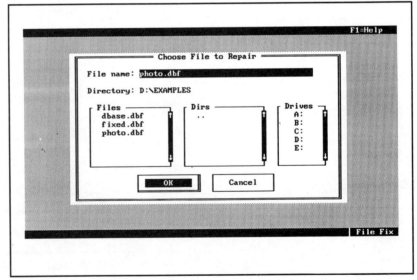

Figure 6.6: Select the file you want to repair from those shown in the Choose File to Repair screen

- Review Damaged Records. If the Fully Automatic recovery mode fails to recover essential records, try this selection. File Fix starts the recovery in automatic mode until it finds a damaged record. You can then view and manually repair the record yourself.

- Review All Records. This last mode let's you review every record before it is written to the fixed file. You can choose to accept, reject, or manually repair each of the records. If the data seems to be out of alignment, select Shift and then use the arrow keys or the mouse to realign the columns. At any point in the recovery, you can select Mode to change to another repair mode. Review All Records is more time consuming than the other modes, but it is essential for badly corrupted databases.

If you see the message:

Contents of Field Invalid

character data might be showing up in a numeric field. You may have to change this field or earlier fields in the file, or change the data itself.

Three other check boxes appear on the Repair dBASE File screen. These offer further options in the repair process:

- Use Clipper Field Limits. Only use this selection if the database was created by Clipper; otherwise, leave this selection off.

- Fix Shifted Data Automatically. This option is on by default. If you turn off this option, File Fix runs faster, but it doesn't check data alignment.

- Strict Character Checking. Turn on this option unless you are repairing a file that contains special graphics characters. Files created by dBASE do not contain these special characters.

After you have made your selections from this screen, move the highlight to the Begin box, or click on the box with the mouse. In this next example, we will work with the file PHOTO.DBF. In Figure 6.7, you can see that the recovery process has started and that PHOTO.DBF will be repaired as the file FIXED.DBF. In a dBASE file, the file header contains vital information concerning the layout of the rest of the file, including the version of dBASE that made the file, and the names, order, lengths, and types of the fields in the database file. The message on the screen in Figure 6.7 indicates that this file header is intact. Choose Review Fields to examine the database field definitions, or select Skip Review to continue with the automatic recovery process.

Figure 6.8 shows the final Repair dBASE File screen for the file PHOTO.DBF. There were 953 bytes of the file recovered, and no data was lost from the file. Choose Printer or File to generate a report of the repair of PHOTO.DBF, or choose No Report.

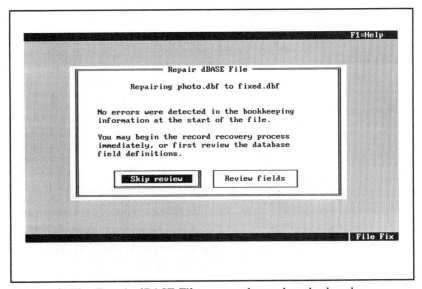

Figure 6.7: The Repair dBASE File screen shows that the header information is intact

REPAIRING A DAMAGED FILE HEADER

If the dBASE file header is damaged, File Fix asks for your help in reconstructing the data. The Repair dBASE File screen displays the message:

The bookkeeping information at the start of the file is severely damaged or missing.

Your assistance is required to reconstruct the database field definitions.

Select **Review Fields** to proceed with the recovery. The next screen shows the current data structure for the dBASE file, as well as the total number of records in this database. Select **Revise** to review the structure, or **Cancel** to return to the File Fix main menu. There are two ways that you can make a repair to the database structure:

- **Import.** If the dBASE file header is damaged, the easiest way to repair it is to import the header information

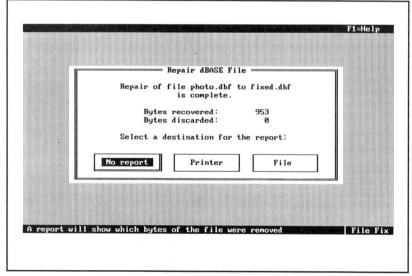

Figure 6.8: The Repair dBASE File screen indicates all the data was recovered from the file

from an undamaged file that shares the same database structure. You can use a backup version of the file for this, or even an earlier version with an identical structure. If you choose Import, enter the path name and the file name for the file you want to import, or move the cursor to the correct entry in the Files box in the Choose Import File window.

Use a database printout, if you have one, as an aid while you manually reconstruct the file structure.

- Edit. If you cannot import a header from an un-damaged file, choose Edit and make the corrections by hand. Editing the file consists of three steps:

  - **Find the start of the data**. Use the left and right arrow keys to move the data from left to right, or enter the position directly into the File Position box. Hold down the Ctrl key and press the right or left arrow keys to move though the data ten characters at a time. You might have to skip past some of the damaged data. Be sure that the first character of good data from the first field is aligned with the left side of the box. Also, be sure you are using real data and not one of the field names.

  - **Establish the size of the record**. For this part of the process, use the left and right arrows to increase or decrease the record size. Align the first character of data from the first field of every record with the left side of the box.

  - **Redefine the fields**. Finally, use the left and right arrow keys to increase or decrease the field size. Change from field to field with the up and down arrow keys. After you have aligned everything, you can edit the specific field names and their data types. Press the Ins key to insert new fields, the Del key to remove fields, and the spacebar to *tag* fields. After you have tagged a field, use the up and down arrows to move it to its new position.

AN EXAMPLE DBASE FILE REPAIR

Repairing a dBASE file is a rather complex process; the following example will help clarify the procedure. Let's assume that the file ADDRESS.DBF has a problem, and dBASE has refused to process the file. Start File Fix, choose the **dBASE** option, and enter the file name into the **File Name** box, or move the highlight to the **Files** box and select the file there. Choose **Fully Automatic** from the Repair dBASE File window, and select the **Begin** box or click on it with the mouse. The next window alerts you that the file header is damaged. Your first option is to review the fields in the ADDRESS.DBF file, as shown in Figure 6.9.

There are five fields, or different types of entries, in this file, and the number of each field is given in the first column. The next column lists the *field name,* which is often the name of the prompt you see on the screen as you are entering data into a new record. The *field type* is shown next. Entries here can include character, numeric, date, memo, or logical data. The last

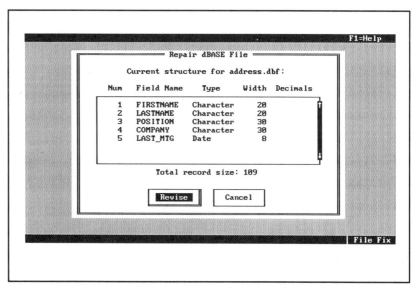

Figure 6.9: The current structure for the ADDRESS.DBF file is displayed field by field

two columns detail the width of each field in characters and the number of decimal places for any numeric entries.

If this structure is incorrect or badly damaged, you can choose to import a new header from another file, or you can edit the current one by hand.

Choose Import to open the Choose Import File window in which you can type in the name of the file you want to use, or you can select it from the list of files shown in the Files box.

If you choose to correct the data by hand, choose Edit, which displays the screen shown in Figure 6.10. Move the data in the central window with the left or right arrow keys until the first character of the word Michael is at the extreme left side of the window. This marks the beginning of the data in the record. You might have to move past some corrupted data first. Now move down a line in the window and perform the same operation for the next entry. Align the name Pamela with the left side of the window. Now, all the entries in this display are aligned vertically, and the data is starting to make some sense, as shown in Figure 6.11.

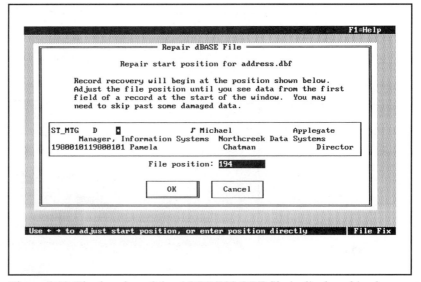

Figure 6.10: The header of the ADDRESS.DBF file is displayed in the central window

The next screen lets you change the sizes of the individual fields. Again, use the left and right arrow keys to adjust the data if necessary. If you make a mistake choosing the start of the data record, select the Restart box below the main window to redisplay the screen shown in Figure 6.11 so that you can establish a new start position. To work with the individual fields, select Edit, and you will see the display shown in Figure 6.12.

To edit a field, use the up and down arrow keys to highlight the field you want to work with, then select the Edit box or click on it with the mouse. The Edit window opens to the right of the original window and provides several options. You can edit the actual field name; specify the field type as character, numeric, logical, date, or memo; change the field width; and, if the field is numeric, alter the number of decimal places.

Use the Edit screen to change any of the field characteristics to their correct settings; then choose the OK box, or click on it with the mouse to continue with the repair. File Fix now shows you the new file header structure. If you accept it, File Fix proceeds with the recovery of the rest of the file. If you are still

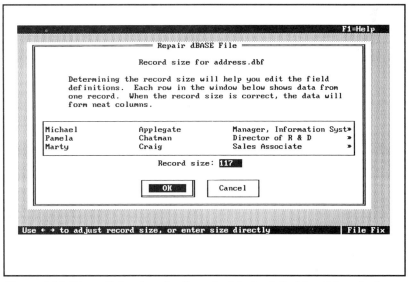

Figure 6.11: Now all the data is aligned with the left side of the window

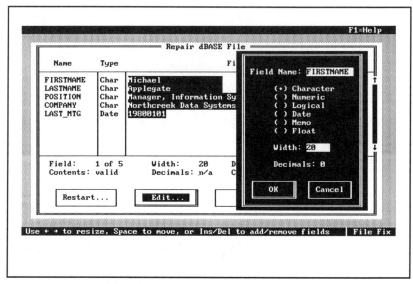

Figure 6.12: Using the Edit window you can change the field name, alter its type, and change the width or the number of decimals if the field is numeric

uncertain about the file structure, select Cancel to return to the editing screens.

If you see the following messages on the screen:

The Sum of the Field Sizes Do Not Agree

or

The Field Definitions Do Not Agree

a conflict exists between the file header and the actual data in the file. You will have to repeat the previous editing steps until File Fix no longer displays these messages.

File Fix uses a percentage-complete display to show the recovery taking place. Finally, it displays a summary screen that lists the amount of data recovered and the number of bytes discarded. Choose between Printer and File for the report destination, or choose No Report to end your session with that file.

Finally, the File Fix window opens and asks if you want to repair any more files. Select **Yes** if you have more files to work on, or select **No** or press Esc to return to the NORTON program shell or to return to DOS.

USING FILE FIX FROM THE DOS PROMPT .

You can also use File Fix directly from the DOS prompt. Simply type:

FILEFIX *filename*

in which *filename* is the file you want to repair. File Fix skips the opening screens when you load it with a file name. File Fix uses the file name extension to determine which application program created it; therefore, the program knows knows how to correct the problems in the file.

FileSave (FILESAVE)

Protecting Files

CHAPTER **7**

HAVE YOU EVER WANTED TO DELETE A FILE THAT YOU were not quite sure about, but that you didn't think you would need again? The FileSave utility lets you delete that file with confidence because FileSave delays the deletion. When FileSave is active, it intercepts the DOS commands that usually delete files, and instead of carrying out the delete operations, moves the files into a directory called TRASHCAN. This procedure has the added benefit of protecting the files from being overwritten, which in turn makes them easier to recover if you change your mind and decide that you want to keep them after all. The files are held in the TRASHCAN directory for a period of time that you specify, and then they are deleted. You can also specify the size of the Trashcan. This delayed deletion offers protection against accidentally deleting important files.

The UnErase program can recover files from the Trashcan very quickly. See Chapter 9 for a description of UnErase.

To run FileSave from the NORTON shell program, select FileSave from the main menu. Alternatively, to run the program from the DOS prompt, type:

FILESAVE

Both methods display the opening menu shown in Figure 7.1. This menu offers three major selections—Choose Drives, File Protection, and Purge Files—as well as a Quit option that returns you to the NORTON program (or to DOS).

CHOOSE DRIVES

Selecting Choose Drives from the main menu displays the Choose Drives window shown in Figure 7.2. Use the Tab or

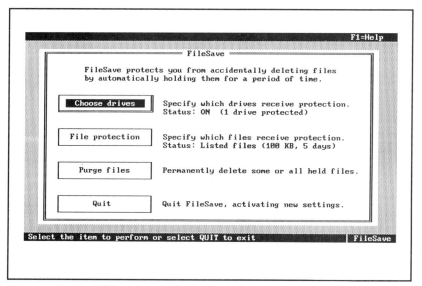

Figure 7.1: The FileSave opening menu screen

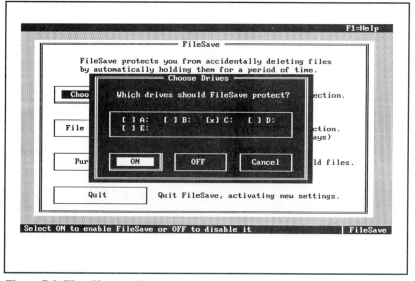

Figure 7.2: The Choose Drives option lets you select the drives you want to protect

The FileSave program includes a terminate-and-stay-resident program. Selecting the ON box loads the resident part of the program into memory.

arrow keys to move from drive letter to drive letter, and press the spacebar or the **X** key to turn on the checkmark for each drive you want to protect. With the mouse, merely click on the appropriate boxes to select the drives. Note that you can also protect network drives.

Move the highlight to the **ON** box and press Enter, or click on the box with the mouse. This actually loads the FileSave program into memory; note in Figure 7.2 that the Status entry opposite the Choose Drives box now indicates FileSave is ON and is protecting two drives.

FILE PROTECTION

Choose File Protection to open the File Protection window shown in Figure 7.3. This option lets you select the files you want FileSave to hold in the Trashcan. Remember, only those files specified in this window are protected by FileSave. Choose one of the following:

To remove file name extensions from the Files list, merely type a space character into each entry.

- **All Files.** This extends protection to all files on the chosen drive or drives. This is the most extensive level of protection and is the one you will probably use most often.

- **Only the Files Listed.** Use this selection if you are sure you only want to protect specific files. You can enter as many as nine file name extensions into the Files area. For example, to protect all of your Lotus 1-2-3 files, enter the extension .WK?; to protect all your dBASE files, enter .DBF; and to protect all your C language source files, enter .C.

- **All Files Except those Listed.** This selection lets you reverse the sense of the previous choice. Enter the file name extensions for those files you do *not* want to protect.

You can also make three other important selections from this screen: one concerned with archive files, and two controlling

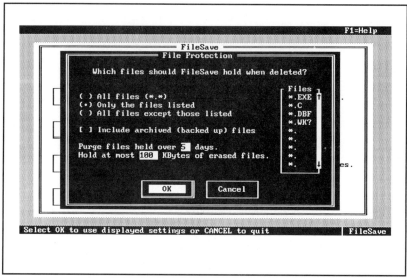

Figure 7.3: Choose the files you want to safeguard in the File Protection window

FileSave's automatic purging function.

- **Include Archived (Backed Up) Files.** FileSave does not automatically save files that have been archived; after all, you can always reload these files from your backup if you need them again. However, if you want to make FileSave include archived files, click on this box with the mouse, or press the spacebar or the X key to put a checkmark in the box.

- **Purge Files Held Over xx Days.** Enter the number of days that you want FileSave to hold your files before automatically purging, or deleting, them. The maximum time is 99 days.

- **Hold At Most xxx KBytes of Erased Files.** Enter the maximum size of the Trashcan in kilobytes. The maximum entry is 9999K. If the Trashcan fills before the specified time period has elapsed, FileSave purges the oldest files as it saves the most recent.

The options you choose here apply to all the drives you selected for protection.

PURGE FILES

FileSave copies the files you delete into the directory called TRASHCAN, giving them names that start with the @ character and end with the .SAV file name extension. The files will be purged automatically as the specified time period expires; however, if you want to remove them earlier, simply choose Purge Files. This selection opens the Purge Deleted Files window, as shown in Figure 7.4.

The files you have deleted are listed in the window, along with their sizes and creation dates and times. Below the window, the screen displays the original path name and the time and date you deleted the file. There are four selections available to you in the Purge Deleted Files window: Drive, Tag, Purge, and Cancel.

- Drive. Select this option to specify the drive or drives from which you will purge files. Choose drives from the list of available drives.

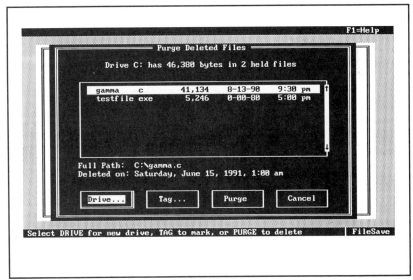

Figure 7.4: The Purge Deleted Files window lets you choose the files to remove from the TRASHCAN directory

- Tag. You can tag a group of files that meet a particular filespec, or you can mark (*tag*) a group of files by specifying a common file name extension. Then you can purge the entire group at once instead of deleting each file one at a time.

- Purge. This selection removes the files you selected or tagged.

- Cancel. Choose Cancel to return to the main menu. Your FileSave settings remain intact.

Using the Purge option is the only safe way to remove files from the Trashcan. Remember, if you use the DOS DEL or ERASE commands to remove them, FileSave will carefully make another copy of them as long as they meet the File Protection criteria.

If you are using FileSave on a network, do not stay in the Purge Deleted Files window for a long period of time. FileSave protection is suspended when this window is open, so if users delete files during this time, those files will not be added to the Trashcan.

The Quit selection returns you to the DOS prompt or to the NORTON program, depending on which method you used to start FileSave.

ADDING FILESAVE TO YOUR AUTOEXEC.BAT FILE

The first time you run FileSave, you should run it from the FileSave main menu as I described above. Your chosen settings are saved in a small data file called FILESAVE.INI. If you add the line:

FILESAVE /ON

to your AUTOEXEC.BAT file, FileSave will load your settings from FILESAVE.INI, and take its place in the memory of your computer without invoking the program's full screen mode. This loads the program with your settings each time you boot up your computer, so you don't have to remember to do it yourself.

After FileSave is loaded, you can examine the program's configuration from the DOS command line by typing:

FILESAVE /STATUS

which displays a summary screen similar to the one shown in Figure 7.5. If you want to unload FileSave from memory, use either the command:

FILESAVE /OFF

or

FILESAVE /UNINSTALL

```
C:\NORTON>filesave /status
FileSave, Norton Utilities 5.0, Copyright 1990 by Peter Norton

FileSave status:      Enabled
Drives Protected:     C: (Trashcan contains 1600K in 2 files)
Files Protected:      Only files with these extensions
                      EXE, C, DBF, WK?
Archive Files:        Not Protected
Files Deleted After:  5 days

C:\NORTON>
```

Figure 7.5: You can access the FileSave status screen from the DOS prompt

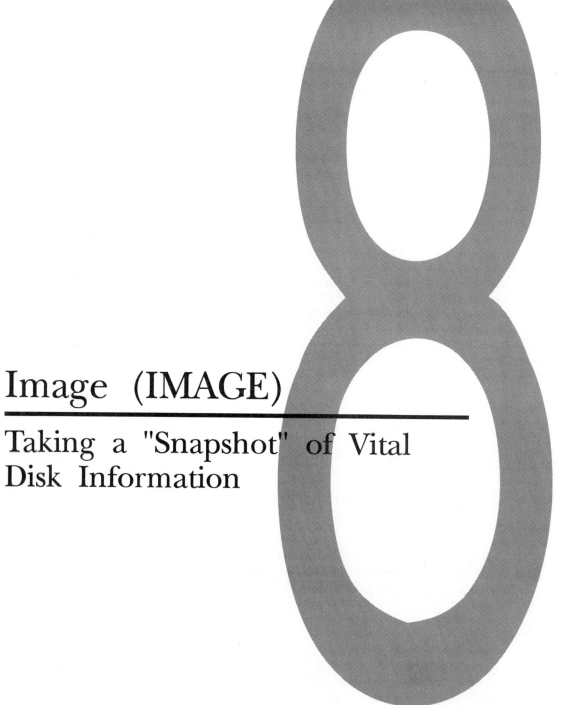

Image (IMAGE)

Taking a "Snapshot" of Vital Disk Information

CHAPTER *8* _____

THE IMAGE PROGRAM MAKES A COPY OF THE SYSTEM area of your hard disk—the boot track, the File Allocation Tables, and the root directory. If you reformat the disk by accident, the UnFormat program uses the information saved by Image to reconstruct the files on your disk.

Although Image and UnFormat can provide a high degree of protection for your files and directories, you should still perform regular backups.

To run Image from the NORTON Shell program, select Image from the main menu. To run the program from the DOS prompt, type:

IMAGE

The program executes very quickly, all you will see is two messages on the screen after the Peter Norton copyright statement. If you run Image on drive C, the first message says:

Updating Image Information for Drive C:

and the second message reads:

Finished Updating Image Information for Drive C:

You cannot use Image to protect a network drive.

as Figure 8.1 shows. Each time you run Image, the program updates two files in the root directory of your disk with copies of the current boot track, the FATs, and all the entries in the root directory. These files, named IMAGE.DAT and IMAGE.BAK, must stay in the root directory if they are to be effective. Do not copy them to another disk or directory. IMAGE.BAK is a backup of the main Image file, IMAGE.DAT; if you don't have the space for two files on your hard disk, run Image with the /NOBACKUP switch. From the DOS prompt, type:

IMAGE /NOBACKUP

```
C:\>IMAGE
Image, Norton Utilities 5.0, Copyright 1990 by Peter Norton

Finished updating IMAGE for drive C:

C:\>
```

Figure 8.1: The Image utility displays two messages on the screen and
quickly performs its task

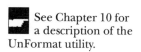
See Chapter 10 for
a description of the
UnFormat utility.

and only the IMAGE.DAT file will be created or updated.

If you accidentally reformat your hard disk, UnFormat uses
the information stored in IMAGE.DAT to recover your files and
directories. Other Norton Utilities such as Speed Disk and Safe
Format also update the IMAGE.DAT file if one is present on
your disk.

In addition, UnErase uses information from IMAGE.DAT to
recover deleted files that have become fragmented or broken
into several small discontinuous pieces.

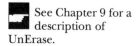
See Chapter 9 for a
description of
UnErase.

You can run Image every time you start your computer by adding the line:

IMAGE /NOBACKUP

to your AUTOEXEC.BAT file.

To ensure that the information in IMAGE.DAT is as accurate
as possible, you should really run Image at the end of your session rather than at the beginning. For example, you can run
Image from a batch file called SHUTDOWN.BAT by including

an Image statement for each hard disk on your system:

```
IMAGE C:
IMAGE D:
IMAGE E:
```

Each time you run SHUTDOWN.BAT, Image will automatically update the IMAGE.DAT files on this three-drive system. Get into the habit of running SHUTDOWN.BAT before you turn off your computer to ensure that the IMAGE.DAT file is as up-to-date as possible. An accurate, up-to-date IMAGE.DAT file increases the chances of a complete recovery of all the files on your hard disk if it is reformatted.

The IMAGE.DAT file made by Image is compatible with the FRECOVER.DAT file created by version 4.5 of the Norton Utilities. The Norton Utilities in version 5 can use either the IMAGE.DAT or FRECOVER.DAT file. If they encounter the FRECOVER.DAT file on your disk, they will rename it IMAGE.DAT in accordance with the latest version of the utilities.

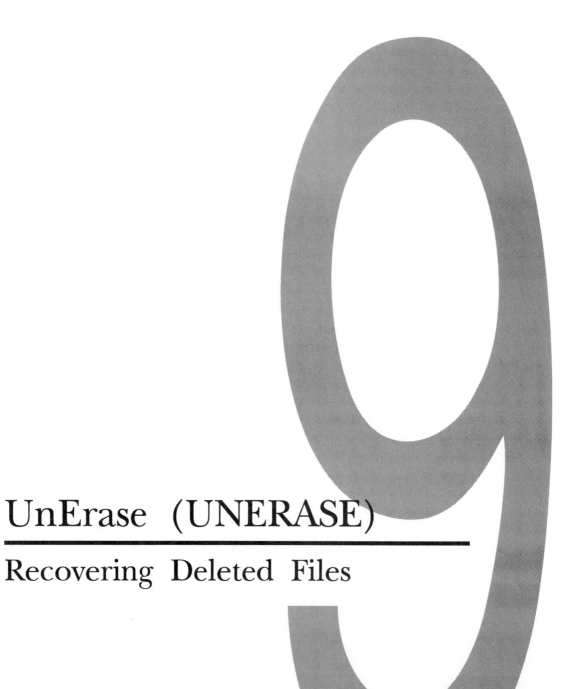

UnErase (UNERASE)

Recovering Deleted Files

CHAPTER **9**

DELETING FILES IS EASY, SOMETIMES *TOO* EASY. IF YOU use wildcards in file names in a DEL operation, you might specify more files than you intended and end up deleting too many files, maybe even the entire contents of a directory. For example, both EDLIN and WordStar create .BAK files when files are modified and saved. Most people delete these files to save space, relying on their backup disks for copies of the original files. Suppose, in this case, you mistype:

DEL *.BAK

as:

DEL *.BAT

Instead of deleting your .BAK files, you have just deleted all your batch files.

Careful disk organization can help prevent some of these accidental erasures. To protect your batch files, for example, you should keep them in a separate directory, away from your EDLIN or WordStar files. No matter how good your organization is, however, sooner or later you will accidentally erase a file or want to recover a file that you erased intentionally. This is where the Norton Utilities come into play; the product is probably most famous for its ability to restore deleted files.

WHAT REALLY HAPPENS WHEN YOU DELETE A FILE?

Before describing how the UnErase utility does its job, I need to explain precisely what happens when you delete a file. When you use DEL or ERASE on a file, the file's entries are cleared from the FAT. DOS also changes the first character of the file name in its directory to a Greek lowercase sigma character (ASCII E5 hex, or 229 decimal) to indicate to the rest of the DOS commands that the file has been erased. However, the file's entry, including its starting cluster number and its length, remains in the directory, hidden from view by DOS's inclusion of the sigma character in the file name. The data itself remains in its original location on the disk. No data is changed until DOS is instructed to write another file over its clusters. Thus, the first cluster of a file can be found and recovered quite easily as long as it has not been overwritten.

To illustrate this process, create a small text file on a blank formatted floppy disk by typing:

```
COPY CON A:MYFILE.TXT
This is a short example of text.
```

Press F6 to terminate your text input, and then press Enter to close the file. Use the Disk Editor program to look at the directory entry for this file by typing

```
DISKEDIT A:
```

The result is shown in Figure 9.1.

The first line of the display shows the length of MYFILE.TXT (34 bytes) and its creation time and date. Note also that its archive bit is set, which tells DOS that the file should be backed up the next time the BACKUP command is run, or XCOPY /M is executed.

Leave Disk Editor and return to DOS by pressing Esc or clicking on Quit on the menu bar. Delete MYFILE.TXT by typing:

```
DEL MYFILE.TXT
```

Now rerun the Disk Editor program and display the root directory again. Notice that the file name's first character has been changed to a sigma character (see Figure 9.2).

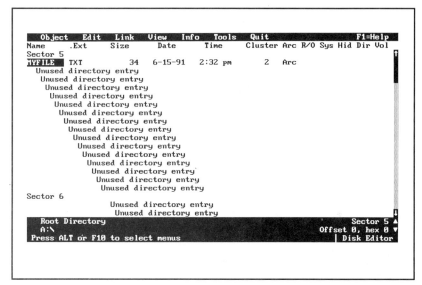

Figure 9.1: Displaying the root directory in directory format

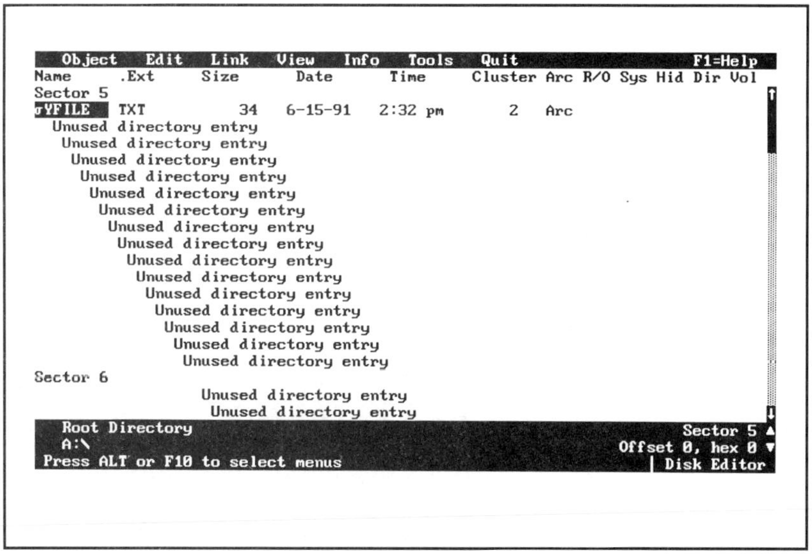

Figure 9.2: Displaying the file entry of the deleted file MYFILE.TXT

If you try to make a DIR listing of this disk, however, you will see only an empty listing.

WHAT HAPPENS WHEN YOU ADD A NEW FILE?

To learn how to reduce file fragmentation, see the discussion of the Speed Disk utility in Chapter 13.

When you add a new file to your disk, DOS looks for the next available cluster of free disk space. If the file is small enough to fit into this space, DOS simply inserts it. However, if the file is larger, DOS splits it up into several pieces, recording it into clusters that are not numbered consecutively. In other words, the file becomes *fragmented*.

Thus, saving a new file on the disk destroys a deleted file's data. If the new file is larger than the old one, the old file is completely obliterated. If the new file is smaller than the old one, some unknown amount of the old file will remain on the disk until it is finally overwritten during another write-to-disk operation.

Do not save anything after you delete a file or files inadvertently, or you may be unable to recover the file(s).

The most important point to remember about file recovery is you must not save anything on the disk until you have completed the recovery operation. Do not even install the Norton Utilities on your hard disk; instead, you should run UnErase from floppy disk number 1. Install the complete Utilities package on the hard disk only when the recovery is completely finished. By following this rule, you will not overwrite the erased file's data, and you will increase the chances of a complete recovery.

USING UNERASE TO RECOVER DELETED FILES

If the deleted file is a short file or is on a floppy disk, there is an excellent chance that UnErase will be able to restore it on the first attempt. If the file is badly fragmented, or part of it has been overwritten by another file, the chances of a complete recovery are substantially less. To demonstrate UnErase, let's try to recover the file MYFILE.TXT that we previously created and deleted on drive A.

To run UnErase, select it from the list of programs in the NORTON program main screen, or at the DOS prompt, type:

UNERASE A:

UnErase can recover deleted files from a network drive only if FileSave protection is in place for that drive.

The main UnErase screen is shown in Figure 9.3. In the center of the screen you can see the information for the file you just deleted, MYFILE.TXT; notice, however, that the screen shows the first character of the file name as a ? character. This reminds you that UnErase does not know what that first character should be (recall that DOS replaced this character with the sigma symbol), and you will have to supply the original character during the next part of the recovery process. (If you are using the FileSave utility, you will see the complete file name, with no missing letters.) Also in the display you can see the file size, creation date and time, and the prognosis for recovery, which in this case is described as good.

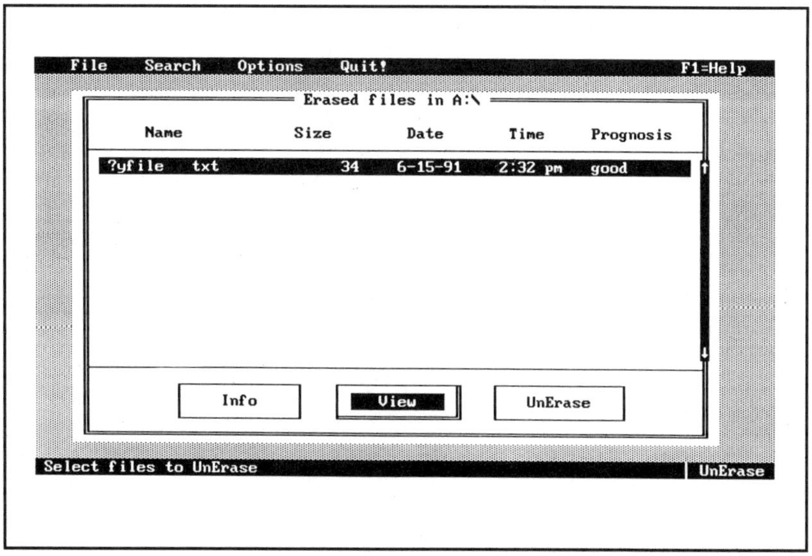

You will always be able to recover a file protected by the FileSave utility.

Figure 9.3: The main UnErase screen lists information about deleted files

To see more information about this file, choose the Info box below the main window. This displays a screen similar to the one shown in Figure 9.4. Figure 9.4 shows the file name, creation time and date, as well as the file size in bytes, and the file attributes. All of this information helps you to identify this file as the correct file to unerase. The recovery prognosis is shown, along with the starting cluster number and the total number of clusters in the file. UnErase describes the chances of recovery, or *prognosis,* of a file as Excellent, Good, Average, or Poor, in decreasing order of the likelihood of a successful recovery. (This column also might display the messages Not Applicable, Recovered, or DIR depending on the status of the recovery process.)

UnErase also displays a short message describing the current status of the file. This message may be relatively optimistic about the recovery, such as:

This file can be recovered in one piece,
but it may not contain the correct data.

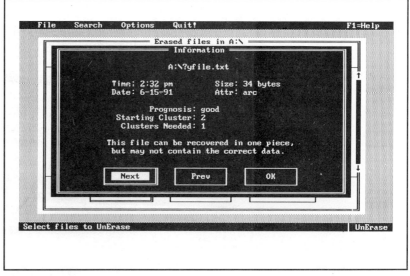

Figure 9.4: The Information screen displays details about the deleted file

See Chapter 19 for a description of file attributes.

or rather more ominous, as in the following case:

The first cluster of this file
is now being used by another file.

The message is directly related to the entry in the prognosis column.

Choose View to look at the contents of the file as text or in hex. For the example MYFILE.TXT, you will see a display similar to the one shown in Figure 9.5. The View selection shows that the original data is still on the disk. Use the Text or Hex box to change the format of the display. The hex view shows the numeric values of the bytes on the left, and the equivalent ASCII characters on the right. Figure 9.5 shows the file in hex view. Select the Next or Previous box to examine other deleted files on the disk, or select OK to return to the main UnErase screen.

To unerase the file, choose the UnErase option, and you will be prompted to supply the first character of the file name. Use the correct character if you can remember it; otherwise, use any

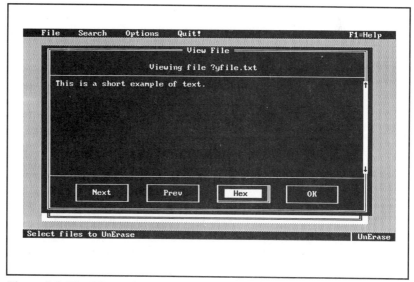

Figure 9.5: The View selection lets you look at the contents of the file as text or in hex

character as the first letter. Remember, you can always use the Rename option from the File pull-down menu or the DOS RENAME command to change the name later. As soon as you type the first character, the file is unerased, and the Prognosis column displays the status as RECOVERED.

If you want to recover several files from the same directory, you can use the Select Group option from the File pull-down menu. Alternatively, you can use the large + key on the numeric keypad. The Select window opens and prompts you to select the files. You can use file names, extensions, or any of the DOS wildcard characters to specify the files. For example, specify *.* to recover all of the deleted files in the directory, or specify *.WK? to recover only your Lotus 1-2-3 spreadsheet files. When you select OK to return to the main UnErase screen, you will see arrowhead characters to the right and left of the files matching your file specification. To remove files from the list press the - key on the numeric keypad, or choose Unselect Group from the File pull-down menu.

After your selection is complete and you choose the UnErase box, a window opens to confirm the number of files you want to attempt to recover. This window also asks if you want to be prompted to supply the missing first character of the file name. When this box has a checkmark, UnErase prompts you to supply a beginning character for each file. If you clear the checkmark from the box, UnErase does not prompt for a character— it simply inserts the first letter of the alphabet that results in a unique file name for each file. These names might look a little strange at first because most of them will begin with the letter A or B. You can use the Rename command from the File pull-down menu to change the names to something more appropriate.

There are several options in the File pull-down menu that you can use to look at erased files in other directories or on other disks. If you want to change to another drive, select Change Drive (Alt-D) and choose a drive from the list in the Change Drive window. Use View Current Directory (Alt-C) to display files in the current directory, or use View All Directories (Alt-A) to look at all the erased files on the current drive. To change to a specific directory, first select Change Directory (Alt-R); then locate the appropriate directory in the graphical display of directory names, or type the first few letters of the name into the Speed Search window. Remember that the Change Directory screen does not show deleted directories.

If the main window displays a large number of files, you can use the selections from the Options pull-down menu to arrange the files in the most convenient order. You can sort the files by name, extension, time, size, or by prognosis, and you can choose to include or exclude existing files in the directory that have not been erased. A checkmark appears next to your current selection in the menu. This sorting applies only to the files shown in the main UnErase window; the order of the files on your disk remains unchanged.

You have now completed a simple file recovery by unerasing MYFILE.TXT. As long as you start the recovery process soon after you have deleted the file, and the file is not badly fragmented or overwritten, the chances for recovery are usually quite good.

MANUALLY UNERASING FILES

Now that you are familiar with unerasing files automatically, you are ready to learn how to unerase files manually. You should only use manual recovery methods if the automatic recovery mode did not work. Although it is considered an advanced technique, always remember that UnErase will provide help at every stage. In the following example, we will delete the READ.ME file supplied with the Norton Utilities, and then we will use UnErase's manual recovery methods to restore the file. First, change to the Norton directory on your hard disk. Then type:

TYPE READ.ME|MORE

to display the beginning of the READ.ME file, as shown in Figure 9.6.

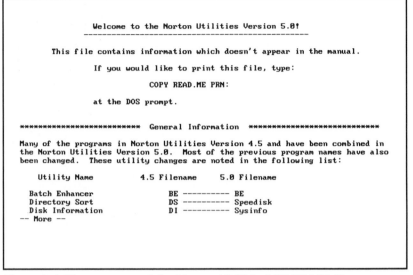

```
                Welcome to the Norton Utilities Version 5.0!
            -------------------------------------------------

        This file contains information which doesn't appear in the manual.

               If you would like to print this file, type:

                           COPY READ.ME PRN:

           at the DOS prompt.


    ****************************  General Information  *****************************

    Many of the programs in Norton Utilities Version 4.5 and have been combined in
    the Norton Utilities Version 5.0.  Most of the previous program names have also
    been changed.  These utility changes are noted in the following list:

       Utility Name          4.5 Filename     5.0 Filename

       Batch Enhancer          BE ---------- BE
       Directory Sort          DS ---------- Speedisk
       Disk Information        DI ---------- Sysinfo
    -- More --
```

Figure 9.6: The contents of the Norton Utilities' READ.ME file

Press Ctrl-C to break out of the display, and then erase the READ.ME file by typing:

DEL READ.ME

To restore READ.ME, start UnErase from the DOS prompt by typing:

UNERASE

or select UnErase from inside the NORTON program. The top of the screen shows that you are in the NORTON directory, and a line within the window describes the ?EAD.ME file.

Position the highlight over the ?EAD.ME file, and then press Alt-M or choose Manual UnErase from the File pull-down menu. UnErase asks you to enter a character to complete the file name. Enter an R and you will see the Manual UnErase screen shown in Figure 9.7.

At the left side of the Manual UnErase screen, the File Information box displays information about the READ.ME file, including

If you want to un-erase the file to a new name, press Alt-F and then T.

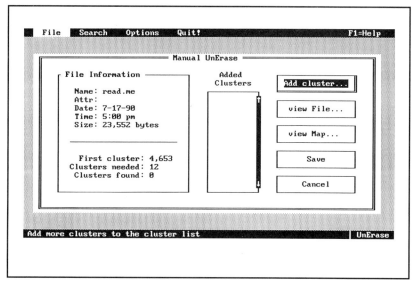

Figure 9.7: The Manual UnErase screen provides detailed information about the erased file

the file name, file attributes, the file creation date and time, and the size in bytes. Below this information is the starting cluster number for READ.ME from the FAT. Next, the **Clusters needed** field reports the number of clusters that the file occupied before it was deleted; this represents the number of clusters that you have to recover to unerase the file. On the last line, the **Clusters found** count keeps track of the clusters you add to the file. This number is zero now, but it will increase as you recover clusters and add them to the file.

In the center of the screen, the **Added Clusters** box displays the actual cluster numbers as you add clusters to the file.

·From the selections at the right of the screen, choose **Add Cluster**, and you will see the display shown in Figure 9.8.

You use the Add Clusters screen to specify the clusters you want to include in the file you are recovering. Use the arrow keys to move the highlight from one box to another. Not all the clusters in the original file may be recoverable, of course.

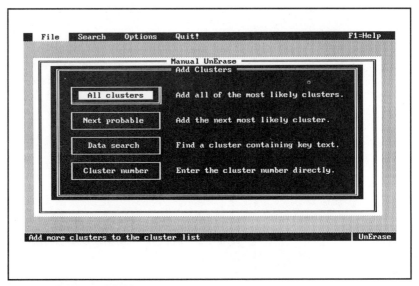

Figure 9.8: The Add Clusters screen

To find the file's clusters, you can choose from the following options:

- **All Clusters** automatically adds the most likely clusters to the file and provides the most straightforward method of recovering the file's data.

- **Next Probable Cluster** lets UnErase choose the next likely cluster to include. (Clusters are chosen one at a time.)

- **Data Search** lets you enter a search string of as many as 28 characters in either ASCII or in hex. If you enter the search string in ASCII, it is translated into its hex equivalent and displayed in the hex window. To enter the search string in hex, use the Tab key or the arrow keys to move to the hex box, and type in the search characters. Place a checkmark in the **Ignore Case** box to find the search string irrespective of case, or clear the checkmark to make the search case-specific.

- **Cluster Number** requires that you know which cluster to add. At the top of the Add Cluster Number screen,

UnErase lists the valid range of clusters for your drive. You can specify a single cluster or a range of clusters. Enter a starting cluster number and an ending cluster number. If the range you specify contains clusters already in use in another file, UnErase finds the first free cluster within the range.

The simplest way of finding the data for the file is to select All clusters. Choose that option now. The program will find all the clusters that the READ.ME data occupies and list them in the Added Clusters box. Before completing the recovery process by actually saving the file, you can examine the information contained in the found clusters or even remove or rearrange the clusters.

VIEWING OR UNSELECTING FOUND CLUSTERS

Be sure that the highlight is on the first cluster in the Added Clusters box, and select View File to examine the contents of this cluster. You will see a display similar to the one shown in Figure 9.9, but remember that your cluster numbers will be different because they refer to your own disk. Figure 9.9 shows the data as text; to see the display in hex, select or click on the Hex box. Use the up and down arrow keys, the PgUp or PgDn keys, or click on the scroll bars to move through the file. Cluster boundaries are marked in the file. Compare this figure with Figure 9.6 to confirm that what you see is indeed the start of the READ.ME text file. Select OK to return to the main Manual Un-Erase screen.

Select View Map to see the relative location and size of the data you have recovered so far. This information for our example is shown in Figure 9.10. The space occupied by this file is shown as an F character. Disk space occupied by other files is shown as a block with a dot in the center, and unused disk space is shown as a solid block. Select OK to return to the main screen.

You can move a cluster within the Added Clusters box if you are unhappy with its current location. Move the highlight to the

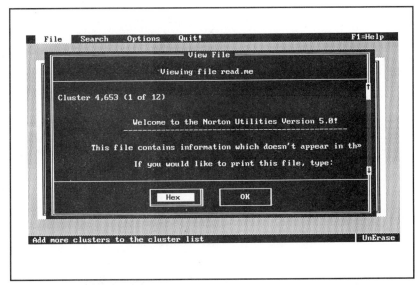

Figure 9.9: View File shows the contents of the first cluster in the
READ.ME file

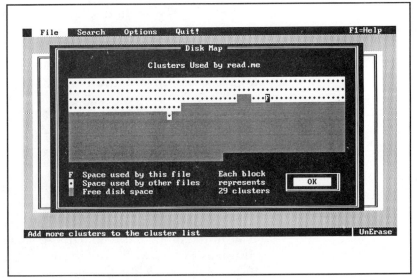

Figure 9.10: The Disk Map display shows the size and location of the
clusters you have recovered so far

Added Clusters box, position the highlight on the cluster you want to move, and press the spacebar. A small arrowhead appears to the right of the cluster number and confirms your choice. Now, use the up and down arrow keys to move the cluster to a new location in the list. Press the spacebar again to unselect the cluster at its new location. Select View File again to be sure that this new position is consistent with the rest of the file's contents.

Now that you're sure that you have selected the correct clusters to unerase, use **Save** to complete the recovery process. This menu selection stores the data in the READ.ME directory entry and also restores the FAT data so that DOS can find the file again. Recovery of READ.ME is now complete.

RECOVERING PARTIAL FILES

Often, recovering files is not as straightforward as it was in the previous examples. DOS may have overwritten all or part of the erased file with another file before you realize that you want to recover the erased file. Several factors determine whether recovery is possible, including the length of the new and erased files, and the existence or nonexistence of the erased file's directory entry.

If the file has been partially overwritten, you still might be able to recover some portion of the file, but there is a good chance that its original directory entry will have been overwritten. If this is the case, you can use Create File from the File pull-down menu to create a new directory entry to use with the recovery process. You can now use Manual UnErase to search for clusters to add to the file. Note that in this kind of recovery, the Add Cluster screen contains only three selections: **Next Probable, Data Search,** and **Cluster Number.** You cannot use automatic recovery techniques under these circumstances.

If you are recovering files from a badly damaged disk, you probably don't want to store the recovered clusters on the same disk. Select the UnErase To option from the File pull-down menu to save the file to another disk. Choose the drive from the list of available drives shown in the UnErase To window, or merely type the letter of the drive you want to use. At the end of your recovery attempt, the clusters will be written to the drive you selected.

The single most important aspect of this kind of file recovery is how much you know about the contents of the erased file. If you know nothing about the file, it may be impossible to determine whether you have recovered it completely. If the file is a program file, running only the recovered portion can lead to unpredictable—and unpleasant—results. The only safe way to proceed in this case is to delete the partial file, and restore the entire file from your backup set.

SEARCHING FOR LOST DATA

If you can't remember which directory an erased file was in, or if you are unable to recover the directory it was in, you can use the selections in the Search pull-down menu to locate clusters containing certain types of data. The Search menu contains the following options:

- For Data Types lets you choose from normal text, Lotus 1-2-3 and Symphony, dBASE, or Other data types. Use the spacebar to make your selection, or click on the appropriate box with the mouse. Select Stop to abandon the search.

- For Text lets you enter a text search string. If you check the Ignore Case box, both upper- and lowercase strings are checked. The text you are searching for is shown at the top of the Search Progress window. A percentage-complete display shows the progress being made by the search. Select Stop to abandon the search.

  As the search proceeds, the screen shows a list of the file fragments. UnErase names these fragments FILE0001, FILE0002, and so on. You can press Esc to stop the search at any time; then you can highlight a file fragment, and use View to examine it. If the file fragment is the beginning of a file you want to recover, select UnErase.

- For Lost Names searches for inaccessible file names. Files may be lost if the directories that they were in are overwritten. Names of erased files are displayed on the screen; when you see a file name you recognize, highlight the file name, and select the UnErase box in the lower right corner of the screen.

- Set Search Range lets you specify the starting and ending cluster numbers for the search. The range of valid cluster numbers is shown on the Search Range window. You can use this selection to restrict the area of the disk that will be searched if you have an idea of where the missing file is located on the disk. You probably should use this selection first to restrict the search, and then specify the type of data you want to search for with one of the other selections.

- Continue Search resumes an interrupted search so you don't have to reenter the search criteria.

To save the file fragments found in this way, use the Append To selection from the File pull-down menu. Append To adds these clusters to an existing file.

Sometimes you can speed up the cumbersome process of finding pieces of files by using the Disk Editor, particularly if you *know* a file fragment is on the disk but UnErase is having trouble finding it. The main Disk Editor screen lists deleted files as well as directory entries and current files, and it also lists the starting cluster number for all the entries. You can use that information to restrict the search in UnErase, or alternatively, you can ask Disk Editor to search for the data instead. Merely select Cluster (Alt-C) from the Object pull-down menu, specify a starting cluster number, and then look through the clusters for data that you recognize. You can also use the Find and Find Again selections from the Tools pull-down menu to search for a text string automatically.

RECOVERING AN ERASED DIRECTORY

To recover files, you must sometimes first recover a directory so that you can gain access to the files. Note that if a directory contains *any* files, it cannot be deleted.

You can use UnErase to restore deleted directories; in fact, the procedure is the same as for restoring deleted files. After you have recovered the directory, you can restore all of its files.

DOS removes a directory in the same way that it removes a file. The first character is set to the same special character, and the removed directory's entry remains in its parent directory (unseen, of course), exactly like a removed file's entry. UnErase lists directories that have not been deleted using their full name in capitals, and lists the names of deleted directories in capitals with a question mark as the first character.

Let's look at an example to review this procedure briefly. Suppose you erased all your spreadsheet files that were in the 123 directory on drive C, erased the directory itself, and then realized that this was not the directory you had intended to delete. The UnErase program will not be able to find the spreadsheet files to restore them, because their names, starting cluster numbers, and file lengths are all stored in the 123 directory that has also been deleted. You must first recover the directory before attempting to recover the files. To run UnErase on the 123 directory, change to the directory that was the parent of the 123 directory (root, in this example) and type:

UNERASE

This displays the screen shown in Figure 9.11.

UnErase asks you for the first character of the file name, or uses information provided by FileSave to complete the entry. After you have recovered the directory, you can proceed to recover the files that were in the 123 directory. Because the files were all small, each a single cluster, your chances of recovering them are relatively good. Select Change Directory from the File pull-down menu and using the graphical directory display, change to the recovered 123 directory. Select each of the files

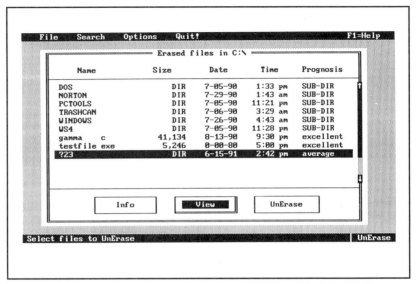

Figure 9.11: Unerasing a directory before recovering the files in that directory

individually, or if you want to recover all of them at the same time, use Select Group to specify all the files.

As you now know, file recovery is by no means certain. Many aspects of the process influence the success of any recovery attempt, most of which you examined in this chapter. Although the file-recovery process can be more difficult than was shown in this chapter's examples (for example, recovering program files can be messy), you should have enough knowledge of the Norton Utilities' UnErase program to attempt difficult recoveries on your own. Chances are the file can't be recovered if you can't rescue it with the Norton Utilities.

UnFormat (UNFORMAT)

Undoing the Accidental
Formatting of a Hard Disk

CHAPTER **10** _____

IN THIS CHAPTER I DISCUSS SOME OF THE MISHAPS THAT can befall your data and the means by which you can recover from them. Both floppy and hard disks can be mechanically damaged by careless handling, files can be deleted accidentally, and disks can be reformatted inadvertently. The Norton Utilities programs provide several elegant solutions to these problems, but there are preventive steps that you should become familiar with; following them helps reduce the impact of these problems.

TAKING CARE OF YOUR DISKS

Extended use can cause both hard and floppy disks to deteriorate. Floppy disks are especially prone to damage through mistreatment and careless handling.

SAFEGUARDING FLOPPY DISKS

The following suggestions for handling floppy disks will help you protect your data and prevent problems:

- When you are not using a floppy disk, keep it in its jacket in a disk storage tray or in its box.
- Do not expose floppy disks to high temperatures; for example, do not leave them on a window sill, on top of your monitor, or in a car parked in the sun. The disks will warp and become unusable.

- Keep disks away from magnetic fields, such as motors, paper clip holders, stereo speakers, magnetized screwdrivers, and magnetic keys.

- Do not touch the recording surface of the disk. This can transfer dirt and body oils to the disk's surface and destroy data.

- Label all your disks. Write on the label before attaching it to the disk. If you must write on the label after it is on the disk, use a soft felt-tip pen—not a ballpoint pen or a pencil. Add a volume label to each of your disks.

- Keep backup copies of all distribution disks, preferably in a different place from the original disks. Often, a local company will specialize in archiving data. Such places use precisely controlled temperature and humidity to ensure long life to the media in storage. They also usually have excellent security and fire protection.

PROTECTING HARD DISKS

Your hard disk is not immune to problems either. The following suggestions relate to its care:

- When you are using the hard disk, do not move the disk unit (if the drive is external) or the computer cabinet (if the drive is internal).

- Before you turn off your computer or move the system, use a head-parking program to stabilize the heads on the hard disk.

- To protect your system against power outages or "brownouts," use a voltage regulator, a surge suppressor, or a small uninterruptable power supply (UPS).

- Do not obstruct the air flow to the back of the computer; the air flow cools your system.

- Keep the card slots at the back of your computer covered. If you remove a card, replace the plate. An open slot directs hot air over the motherboard.

- Perform timely backups.

RECOVERING FROM FORMATTING PROBLEMS

One of the most appalling prospects for a hard-disk user is accidentally reformatting a hard disk, an operation that destroys all data and programs. With UnFormat, however, you can now recover data from a reformatted hard disk. Some PC manufacturers have even invented another command for formatting the hard disk, just to make reformatting more difficult to do by accident. The Norton Utilities provides the Safe Format program, which not only helps to protect your hard disk from being inadvertently reformatted, but can also speed up the formatting process.

USING UNFORMAT

Some versions of DOS, including Compaq DOS 3.1, and DOS 2.11 from AT&T, actually overwrite all the original data when they format a hard disk. UnFormat cannot recover files under these circumstances.

When you run the DOS FORMAT command on a hard disk, it clears the root directory and the FAT of their entries, but it does not overwrite the data area on the disk. The data is still there, but because the root directory and the FAT have been cleared, you normally have no way of getting to it. The UnFormat program provides an easy way of recovering these files. Note, however, that UnFormat will not recover floppy disks formatted with the DOS FORMAT command because the data is overwritten. However, UnFormat *can* recover floppy disks that have been formatted using the Norton Utilities Safe Format program.

Include the Image utility in your AUTOEXEC.BAT file so that IMAGE.DAT is updated regularly.

You should run the Norton Image program as a part of your daily operation. Doing so creates a file called IMAGE.DAT (and a copy called IMAGE.BAK) that UnFormat can use to recover the disk. Although these files' entries will be cleared from the root directory and FAT if the hard disk is reformatted, running the UnFormat program from a floppy will let you recover their data and thereby recover your hard disk completely. You should add a separate Image statement for each logical disk drive on your computer. For example, if you have a large hard disk divided into three logical drives, C, D and E, you need three Image statements in your AUTOEXEC.BAT file. Add the lines:

```
IMAGE C:
IMAGE D:
IMAGE E:
```

to protect all three disk drives.

IMAGE.DAT is compatible with the FRECOVER.DAT file made by the Norton Utilities version 4.5. UnFormat searches for either file. If it finds FRECOVER.DAT, UnFormat renames the file IMAGE.DAT.

After Image has created these files, you cannot delete them by accident—they are read-only files. If you try to delete them with the DOS DEL or ERASE command, you will receive an "Access denied" error message. The IMAGE.DAT file is also used by the UnErase program when you recover files and directories.

If you run UnFormat on a hard disk when the information contained in IMAGE.DAT is not up-to-date, the recovery will be incomplete. If you have added or removed files and these changes were not stored in IMAGE.DAT, UnErase will not know about them. For example, if you deleted files, UnFormat will assign data to those files even though they no longer exist. Furthermore, data in files created since IMAGE.DAT was updated will not be recovered. After UnErase has done all it can to recover data with an outdated IMAGE.DAT file, run Norton Disk Doctor II (NDD) to sort out the few remaining file fragments.

You can run UnFormat from a network, but you cannot unformat a network fileserver.

If your hard disk has been accidentally reformatted with the DOS FORMAT command, insert the floppy disk that contains UnFormat into drive A (Norton disk #2 if you use 5¼ inch floppy disks, or disk #1 if you use 3½ inch disks.) You have to run UnFormat from a floppy disk because your hard-disk copy of UnFormat can't be accessed. Do this immediately—before loading any backup copies to the reformatted hard disk. If you try to load programs first, you may overwrite the IMAGE.DAT file, in which case a complete recovery will be impossible.

⊙ Always run
UnFormat on an
accidentally refor-
matted hard disk
before writing anything
else to the disk—other-
wise you may overwrite
IMAGE.DAT, making
recovery difficult.

The UnFormat program is automatic and easy to use. You don't need to select options from pull-down menus; simply choose from two or three simple alternatives shown on the screen. To run the program, select UnFormat from the menu in the NORTON shell program, or at the DOS prompt, type:

UnFormat

The program displays the startup screen shown in Figure 10.1.

Choose Continue to change to the drive selection window from which you can select a drive to unformat. In this example, we will use drive E.

The next window asks if you used IMAGE to save IMAGE.DAT for drive E. Answer Yes if you did or if you are not sure. If you answer No, the disk will be unformatted from scratch.

RECOVERING DATA WITH IMAGE.DAT If you previously used the Image utility to save a copy of the system area of your disk, recovery after an accidental format should be fast and easy. The next window that opens is a warning screen that

▨ The combination
of an up-to-date
IMAGE.DAT file and a
complete set of current
backup disks greatly in-
creases the chances of a
complete recovery of
all the files on your
reformatted hard disk.
Be prepared.

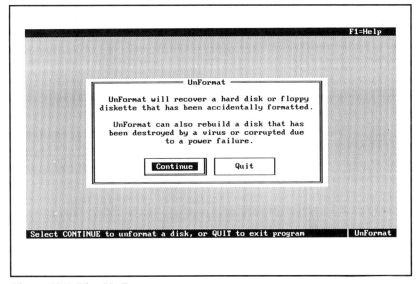

Figure 10.1: The UnFormat startup screen

contains a list of the files in the root directory of the selected drive. These files will be lost if you unformat the disk.

Next UnFormat looks for a copy of IMAGE.DAT on the disk. If it finds a copy, it opens the IMAGE Info Found window, as shown in Figure 10.2.

The window shows both the most recent time that Image saved the IMAGE.DAT file and the previous time, and asks you which version you want to use to unformat your hard disk. If you want to use the most recent copy of IMAGE.DAT to recover the contents of your disk, select Recent. If you want to use the previous copy, select Previous; otherwise, select Cancel. If damage occurred to your disk after the last IMAGE.DAT file was created, you may not always want to use the most current version of this file to recover the hard disk. Obviously, any changes you made to the disk after the IMAGE.DAT file was created will not be recovered.

Restoring the data will overwrite the current data; if this is acceptable, select OK to continue. UnFormat now gives you the choice of a "full" restore or a "partial" restore.

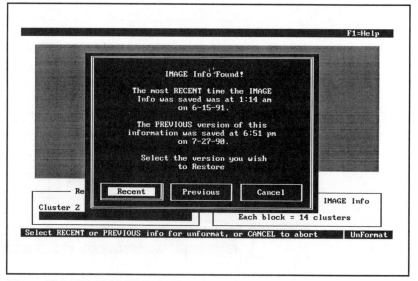

Figure 10.2: The IMAGE Info Found window displays the time and date the IMAGE.DAT file was made

- Full restores the entire system area, including boot record, FAT information, and the root directory. If you are unsure of how to proceed at this point, selecting Full is safest option.

- Partial lets you select the parts of the system area you want to restore—Boot Record, File Allocation Table, or Root Directory.

UnFormat reconstructs the data, and then opens the window shown in Figure 10.3. In Figure 10.3, the program informs you that drive E has been successfully restored and advises you to run NDD with the /QUICK switch selected as a final precaution against lost clusters or cross-linked files. If NDD reports errors on your disk, the errors are a result of creating files after you last ran the Image utility. In other words, IMAGE.DAT was not completely up-to-date.

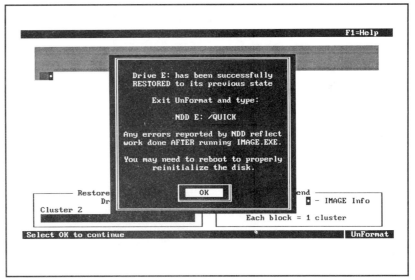

Figure 10.3: The final UnFormat window shows that the process is complete

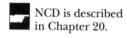 If you are prompted for a DOS disk during the recovery process, copy COMMAND.COM to your root directory to make the hard disk a bootable disk.

NCD is described in Chapter 20.

UnFormat cannot recover files in the root directory; however, it can recover files in all other directories.

RECOVERING DATA WITHOUT THE IMAGE.DAT FILE If you do not have a copy of IMAGE.DAT, you can use UnFormat to recover much of the data on your hard disk.

In the IMAGE Info Found screen, choose **No**. UnFormat then shows a map of the disk and displays the progress made during the unformatting process. When UnFormat is finished, subdirectories will be called DIR0, DIR1, DIR2, and so on. Use Norton Change Directory (NCD) to rename the directories appropriately. If you want to boot from this disk, use the **Make a Disk Bootable** selection from the Disk Tools program. All the files in your root directory will be missing. Use the manual UnErase techniques described in Chapter 9 to recover these files.

Remember to run NDD to find any remaining file allocation errors when UnFormat has finished. Then, check to see if all your files and subdirectories are on the hard disk.

Finally, copy any of the files that you need for normal operation to the root directory. Be sure that AUTOEXEC.BAT, CONFIG.SYS, and COMMAND.COM are all present. If they are not there, copy them to the root directory from your backup floppy disks.

UnFormat returns to the opening screen to ask if you want to UnFormat another disk. Select **Quit** to return to the NORTON shell program or to DOS, depending on how you started the program.

P art III shows you how to optimize your computer system so that it runs at peak efficiency.

Chapter 11 explains how Calibrate assesses the performance of your hard disk and lets you alter the interleave factor for faster performance. Chapter 12 describes how the Norton Utilities disk cache programs speed up disk access by making often accessed data more readily available. In Chapter 13, you learn how to increase the performance of your hard disk by reducing file fragmentation with the famous Norton Utilities Speed Disk program.

PART

Optimization

III

11

Calibrate (CALIBRAT)

Optimizing the Speed of Data Transfer to a Hard Disk

CHAPTER **11** _____

CALIBRATE TESTS THE INTERLEAVE FACTOR OF YOUR hard disk and tries to increase disk performance by changing it to a different value. If the analysis indicates that another interleave factor will result in improved disk access time, Calibrate can perform this optimization for you.

The *interleave factor* is the order in which the sectors were arranged on your hard disk by the initial low-level format. Because data can be read from or written to a hard disk much faster than the computer can read it from the disk controller, the interleave factor is used to keep the disk running in step with the computer. Numerically sequential sectors are not always contiguous; they might be separated by a predetermined number of physical sectors. If your hard disk is set at the wrong interleave factor, your system cannot operate at its optimum speed.

Changing the interleave factor on your hard disk is a one-time operation. Before Calibrate became part of the Norton Utilities, performing this operation was always a complex procedure. First, you had to determine an optimum interleave by some method. Next, you needed to back up all the files from your hard disk, run a low-level format program such as Disk Manager or use Debug to access the low-level format on your hard disk controller, and then run FDISK to partition the disk. Only after you used FORMAT to lay down a new boot track, root directory, and FAT, could you finally reload all your files and data onto the hard disk from your backup. Calibrate changes all that.

Calibrate determines the current interleave factor and indicates the possible speed increase you will see if that factor is less than the optimum setting.

The interleave factor is described in Chapter 2.

Calibrate will not work on network drives.

CH. 11

If you think there are any incompatibilities between your hardware and Calibrate, back up your hard disk before you change the interleave factor.

If you decide to change to the new interleave factor, Calibrate will reformat your hard disk in a nondestructive way. This saves you from having to back up all your files first.

Do not load any TSR (terminate-and-stay-resident) programs before you use Calibrate; in fact, it is a good idea to boot up from a floppy disk containing DOS, so that you are using only the basic DOS system with no additional resident programs. Calibrate is completely automatic in use—merely select or click on the Continue button to advance to the next stage, or select Stop to abandon the procedure.

To start Calibrate, select it from the menu in the NORTON shell program, or if you want to start Calibrate directly from the DOS prompt, type:

CALIBRAT

The opening Calibrate screen is shown in Figure 11.1.

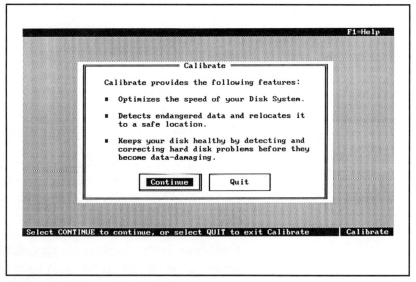

Figure 11.1: The opening Calibrate screen

Calibrate performs the following functions:

- It measures and changes the sector interleave factor on your hard disk to improve disk access times.

- It finds bad sectors and moves the information contained in them to a safe location on your disk.

- It finds bad unused sectors and marks them so that they will never be used by DOS.

After the Select Drive window opens, select the drive you want to test and optimize. If you have a hard disk divided into several partitions, you should run Calibrate on all of the partitions. Calibrate only works on physical drives; it cannot work with:

- floppy disks

- Iomega Bernoulli Boxes

- RAM disks

- drives specified in DOS ASSIGN or SUBST commands

- Novell file server systems

- disk controllers that do not allow interleave modification, such as the Small Computer System Interface (SCSI)

- drives with controllers that translate the number of sectors per track, such as many Enhanced Small Device Interface (ESDI) controllers

To ensure that Calibrate is compatible with your disk system, the program executes four sets of checks before proceeding further. Figure 11.2 shows the four types of tests that Calibrate performs.

Each of these tests consists of many smaller tests as described in the next four sections.

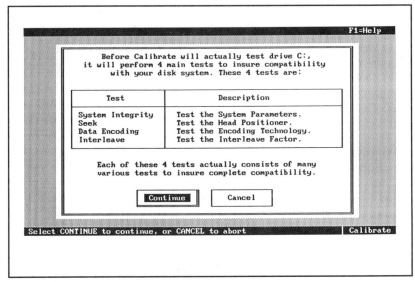

Figure 11.2: The Calibrate utility runs four sets of tests to ensure compatibility with your disk system

SYSTEM INTEGRITY

The System Integrity Tests screen is shown in Figure 11.3.

- Memory Tests check your system memory for errors. The DMA (Direct Memory Access) test checks the DMA hardware for problems because Calibrate cannot work with a defective DMA controller. The controller test checks the memory on your disk controller card.

- Disk Tests check the logical and physical characteristics of your hard disk system. If you are using a disk caching program, Calibrate will find it.

- System Tests check the hardware clock and ensure that the CMOS hard disk configuration data actually matches the characteristics of your hard disk. (This test does not apply to PC/XTs because they do not have a CMOS configuration.)

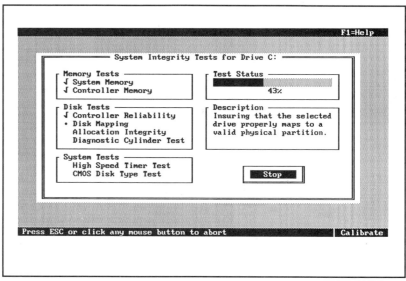

Figure 11.3: The System Integrity Tests screen

Use System Info to examine the settings in your CMOS configuration.

When these tests are complete, Calibrate advances to the Seek tests.

SEEK TESTS

The Seek tests display is shown in Figure 11.4.

The center of the screen displays a simulated single-disk platter and its read/write heads. As the test proceeds, the "disk heads" on the screen move to demonstrate how the actual disk hardware is being tested inside the sealed enclosure. An analog display in the lower portion of the screen indicates the progress being made throughout the test set.

If you run Calibrate from the DOS prompt using the /NOSEEK switch, you can bypass the Seek tests.

The tests being performed are listed above the graphic. Watching these tests will give you a good idea of your hard disk's performance:

- BIOS Seek Overhead is a measure of the amount of time your system spends executing code that communicates to your hard disk controller.

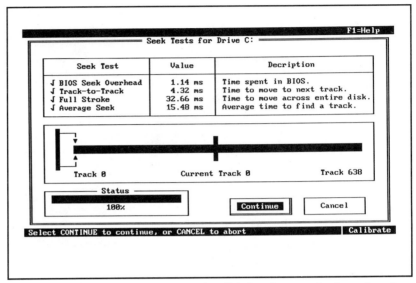

Figure 11.4: During the Seek tests, the disk heads move backward and forward very quickly

- Track-to-Track is how long it takes for the disk heads to move from one track to an adjacent track, settle, and start reading data.

- Full Stroke measures the time it takes to move the heads from one side of the disk (or partition) to the other.

- Average Seek is calculated as the average time of a series of random movements.

In Figure 11.4, BIOS Seek Overhead is calculated at 1.14 ms, Track-to-Track access time is 4.32 ms, Full Stroke is 32.66 ms, and the Average Seek time is 15.48 ms.

DATA ENCODING

The Data Encoding Tests screen is shown in Figure 11.5. The following tests evaluate the physical characteristics of the

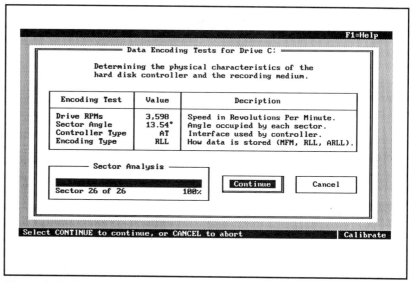

Figure 11.5: The Data Encoding Tests screen

disk controller and the format of the data:

- Drive RPMs indicates the speed that the disk is spinning in revolutions per minute. Most disks revolve at about 3,600 RPM, but several high performance disks revolve faster.

- Sector Angle indicates the angular size of the sectors.

- Controller Type identifies the type of disk controller as XT, AT, ESDI, or SCSI.

- Encoding Type identifies the actual format used to record data onto the disk from the three most common types: MFM (Modified Frequency Modulation), RLL (Run Length Limited), or ARRL (Advanced Run Length Limited). RLL uses data compression techniques to pack about 50 percent more data into the same space as MFM, and ARRL can store up to 100 percent more data than MFM.

INTERLEAVE

If your disk hardware passes all the previous tests, Calibrate next checks the interleave factor currently being used on your hard disk system. The next screen shows a bar chart that depicts the results of Calibrate's tests. Different interleave factors are shown along the bottom of the screen, and the number of disk rotations needed to read the next numbered sector are shown on the left side of the screen. This chart is shown in Figure 11.6.

The current and the optimum interleave setting are both shown on the graph; the optimum setting is the smallest bar on the graph and is enclosed in a box. At the top of the graph you will see the calculated speed increase that will result from changing to the optimum setting. If your disk is already configured for its optimum interleave setting, there is no reason to change it; your disk system is working as fast as it can.

Use the arrow keys or the mouse to move the box to one of the other bars on the screen. As you do so, the message at the top of the screen changes to reflect the speed increase or

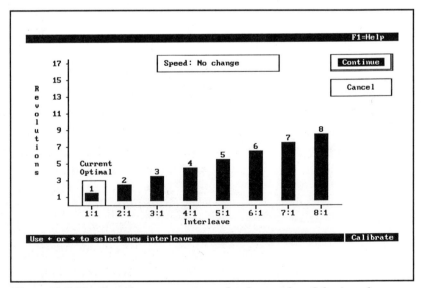

Figure 11.6: The Interleave screen graphs the results of the interleave tests

decrease that changing to that interleave will produce.

If your computer cannot display this interleave chart, it will open a dialog box telling you that Calibrate cannot modify the interleave on your drive. Calibrate then continues to the pattern testing portion of the program.

PATTERN TESTING

During this final phase of the program, Calibrate performs several operations on your hard disk:

- It reads the data from a complete track into memory

- It formats that track using the new interleave factor

- It writes a set of test patterns into each sector, and rereads the data to verify that it is correct (you can specify the intensity of these tests)

- Finally, it writes the original data back to the track again

The Pattern Testing selection screen is shown in Figure 11.7. You can select from four levels of pattern testing:

- **No Pattern Testing.** No pattern testing is done with the low-level reformatting of the disk. This is obviously the fastest way to change the interleave factor on your disk system, but it is also the least rigorous.

- **Minimal Pattern Testing.** Minimal level writes five different test patterns into each sector and reads them back as a verification check.

- **Standard Pattern Testing.** Standard level writes 40 different patterns into each sector, one pattern at a time. This is usually an adequate level of testing.

- **Rigorous Pattern Testing.** Rigorous testing is a stringent and time consuming test. It writes 80 different test patterns into each sector, reading each one back before moving to the next pattern. Run this advanced level of testing if you have doubts about your hard disk, if DOS has reported disk read errors such as "Sector read error on drive *x*," or if you have recently installed a new hard disk.

Choose the appropriate level of testing with the mouse or the arrow keys and the spacebar; then click on or choose **OK**. The more testing you do, the more secure you can feel about the integrity of your hard disk system. When Calibrate finds a bad sector, it marks the cluster containing the sector and does not write any data into that cluster when the reformatting is complete. Any data that was in this cluster is written to a safe area of the disk. Almost all hard disks contain a small number of bad sectors, so don't be surprised if Pattern Testing finds these.

This entire testing and reformatting process can take many hours, varying according to the size and speed of your disk system and the level of pattern testing you choose.

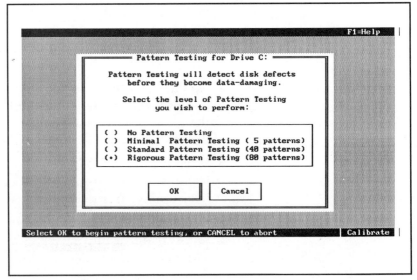

Figure 11.7: The Pattern Testing selection screen lets you specify the level of testing to use

Next you will see the Pattern Testing and Reformatting screen as shown in Figure 11.8.

This screen is similar to the disk map used by Speed Disk; each portion of the disk is represented by square characters on the screen. The **Legend** box at the lower right of the screen explains what the different characters represent. You can monitor the program's progress by noting the character at the cursor, which indicates pattern testing, verifying, or reformatting. Not only does the main screen highlight reformatted clusters, it also displays a percent completed display at the lower left of the screen. The current time and the estimated completion time are also shown to let you know how long this process will take. The current and total number of tracks on the disk are also shown.

Reformatting with the rigorous level of pattern testing can take many hours, so you can turn off this disk map display by pressing the spacebar. In its place, the program displays only the percentage of the operation completed and a message indicating that you can press the spacebar to return to the full display. This small message window moves around the screen as

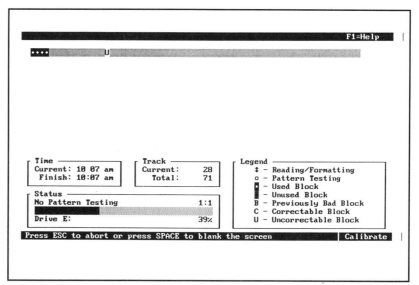

Figure 11.8: The Pattern Testing and Reformatting screen shows the progress being made

Calibrate runs to prevent the disk map display from creating a shadow in the phosphor of your monitor.

Next, you will see the Calibrate report on the screen, as shown in Figure 11.9.

Use the arrow keys or the scroll bars to move through the report. You can also send the report to your printer or save it to a disk file for later review. If you choose Save As, a window opens to let you specify a file name for the report. Finally, you return to the Calibrate Select Drive window to choose another drive for optimization. Select a drive, or choose Cancel or press Esc to return to the NORTON shell program or to DOS.

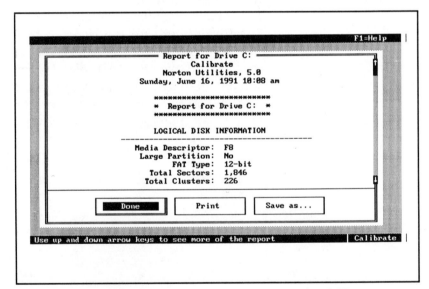

Figure 11.9: You can use the arrow keys to examine the Calibrate report on the screen

RUNNING CALIBRATE FROM THE DOS PROMPT

You can run Calibrate from the DOS prompt in several different ways. To bypass the Calibrate Select Drive window, specify

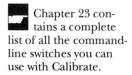
Chapter 23 contains a complete list of all the command-line switches you can use with Calibrate.

the drive letter for optimization on the command line by typing:

CALIBRAT C:

To avoid running the Seek tests, add the /NOSEEK switch to the command line:

CALIBRAT C:/NOSEEK

If you are using Calibrate as a diagnostic tool to test your disk drive, you can specify the level of pattern testing you require by typing:

CALIBRAT C:/PATTERN:n

in which n is the level of testing you want to use. Specify n as either 0, 5, 40, or 80.

Norton Cache (NCACHE)

Improving Computer Performance with a RAM Buffer

CHAPTER **12**

You should use only one cache program at a time.

WHEN YOUR APPLICATION PROGRAM NEEDS DATA FROM the disk, it asks DOS to find it. DOS reads the data and passes it to the application program. If you are updating your database, for example, this can mean that the same data is requested and read many times during the update. A *disk cache* program mediates between the application and the hard disk controller. Now, when the application program requests data that is on the disk, the cache program first checks to see if the data is already in the cache memory. If it is, the disk cache program loads the data from the cache memory rather than from the hard disk. If the data is not in memory, the cache program reads the data from the disk, copies it into the cache memory for future reference, and then passes the data to the application program. Figure 12.1 shows how a disk cache program works.

If you primarily work with programs such as word processors that do not read data from the hard disk often, you will see a modest speed increase from the disk cache; however, if you use a database or a language compiler that continually reads the disk, you will see a startling increase in speed. Because a database program often needs to read the same file (such as an index) many times during an update, chances are good that the data is already in the cache. If your system includes extended or expanded memory, the cache program can locate its cache buffer in extended or expanded memory, thus using only a small amount of conventional memory for the program that controls the cache. A disk cache program can let DOS read and write to a floppy disk 50 times faster and can make hard disk access 10 times faster.

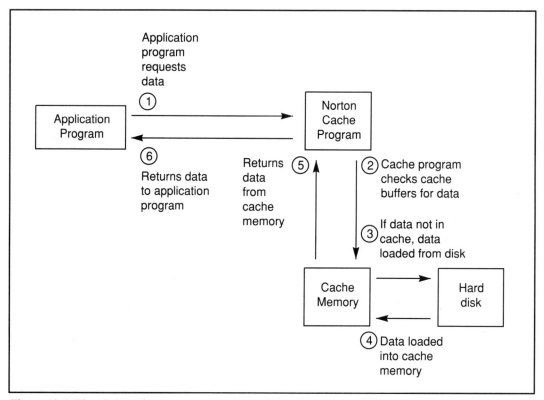

Figure 12.1: The disk cache program mediates between your application program and the hard disk controller

Because computer users constantly face choices between increasing speed but using more memory, the Norton Utilities provides two disk caching programs—NCACHE-S (the S signifies *small*) and NCACHE-F (the F signifies *fast*). To decide which you should use, you must examine both your hardware and the way in which you use your computer.

NCACHE-F is best suited for a 80286 or 80386 computer with expanded or extended memory available. NCACHE-F buffers both disk reads and disk writes, and it can delay writes until after reads.

NCACHE-S conserves memory usage, so if you have little memory available or are using an XT, this is the cache program for you. It buffers read requests but does not buffer writes. You can also configure it to take less than 5K of DOS memory.

LOADING NCACHE

You can configure the Norton cache program during the initial installation of the Utilities, or you can load it from the DOS prompt by typing the name of the program followed by any parameters you want to use. To be sure the cache program is loaded every time you boot your computer, add a command to your CONFIG.SYS file that uses the following format:

DEVICE=C:\NORTON\NCACHE-F.EXE *parameters*

or

DEVICE=C:\NORTON\NCACHE-S.EXE *parameters*

assuming that the two cache programs are in the NORTON directory on drive C. Alternatively, you can install the cache by adding a line similar to the following to your AUTOEXEC.BAT file after the PATH statement:

NCACHE-F *parameters*

or

NCACHE-S *parameters*

The difference between these two installation techniques is that if you load the program with CONFIG.SYS you cannot uninstall the cache. However, you *can* uninstall the cache if you load the program from the DOS prompt or as the last TSR program in your AUTOEXEC.BAT.

After you have loaded one of the caches, the program immediately displays the cache status screen. (For a complete description of this screen, see the last section of this chapter.)

CONFIGURING THE CACHE

You can use several options to configure the cache programs to your own working environment. The following parameters apply to both NCACHE-F and NCACHE-S.

- BLOCK=*nnn.* Sets the size of the cache blocks. Larger blocks allow the cache table to be smaller, and smaller blocks mean the cache buffer is used more efficiently. Use small blocks if you work with a lot of small files.

The next three sets of options tell the cache how much and what kind of memory is available for it to use. If you specify a positive number, the cache will use this amount of memory; if you specify a negative number, the cache must leave this amount of memory free for other application programs.

- EXT=*nnn.* Use this amount of extended memory (in kilobytes) for the cache.

- EXT=–*nnn.* Leave this much extended memory (in kilobytes) free for other application programs. If you do not specify a number, the cache program will use all extended memory.

- EXP=*nnn.* Use this amount of expanded memory for the cache.

- EXP=–*nnn.* Leave this much expanded memory free. If you do not specify a number, the cache program will use all expanded memory.

- DOS=*nnn.* Use this much DOS memory.

- DOS=–*nnn.* Leave this much conventional memory free. If you don't specify a number, the cache program will create a 128K cache. If you have extended or expanded memory, do not use this option because it reduces the amount of conventional memory available to your application programs.

- INI=*path*. Specifies the path to use to find the parameter file containing the installation options.

- RESET. Resets the cache statistics shown on the status screen.

- HELP or ?. Displays a help screen.

- STATUS. Displays a status screen that details cache statistics. This status screen is described in the last section of this chapter.

- UNINSTALL. Removes the cache if it was loaded from the DOS prompt or by AUTOEXEC.BAT. You cannot remove the cache if you loaded it using CONFIG.SYS.

- USEHIDOS YES/NO. High memory is provided by memory managers such as QEMM or 386-to-the-Max, and using it can cut the requirement for main DOS memory to as little as 12K. The usual default is NO.

- USEHMA YES/NO. XMS High Memory is made available by extended memory managers such as HIMEM.SYS or EME.EXE. The default is YES.

- SAVE. Saves the current cache configuration as the default setting.

- PRINT. Copies the display to the printer.

- PAUSE. Pauses display scrolling.

The following parameters only apply to NCACHE-F:

- DELAY=*ss.hh*. Specifies a time delay in seconds and hundredths of seconds to delay disk writes. If you use a cache with a program on a floppy disk, do not remove the floppy from the drive until you clear the write buffer with the F option; otherwise, you will lose data. If this data includes an update to the FAT, the results could be devastating. The default is no delay.

- QUICK ON/OFF. If QUICK is set to ON, and the Intelli-Writes switch (I) is also on, DOS prompts are displayed even if the current disk operation is not complete. If you use this setting and use a cache with a floppy disk drive, be sure that all write operations are complete before you remove the floppy disk; otherwise, you may lose data. The default is QUICK=OFF, which completes all write operations before returning the DOS prompt.

The following options apply to both cache programs. For those options with a +/− designation, the + sign enables the option and the − sign disables the option.

- +/− A. Turns disk caching on or off.

- +/− C. Enables or disables the caching of additional data.

- F. Flushes, or empties, the cache. All remaining writes are written to disk before the buffer is reinitialized.

- G=*nnn*. Specifies the Group Sector Size, which limits the number of sectors loaded into the buffer from each read. The default is 128, equivalent to 64K.

- +/− W. Enables or disables write-through caching. If you enable this setting, the cache copies writes to the disk and to the cache. If you disable it, writes are not copied to the cache. This option has no effect if Intelli-Writes are on.

These final options only apply to NCACHE-F.

- +/− I. Enables or disables IntelliWrites. Turning on this setting accelerates disk writes and returns control to the application program before the write is complete.

- R=D*nn*. Specifies how many sectors ahead the cache should read. R=*nn* always allows read ahead, and R=D*nn* allows read ahead only if the sectors are sequential and not random. R can be set to a value between 0 and 15. R=0 and R=D0 disable the read ahead setting.

- +/– S. Enables or disables SmartReads. Enabling SmartReads allows the cache to read additional data before writing data. This almost always improves the performance of your computer, because programs usually make more reads than writes. If you turn off SmartReads, all data must be written to the disk before any new data can be read.

CACHE CONFIGURATION EXAMPLES

Now that you know all the options for the two cache programs, let's look at how you might use them on your computer system.

If your computer is an PC/XT or a laptop with no extended or expanded memory, you will have to balance the speed increase gained through using the cache against the memory space lost to the cache program and the cache buffers themselves. The best solution is to use NCACHE-S, which minimizes the amount of memory used by the cache program and limits the size of the cache buffers themselves. To do this, add the following line to your AUTOEXEC.BAT file:

NCACHE-S DOS=64 G=40

This limits the amount of memory used to 64K, an amount large enough to be useful, but not too large to prohibit other application programs from running. G=40 prevents the cache from filling up every time a read is made. You should determine the best setting for G by experimentation, but a setting of G=40 is equivalent to 20K.

If, on the other hand, you have an 80386 computer with several megabytes of RAM, you should use NCACHE-F to optimize speed at the expense of using some memory space. To create a 500K cache using SmartReads and IntelliWrites, add this line to your AUTOEXEC.BAT file:

NCACHE-F EXP=500 +S +I

If you are using the 386-to-the-Max memory manager, you can use the following line instead:

NCACHE-F USEHIDOS=YES EXP=500 +S +I

If you are concerned about removing a floppy disk from its drive before all the writes are complete, you can use the cache only on your hard disk and have your floppy disks work as usual; simply add the line:

NCACHE-F EXP=500 a: –a b: –b

to your AUTOEXEC.BAT file.

UNDERSTANDING THE CACHE STATUS SCREEN

If you want to see how your cache is performing, you can use the STATUS parameter from the DOS prompt to display the Norton Cache Status screen. An example of this screen for NCACHE-F is shown in Figure 12.2.

The Status screen for NCACHE-S is similar to the screen in Figure 12.2. The program name at the top left corner is different, and fewer cache options are detailed on the screen because NCACHE-S does not include all the options of NCACHE-F.

The top portion of the screen shows how the memory in your computer is being used by the cache program, the cache configuration tables, and the actual cache buffers. This part of the screen also displays the amount of DOS, extended, and expanded memory in use.

The next line, Cache Allocated, shows how full the current cache is. If you have only recently started to use the cache, it might be less than full.

On the next line, you can see details of how the cache is configured, including the status of DELAY and QUICK for NCACHE-F.

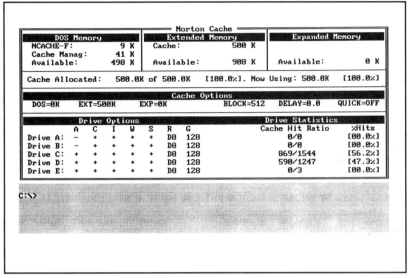

Figure 12.2: The Norton Cache Status screen for NCACHE-F

The last and largest part of the screen displays a table of all the cached drives and their current settings, along with the cache statistics for each drive. At the left side of the screen, the Drive Options section shows which options are in effect for which drives. A plus (+) sign next to the drive indicates that the option in the heading is enabled. In Figure 12.2 neither drive A nor drive B are being cached, and the Drive Options are set as follows:

- A caching enabled for that drive
- C caching of additional data
- I IntelliWrites enabled
- W write-through caching enabled
- S SmartReads enabled
- R read-ahead disabled
- G Group Sector Size value

At the right of the screen, the Drive Statistics section displays the Cache Hit Ratio and the percentage of hits. The Cache Hit Ratio shows how many sectors (not files) were read from the cache against the number actually read from the disk. The higher the Percentage Hits, the more effective the cache settings. Remember that because all data must originally be read from the disk, it is impossible to see a Percentage Hits of 100 percent.

If you change a cache option, the status screen is displayed again with the changed item highlighted. The rest of the settings are shown in normal intensity.

Finally, do not use the DOS FASTOPEN command if you are using one of the Norton Cache programs. FASTOPEN is much less efficient than the Norton Cache programs, and it can sometimes cause problems with other application programs.

Speed Disk (SPEEDISK)

Optimizing Disk Speed by Unfragmenting and Reorganizing Your Files

CHAPTER *13* _____

FILES ARE WRITTEN TO THE DISK IN GROUPS OF SECTORS called clusters. When you write a short file to disk, it occupies the first available cluster. When you write another short file to the same disk, this file occupies the next available cluster. Then, if you modify the first file by increasing its size above that of one cluster and save it under the same file name, DOS cannot push the second file up the disk to make room for the larger first file. Instead, DOS *fragments* this file by splitting it in two pieces, one occupying the first cluster and one occupying the third cluster. This is the way DOS was designed to work.

The potential problem with fragmentation is that the disk heads have to move to different locations on the disk to read or write to a fragmented file. This takes more time than reading the same file from a series of consecutive clusters. By reducing or eliminating fragmentation, you can increase the performance of your disk.

Another benefit of unfragmenting a disk is that DOS is less likely to fragment files that you subsequently add to the disk. If you should delete and then try to unerase any of these added files, your chances of success would be higher because unfragmented files are usually easier to unerase. On the other hand, unfragmenting, or *optimizing,* your disk will probably make it impossible to recover any files that were deleted before the optimization. The reason for this is that Speed Disk "moves" data by rewriting it at new locations and it will probably write over any erased files in the process.

To remove the effects of file fragmentation, all the files on the disk must be rearranged so that they consist of consecutive clusters. You can do this yourself by copying all the files and directories to backup disks, reformatting the hard disk, and reloading all the files back onto the hard disk, but that would be

◉ If you need to recover erased files, do so before you unfragment a disk with Speed Disk.

a tremendous amount of tedious work. It is much easier to use a program designed for eliminating file fragmentation—the Norton Speed Disk utility.

PRECAUTIONS TO TAKE BEFORE RUNNING SPEED DISK ON YOUR HARD DISK

Be sure to make a complete hard-disk backup before you use Speed Disk to reorganize your files.

Before you have Speed Disk actually reorganize the files on your disk, you must take a few precautions:

- Completely back up your hard disk in case your system and the Speed Disk utility are incompatible. Problems sometimes occur because of the enormous number of potential combinations of disks and disk controllers.

Never turn off your computer while Speed Disk is running.

- Do not turn off your computer while Speed Disk is running. The only safe way to interrupt Speed Disk is by pressing Esc. Speed Disk will not stop working immediately but will continue to run until it reaches a convenient, safe point at which to do so.

- Be sure to disable any memory-resident software that might access the disk while Speed Disk is running. For example, some programs save your work to the hard disk at set time intervals. This type of software must be turned off.

If you are using the DOS FASTOPEN utility or any other disk-buffering program, you will probably have to reboot your computer after running Speed Disk. Because Speed Disk changes directory and file locations on the disk when it optimizes the disk, FASTOPEN might not find the files where it expects to find them. If DOS displays the message "File not found" after you run Speed Disk, reboot your computer and try again.

The Norton Disk Doctor is discussed in Chapter 3.

Before running Speed Disk, you should run the DOS CHKDSK command to remove any lost clusters and the Norton Disk Doctor to find and fix any bad sectors on your disk. This gives Speed Disk a clean system to work with.

UNFRAGMENTING YOUR HARD DISK WITH SPEED DISK

Although Speed Disk reports on specific files and directories, you cannot un-fragment only selected files or directories.

You cannot use Speed Disk on a network drive.

Select Speed Disk from the NORTON shell program main menu, or start Speed Disk from the DOS prompt by typing:

SPEEDISK

The program starts with the display shown in Figure 13.1.

Select the drive letter of the disk you want to optimize by using the arrow keys; then move the cursor to the OK box and press Enter. (You can also double click on the drive letter with the mouse.) After Speed Disk reads and analyzes the data on the chosen drive, it visually displays memory usage and informs you which level of optimization is required. Figure 13.2 shows this display for a 33MB hard disk.

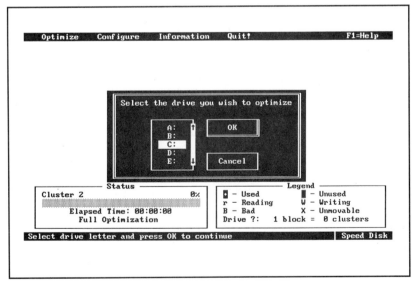

Figure 13.1: The Speed Disk startup screen

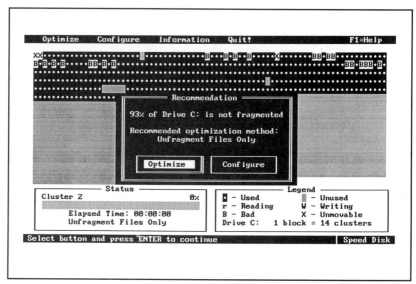

Figure 13.2: A Speed Disk map for drive C

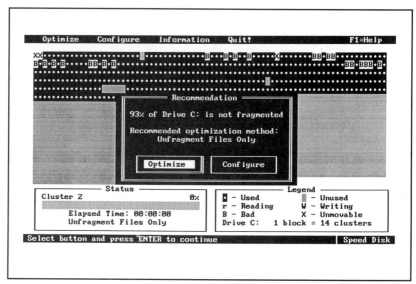 Speed Disk is smart enough to know when optimization is not needed and will display the message "No Optimization Necessary."

In Figure 13.2, Speed Disk shows the percentage of fragmentation for the 33MB hard disk and recommends an optimization method based on this percentage. The two boxes on the screen give you the choice of optimizing your disk or configuring Speed Disk. The first time you run Speed Disk, press Esc to go to the Configure pull-down menu. After you have examined all the possible options you can run the optimization.

The Legend box, at the lower right corner of the screen, defines the graphic characters used to make the disk-usage map. The characters represent the following elements:

- Used Block. The "used block" character designates the area of the disk currently occupied by files. It represents all the directories and files in the data area of the disk.

- Unused Block. The "unused block" character designates the area of the disk occupied by clusters not allocated to files. Speed Disk can consolidate this space and make it available as part of the unused disk space at the end of the files' area on the disk.

- Bad Block. The "bad block" character—an upper-case **B**—represents any bad blocks on the disk. Note that the example disk has several bad blocks.

- Unmovable Block. The "unmovable block" character—an uppercase **X**—marks the position of any files or directories that Speed Disk cannot move. The **X** characters at the upper left corner of the display in Figure 13.2 represent the hidden DOS system files. To avoid interfering with copy-protection schemes, Speed Disk does not move hidden files.

Depending on the size of the current disk, each legend character on the screen represents a specific amount of disk space. In Figure 13.2 each character represents 14 clusters.

The **Status** box at the lower left of the screen displays Speed Disk's progress after you start the optimization. The current cluster number and percentage-complete value are shown as numbers, along with the optimization type and the time that has elapsed so far. The horizontal bar displays the percentage of the operation that has been completed as an analog display.

CHOOSING THE RIGHT OPTIMIZATION METHOD

Speed Disk provides pull-down menus that let you configure the program and make the appropriate optimization selection. Selecting the Optimize pull-down menu displays the following three selections.

Don't start optimizing until you're sure that all options are set correctly.

Begin Optimization (Alt-B) begins the process of unfragmenting the drive. Don't select this option until you're sure that all the other options are set correctly.

Change Drive lets you switch to another drive. It opens a window that is similar to the initial drive selection screen you used when Speed Disk first started. Use the arrow keys to highlight a new drive letter or type in the drive letter and press Enter. With the mouse, simply double click on the new drive letter.

Optimization Method lets you choose the type of optimization that Speed Disk will run on your disk. When you select this choice, the Select Optimization Method window opens, as shown in Figure 13.3.

Choose the method that is best suited to your disk and the way you work with your system; you don't always have to use the same method every time. You can select one of the following radio buttons:

- Full Optimization. This option initiates the most complete optimization offered by Speed Disk. It will give the greatest performance increase, but it is also the slowest of all the sort methods because of the amount of work it does. When you select Full Optimization, all directories are moved to the front of the disk, all (nonhidden) files are unfragmented, and all unused space is collected into one large block at the end of the files on the disk.

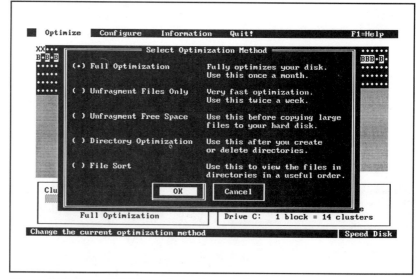

Figure 13.3: Speed Disk's optimization methods

- Unfragment Files Only. This selection unfragments as many files as it can, but leaves some files still fragmented, and may leave the unused space between files untouched. This selection does not move directories. Unfragment Files Only works very quickly.

- Unfragment Free Space. This selection rearranges the files on your disk by filling all the unused space between files. Unused space is then collected and stored at the end of the disk. However, the files themselves are not unfragmented. You can use this selection to create a single block of free space before you install a new software package.

- Directory Optimization. This selection only moves directories. No files are unfragmented, and unused space remains between files. Because this option does relatively little work, it executes very quickly. Use Directory Optimization if you have created or removed directories.

- File Sort. This selection sorts files inside their directories; it does not do any disk optimization. Use the File Sort selection from the Configure pull-down menu to choose the file sort criteria. (This is described in the next section.)

Use the arrow keys or the mouse to choose one of these optimization methods. Next, select the Configure pull-down menu selections to complete the optimization setup.

CONFIGURING SPEED DISK

The Configure pull-down menu, shown in Figure 13.4, contains six options.

- Directory Order. This selection lets you manipulate the order in which Speed Disk arranges the directories. You do this by working with a graphic display of

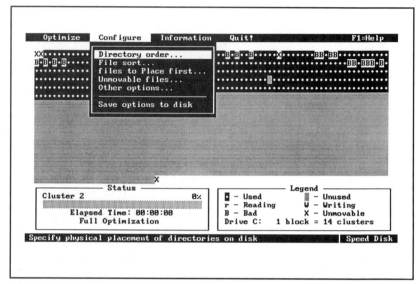

Figure 13.4: Speed Disk's Configure pull-down menu offers six options

the disk's directory, as shown in Figure 13.5. The window is divided into two parts: the Directory List shows all the directories on your disk in a graphical form, and Directory Order shows the sequence in which the directories are arranged. The default directory order is taken from the path you established in your AUTOEXEC.BAT file. To select a directory from the Directory List, use the up and down arrow keys to highlight the directory name, and then press Enter or click on the **Add** box. You will see the directory name appear at the top of the list in the Directory Order display. You can also use the **Speed Search** box to move directly to a specific directory. Use the left and right arrows to move between the two windows. The Directory Order display provides two more options: **Delete** and **Move**.

Delete. To delete a directory from the Directory Order screen, highlight its name, move the cursor to the **Delete** box with the Tab key, and press Enter.

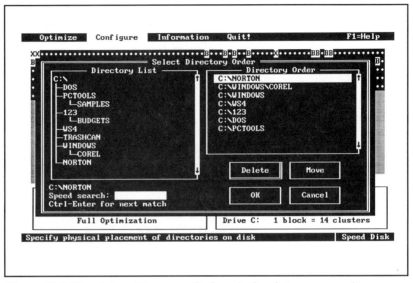

Figure 13.5: The Select Directory Order window lets you organize your
directories

Move. To move a directory, highlight the name, and
use the up and down arrow keys to place the directory at a new location. Press Enter to confirm the
position of the directory.

OK. When you are satisfied with the placement of
directories, select OK to return to the main Speed
Disk screen.

- File Sort. Use this selection to specify the order in
  which you want your files arranged if you chose File
  Sort from the Optimize pull-down menu. The File Sort
  window is shown in Figure 13.6. File Sort will arrange
  your files according to one selection from the Sort
  Criterion list. You can sort by name, extension, date
  and time, file size, or you can choose unsorted. Unsorted does not change the order of your files; it leaves
  them exactly where they are. You can also make the
  sort ascending or descending. Select OK after you have
  made your choice.

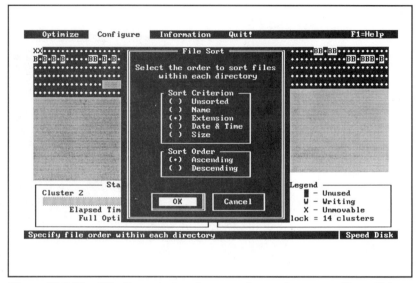

Figure 13.6: The File Sort window lets you choose how your files will be arranged

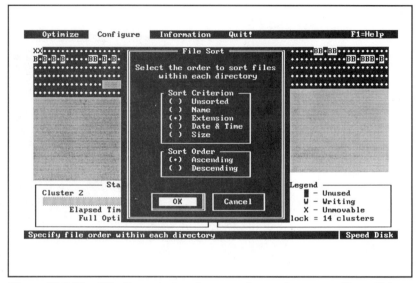
Putting program files near the outer edge of the disk helps prevent fragmentation.

- Files to Place First. This lets you choose which files to put at the "front" (the outer edge) of the disk. Use this option to position your program files, which do not change in size, close to the FAT. The first time this window opens it contains two file specifications: *.EXE and *.COM. You can add or remove files, and you can use the DOS wildcard characters in the file specifications. Position your data files, which do change size when you modify them, after your program files. This arrangement avoids future file fragmentation by preventing space from opening up near the front, or outer edge, of the disk. The Files to Place First window is shown in Figure 13.7. You can use wildcards to help relocate files. For example, to relocate all .EXE files, you would type:

  *.EXE

  into the highlighted box. Use the Delete, Insert, and Move boxes to rearrange the entries in the list.

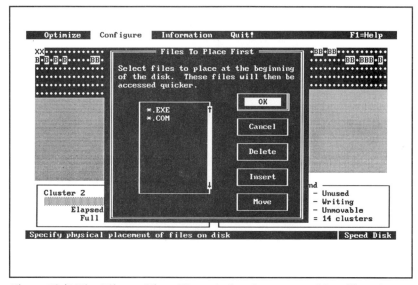

Figure 13.7: The Files to Place First window lets you position files where you want them

Delete. To remove an entry from the list, highlight the entry, move the cursor to the Delete box, and press Enter.

Insert. To insert a new entry, highlight the entry immediately below where you want to make the insertion, move the cursor to the Insert box, and press Enter. A blank space opens for you to add the new filespec.

Move. To move an entry, place the highlight over the entry, position the the cursor in the Move box, and press Enter. Use the up and down arrow keys to move the entry to its new location and press Enter.

After you have completed your entries, select OK to return to the Configure pull-down menu on the main Speed Disk screen.

- **Unmovable Files.** Use this selection to enter the names of files that you do not want to be moved during optimization. This window holds only ten entries, but you can use the DOS wildcard characters to extend the selection to more than ten files.

- Other Options. This selection includes three options. Note that you can choose more than one option from this list:

  Read-After-Write. By default, Speed Disk uses this setting as a check for the optimization process. However, because it is such a rigorous check, it can take up to twice as long to perform the checks as the next selection.

  Use DOS Verify. This selection is faster than the Read-After-Write, but it can be less accurate. You can ensure the highest degree of accuracy by turning on both Read-After-Write and Use DOS Verify.

  Clear Unused Space. Speed Disk can wipe clean all areas of the disk that are not being used to store files or directories. The Clear Unused Space option writes zeros into all the unused clusters on the disk during the optimization process.

- Save Options to Disk. This selection saves the options you have chosen to a small hidden file (called SD.INI) in the root directory of the disk you are optimizing, and returns you to the main Speed Disk screen. The next time you run Speed Disk, these configuration options are loaded from the SD.INI file and used as the default startup settings.

SPEED DISK INFORMATION

The selections in the Information pull-down menu let you look at fragmentation and disk statistics.

Choose Fragmentation Report to check the degree to which a file, directory, or disk is fragmented before you decide whether to start the file reorganization process. Daily and weekly file fragmentation reports show you how fragmentation on your disk is changing over time and tell you how often you should run Speed Disk to get the best results.

The report is shown in Figure 13.8. The left side of the File Fragmentation Report window shows a graphical display of your directory structure, and the right side shows the files in the directory. As you use the arrow keys to change to a different directory in the left window, the file display changes to show the files in the new directory. You can also use Speed Search to enter a directory name. A "percent unfragmented" figure is given for each file in the directory. A value of 100 percent means that the file is not fragmented and that all its clusters are consecutive. A value lower than 100 percent signifies some degree of fragmentation in the file. Files that are moderately fragmented (90 percent or more unfragmented) are shown in red on a color monitor and in bold on a monochrome monitor. Highly fragmented files are bulleted and shown in yellow on a color monitor, and are bulleted on a monochrome monitor.

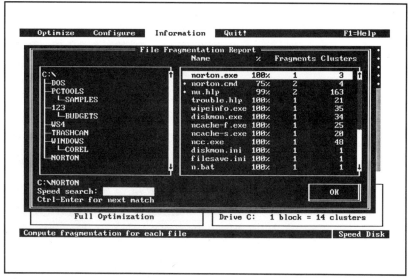

Figure 13.8: Speed Disk reports the percentage of fragmentation for all files in the directory

This window also shows the number of fragments each file or directory is broken into, as well as the total number of clusters the file or directory occupies. File names are shown in lower-case, and directory names are displayed in uppercase.

Select OK to return to the main Speed Disk screen. The other selections in the Information pull-down menu provide useful information about files and disks. You can choose from the following four selections:

- Disk Statistics. Disk Statistics provides detailed information about the drive you selected for optimization. Figure 13.9 shows the statistics for a 33MB hard disk. The statistics include the disk size, the amount of the disk used, the number of files and directories, and the percentage of unfragmented files. Also shown are details about the clusters allocated to movable and unmovable files, the clusters allocated to directories, the number of bad clusters, and the total number of clusters on the disk.

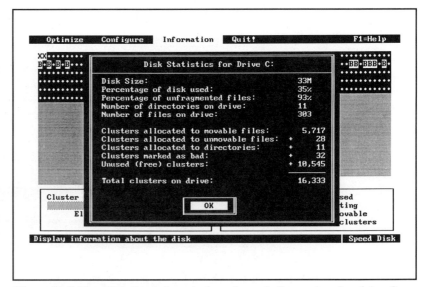

Figure 13.9: The Disk Statistics window shows information for drive C

- Map Legend. This selection opens an information window that shows the characters used on the disk map display while the disk is being optimized. This window, shown in Figure 13.10, is more detailed than the Legend box displayed on the main Speed Disk screen. As the optimization proceeds, you will see different characters on the screen, each one representing a different part of the process. Disk space in use by files or directories is indicated by the block with a dot in the center, and unused disk space is represented by an unfilled block. Bad blocks are represented by B, and clusters occupied by unmovable files are marked with an X. An r character shows the area of the disk currently being read, a W shows clusters being written, and a V shows that the data is being verified. If you selected Clear Unused Space in the Other Options from the Configure pull-down menu, you will see a C character to indicate clearing.

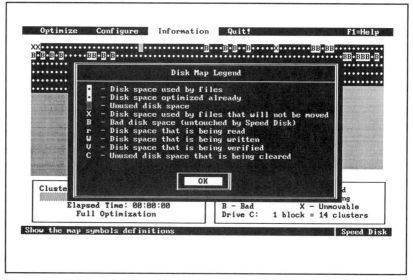

Figure 13.10: The Disk Map Legend shows the characters used during the optimization process

- Show Static Files. This selection opens the Static Files window, which lists all the files that Speed Disk cannot move. Figure 13.11 shows the DOS system files, IBMBIOS.COM and IBMDOS.COM, listed in the Static Files window along with several other files. These two files are position sensitive; they must be at a specific location on your disk, therefore Speed Disk will not move them.

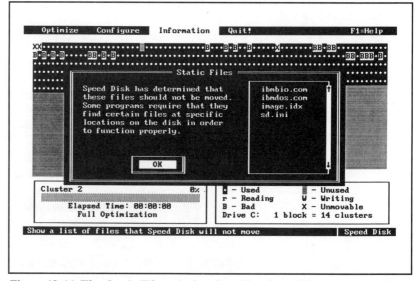
The MS-DOS names for these two files are IO.SYS and MSDOS.SYS.

- Walk Map. This selection lets you use the arrow keys to move around the disk map and display which files occupy which locations on your disk. The cluster range represented by the block character under the cursor is shown at the lower left of the disk map screen. When you find an area of the disk you want to look at more closely, press Enter to open the Contents of Map Block window, as shown in Figure 13.12. If you use a mouse,

Figure 13.11: The Static Files window lists files that will not be moved during the optimization

merely click on the area of the disk you want to examine. The window includes three columns of information: Cluster, File, and Status. The Cluster column lists the cluster numbers, the File column displays the name of the file that occupies that cluster, and the Status column indicates whether the file is fragmented or optimized. You might also see a cluster labeled as "bad," "unmovable," or simply "not used." Use the arrow keys or PgUp and PgDn to move through the display, or click on the scroll bars with the mouse. Press Enter to return to the Walk Map, and press Esc to return to the main Speed Disk screen.

The Quit menu selection returns you to the NORTON shell program or back to DOS, depending on the method you used to start Speed Disk.

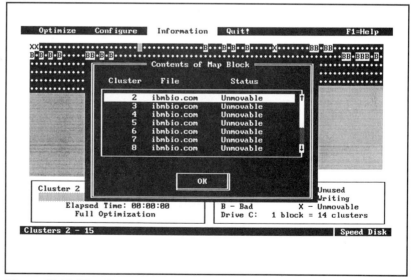

Figure 13.12: The Contents of Map Block window gives details of the chosen cluster range

RUNNING SPEED DISK

Optimization can take a long time, especially if you are unfragmenting an entire disk. Monitor the Status box to get an idea of how long the entire process will take. Press Esc if you need to stop the optimization.

When you are sure that all the options have been set correctly, choose Begin Optimization from the Optimize pull-down menu to start the process. Speed Disk unfragments the selected item or items, collecting all the free space and placing it at the end of the used blocks. The disk usage map shows you this process as Speed Disk works. As data is read from the disk, the r character moves across the screen. When the data is rewritten to the disk, W is used to indicate writing. If you turn the Verify option on, V indicates the progress of the verification process. A C represents unused disk space that is being cleared.

You can press Esc if you want to interrupt Speed Disk, but Speed Disk might not stop instantly—it will take a few moments to complete the current operation and tidy up before stopping. When optimization is complete, Speed Disk beeps the computer speaker to tell you it is finished. This means that you don't have to watch the display during the entire process.

SPEED DISK AND COPY-PROTECTION SCHEMES

Some copy-protection methods that rely on hidden files insist that the hidden files stay in exactly the same place on the disk. For example, Lotus 1-2-3 version 2.01 uses this method. If your copy-protection method uses hidden files and you move them to another location on the disk, your application program will often refuse to work—it thinks you are using an illegal copy. Speed Disk recognizes this problem and does not move hidden files in case moving them interferes with the copy-protection system. In fact, Speed Disk goes further than this: It will not move any .EXE file that does not have a standard file header. All such files are left alone. Also, Speed Disk will not move the hidden files—IBMBIO.COM and IBMDOS.COM or IO.SYS and

MSDOS.SYS—that DOS places at the beginning of all bootable disks. Remember, however, that the only way to be absolutely sure that Speed Disk will not interfere with a copy-protection scheme is to completely remove the software package before running Speed Disk, and then to reinstall it again after Speed Disk is finished.

RUNNING SPEED DISK FROM THE DOS PROMPT

If you run Speed Disk from the DOS prompt, you can take advantage of some of the special Speed Disk switches. For example, if you want to use the Unfragment Free Space option to collect all the free space on your C drive into one large piece, you can do so by typing:

```
SPEEDISK C: /Q
```

from the DOS prompt. Speed Disk runs the optimization automatically, without any prompting. Chapter 23 contains a complete list of the Speed Disk command line options.

Part IV discusses several important computer security issues, including data encryption.

Chapter 14 shows you how to use Disk Monitor to prevent unauthorized activity on your hard disk and how to park the heads on your hard disk system. Chapter 15 details the file-encryption program Diskreet and describes how to use passwords to protect your most important files.

In Chapter 16, you learn how to use a government standard technique for obliterating data from your disks so that the data can never be recovered.

PART IV

Security

Disk Monitor (DISKMON)

Approving Data before It Is
Written to Your Disk

CHAPTER *14* _____

DISK MONITOR PROVIDES THREE KINDS OF PROTECTION
for your disks. Disk Protect prevents unauthorized disk writes,
Disk Light displays the drive letter of the current drive, and
Disk Park moves your hard disk heads to a safe place on the disk
so that you can move your computer without fear of damaging
your hard disk. To start Disk Monitor, select it from the NORTON
shell program menu, or run it from the DOS prompt by typing:

DISKMON

This displays the opening Disk Monitor screen shown in Figure 14.1.

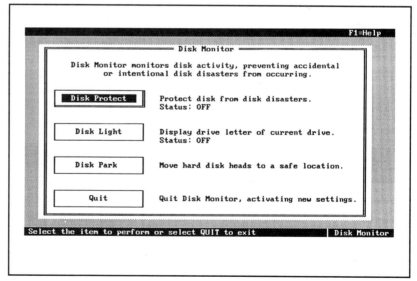

Figure 14.1: The Disk Monitor main menu screen

Use the arrow keys or the mouse to make selections from this screen.

DISK PROTECT

Disk Protect installs a small TSR program that watches over all attempts to write to your disks. This can provide some protection against viruses and also against accidental deletion of files.

Select Disk Protect from the main Disk Monitor screen and you will see the Disk Protect window as shown in Figure 14.2.

You can choose to protect the following areas of your disk:

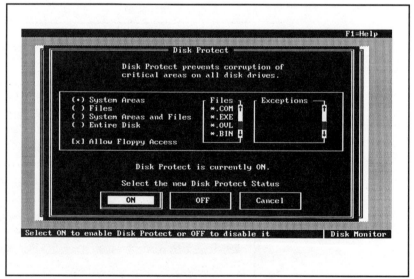

Not even the Norton Disk Editor can bypass Disk Protect.

- **System Areas** protects the hard disk partition table, the boot record, and all the DOS system files including COMMAND.COM. Several viruses are known to attach themselves to COMMAND.COM so this level of protection can prevent such a virus from attacking your system.

Figure 14.2: The Disk Protect window lets you choose the areas of the disk you want to protect

- Files protects all the files shown in the Files list, and disregards the files shown in the Exceptions list. You can insert nine entries in the Files list and 20 entries in the Exceptions list. Note, however, that you can use DOS wildcard characters in any or all of these entries. Directories are not protected, so you can still add or create new files using your applications programs.

- System Areas and Files combines the two previous options.

- Entire Disk effectively write protects your entire disk, including the system area, the FATs, the directories, and the unused free space on your disk. This selection stops all writes to all disks (including RAM disks) unless you manually allow each write yourself.

The Allow Floppy Format checkbox lets you format floppy disks while maintaining all other levels of protection. Press the spacebar or the X key, or click on the box with the mouse if you want to allow floppy disk formatting.

Select ON to turn Disk Protect on, or OFF to turn it off again. After you make your choice, the program returns you to the main Disk Monitor menu where you will see a reminder of your selection next to the Disk Protect Status entry.

When Disk Protect is on and you are using your computer in text mode, you are warned whenever a write is attempted on one of the protected areas of your disks. A window opens on the screen and informs you that a write operation was attempted on a protected area of your disk; Disk Monitor then gives you the choice of entering "Yes" to allow the write to take place, "No" to stop the write operation, or "Disable Protection" to turn the write protection off. Because each write operation is monitored at several different levels, you might have to answer Disk Monitor several times for the same write operation.

If you are using your computer in graphics mode when the write operation starts, perhaps using Windows, Disk Monitor cannot open the message window. Instead it rejects all write attempts and beeps the computer's speaker. You should then see an error message from your applications program because Disk Protect returns a write protection error to the program.

Another approach is to turn Disk Protect off when you know you will be using programs such as Windows, Ventura Publisher, or PageMaker, and then turn it on again when the application ends.

DISK LIGHT

Disk Light installs another small TSR program on your computer. This program displays a small indicator at the top right corner of your monitor when you access your disks. This can be very useful if your computer is positioned so that you can't see the drive lights, if you use a hardcard or work on a network, or if your computer is in a tower configuration on the floor under your desk.

Figure 14.3 shows the Disk Light window. Select **ON** to turn the disk light indicator on, or **OFF** to turn it off again.

You will not see this indicator if your applications program uses graphics mode.

Figure 14.3: The Disk Light window lets you turn the indicator on or off

If you are accessing drive C, you will see C− while data is being read from the disk and C+ while data is being written to the disk.

If you are using one of the Norton Cache programs, Disk Light will show less disk access than you might expect, because many of the reads are made directly from the cache buffer instead of the disk.

DISK PARK

Disk Park moves your hard disk heads to a safe place on the disk, so that you can power down or move your computer without worrying whether your disk heads will crash onto a useful area of the disk. Hard disks have an area designated as the *landing zone* at the far end of the platter, usually the highest numbered cylinder on the drive where no data is ever written. On a hard disk with more than one partition, the heads are placed at the end of the last partition. Many modern disks automatically detect when the power level is falling and move the disk heads to the landing zone themselves.

It is a good idea to park your hard disk heads if you are going to move or ship your computer. Do not use your computer for any other operation after parking the heads, because the disk heads will move to access disk information and will again be positioned over the data area of the disk. You cannot use Disk Park on network drives.

USING DISK MONITOR FROM THE DOS PROMPT

If you want to turn off Disk Protect from the DOS prompt, type:

```
DISKMON /PROTECT−
```

To restore the previous level of protection, type:

```
DISKMON /PROTECT+
```

To turn on Disk Light, type:

DISKMON /LIGHT+

and to turn off the light again, type:

DISKMON /LIGHT–

To park the heads on your hard disk from the DOS prompt, type:

DISKMON /PARK

This displays the following message:

Heads Parked on all drives. Power off the system now.

Turn off your computer immediately. To see how Disk Monitor is configured, type:

DISKMON /STATUS

and you will see a brief message detailing the Disk Monitor configuration.

If you load Disk Monitor from your AUTOEXEC.BAT file and then load other TSR programs after it, you will not be able to recover the memory space Disk Monitor uses until you also remove the other TSR programs. You can still turn off the individual Disk Monitor options, but the small amount of memory (8K) that Disk Monitor uses cannot be released until you uninstall Disk Monitor.

Diskreet (DISKREET)

Encrypting and Password-Protecting Files and Directories

CHAPTER *15* _____

AS AN OPERATING SYSTEM, DOS IS PARTICULARLY WEAK on system security and has virtually no security features built into it. If your computer contains confidential files such as payroll records or personnel files, you may want to consider encrypting them for increased security. Encryption is a process that scrambles the contents of the file into an unreadable jumble that cannot be decoded or decrypted without the original password.

■ Check the READ.ME file on the Install disk for last minute information about Diskreet.

The Norton Utilities contains a powerful encryption program called Diskreet that not only can encrypt or decrypt files, but also can create and maintain encrypted password-protected drives called *Ndisks*. An Ndisk looks like a hidden file to DOS, but it works exactly like a disk drive. You save files to it as you do with a regular disk, but every file that you write to it is encrypted automatically. The Ndisk is protected by a password, and you have to supply this password every time you try to access it. After the Ndisk is open, you use it as you would a normal drive; your files are decrypted as you view, copy, or print them. However, when you close the Ndisk again, it is almost impossible for other people to access the drive without the password.

──── *THE DATA ENCRYPTION STANDARD* ────

Diskreet uses the DES (Data Encryption Standard) to encrypt and decrypt individual files and also as the encryption mechanism to secure the Ndisks. The DES encryption scheme is a *block cipher* that works by a combination of transposition and substitution. It works on blocks of 8 bytes (64 bits), encrypting or decrypting them using a 56-bit user supplied key. Using 56 bits, you can generate about 7.2×10^{16} possible keys. (This algorithm is too long and complex to be reproduced here.)

DES was developed at IBM after years of work. Rigorously tested by the National Security Agency, it was finally accepted as being free of any statistical or mathematical weaknesses. This suggests that it is impossible to break the system using statistical frequency tables or to work the algorithm backwards using mathematical methods. DES is used by federal departments and most banks and money transfer systems to protect all sensitive computer data.

DES encryption provides the following advantages:

- DES is robust—it has remained unbroken despite years of use

- DES completely randomizes the data in a file

- Even if you know some of the original text, you cannot use it to determine the encryption key

- After DES encryption, it is virtually impossible to decrypt the file without the key

If you want to know more about the DES, see the U. S. Department of Commerce/National Bureau of Standards, Data Encryption Standard, Federal Information Processing Standard Publication 46, 1977, which contains full details of the algorithm.

The DES algorithm cannot be shipped outside the U.S.A.

CONFIGURING DISKREET

Before you run Diskreet for the first time, be sure you have installed the Diskreet driver in your CONFIG.SYS file. Assuming that you have installed the Norton Utilities on drive C in a directory called NORTON, you should have the line:

DEVICE=C:\NORTON\DISKREET.SYS

You can load this device driver into high memory if you use HIMEM.SYS, QEMM.SYS, or PCSHADOW.SYS.

in your CONFIG.SYS file. If this line is not present in your CONFIG.SYS file, the selections in the Diskreet Disk and Options pull-down menus will not work, and if you try to use an Ndisk, a window opens telling you that the DISKREET.SYS device driver is not activated.

ENCRYPTING YOUR FILES

To start Diskreet, select it from the menu in the NORTON shell program, or type:

DISKREET

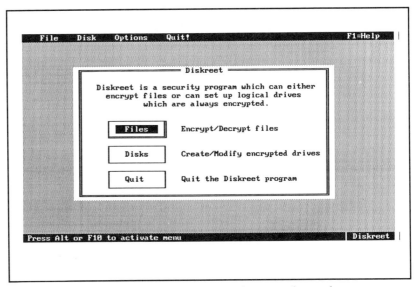 To work with an Ndisk, choose the Disks selection. I describe how to use Ndisks in the next part of this chapter.

at the DOS prompt. The opening Diskreet screen is shown in Figure 15.1.

To encrypt or decrypt a file, choose the Files option. First, you must specify how the file is to be encrypted, so choose the File Options selection from the File pull-down menu. This selection controls all the file encryption options for Diskreet and must be set up before you encrypt a file or files. The File Encryption Options screen is shown in Figure 15.2.

Choose one of the following encryption methods:

- **Fast Proprietary** is a proprietary Peter Norton encryption scheme; it operates faster than DES, but it is less secure.

Figure 15.1: The opening Diskreet screen lets you choose between encrypting or decrypting files or using Ndisks

• DES is a slower method of encryption, but it is the method used by many government agencies and banks, so you know it is secure.

After you have chosen the encryption method, you can further configure Diskreet with four more options:

• Wipe/Delete Original Files After Encryption ensures not only that the original unencrypted file is deleted from your system, but also that the space it once occupied is overwritten with zeros to prevent the file from being unerased later. After the entire file is overwritten, not even Norton's UnErase can recover the file.

• Set Encrypted File to Hidden sets the hidden file bit in the file's attribute byte. This file will not appear in listings made by the DOS DIR command, and cannot be deleted or copied by DOS.

Diskreet does not recognize that some word processors (such as WordStar and Microsoft Word) make backup files with the same file name of the original but a different extension. Diskreet will not overwrite these files. For complete security, use an Ndisk in which all files are encrypted.

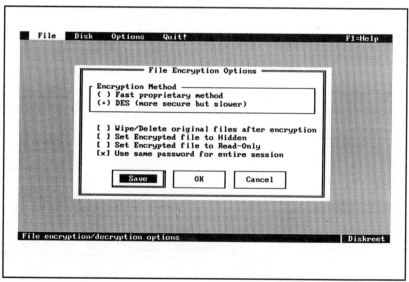

Figure 15.2: The File Encryption Options let you choose how to encrypt a file

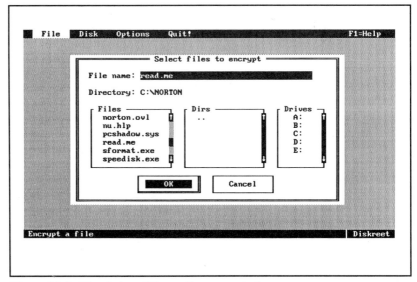

See Chapter 19 for a complete discussion of file attributes.

- **Set Encrypted File to Read-Only** sets the read-only bit in the file's attribute byte, so that the file cannot be edited, changed, or deleted from your disk.

- **Use Same Password for Entire Session** requires that you enter a password only once, instead of for each file that you want to encrypt.

After you make your selection, choose the **Save** box to save these settings for future Diskreet use. A small window opens to confirm the file was saved to the right drive.

Next choose Encrypt (Alt-E) from the File pull-down menu to continue with the encryption process. The Select Files to Encrypt window opens as Figure 15.3 showsIf you only want to work with a single file, either enter the file name directly into the **File Name** box or move the cursor to the Files area and choose a file from those listed in the current directory. You can also enter file specifications using the DOS wildcard characters if you want to work with several files from the same applications

Figure 15.3: The Select Files to Encrypt window

program. You can encrypt all your Lotus 1-2-3 spreadsheet files if you enter *.WK?, or all your dBASE database files if you enter *.DBF. The example in this chapter uses the READ.ME file that was installed with the Norton Utilities to demonstrate how completely scrambled the resulting file will be. You can also change to other directories and drives with the two other selections in this window.

Lastly, details about the file you want to encrypt are shown in the File Encryption window for your final approval. Note that the extension of the file name will be changed to SEC (for secure) after the file is encrypted.

You must be careful if you encrypt files with different extensions but the same names; Diskreet might overwrite these files, causing data to be lost. For example, if you turn on **Wipe/Delete Original Files After Encryption** from the File Encryption Options window, and you try to encrypt three files called CHAPTER.ONE, CHAPTER.TWO, and CHAPTER.THR, the first file will be encrypted to CHAPTER.SEC, but so will the second and the third files. However, Diskreet doesn't overwrite the files immediately; it first opens a window that displays the message:

FILE D:\NORTON\CHAPTER.SEC ALREADY EXISTS

and gives you the choice of overwriting the file or canceling the encryption operation. If you answer "yes" to overwrite the file, the first file is overwritten by the second. You can prevent this by being sure that all file names are unique, instead of relying on the extension itself.

The final part of the encryption mechanism requires that you supply the key, or password, to be used for the encryption. It is worth digressing here to discuss how to choose an appropriate, yet secure, password.

CHOOSING YOUR KEY OR PASSWORD

Diskreet uses two levels of passwords for protection: *main* and *specific*. A password can be a combination of as many as

If you turn on Wipe/Delete Original Files After Encryption, and then encrypt files with the same name but different extensions, files might be overwritten and lost.

40 alphabetic or numeric characters; however, it is not case sensitive. For example, computer, Computer, and COMPUTER are all the same password. Your password should be longer than six characters, because passwords of six or less characters are too easy to guess.

Consider the following advice when choosing your keys:

If you forget the password you used to encrypt a file, you will *never* be able to decrypt the file, so be very careful.

- Don't choose a key which others might easily guess
- Don't lose your keys
- Don't tell other people about your keys

The worst keys are the obvious ones, initials, place names or people's names, phone numbers, birth dates, or complete English words; there are a limited number of words in the English language and a computer can try them all very quickly. The best keys are longer rather than shorter, and usually contain a combination of letters and numbers. Your key should be easy for you to remember but meaningless to anyone else.

For security reasons, as you type your password, Diskreet displays the * symbol instead of the character you enter. It then asks you to confirm your key by typing it a second time. If you type the password incorrectly, Diskreet opens an error window with the message:

THE ENTERED PASSWORDS DO NOT MATCH
MAKE SURE THAT YOU REMEMBER THE PASSWORD
AND THAT YOU TYPE IT IN CORRECTLY

and returns you to the password window so that you can enter your password again. As the file is actually being encrypted, another window opens displaying an analog bar graph of the percentage of the operation that is complete. The final Diskreet window announces that the encryption is complete.

If you use the Disk Editor to look at the contents of READ.SEC, the only thing you will be able to recognize is the Peter Norton Computing Inc CRYPT signature at the beginning of the file. Figure 15.4 shows the READ.SEC file displayed in the

Disk Editor hex viewer. The first 10 characters in the file are a special signature that allows Diskreet to recognize a file encrypted by the Norton Utilities rather than by another encryption program.

Do not encrypt applications that use some sort of copy-protection scheme. Diskreet will encrypt the file, but the application will not run if certain information is not accessible.

You can use the normal DOS commands to copy, delete, back up, and restore encrypted files; you can even use other Norton Utilities, such as Speed Disk, with encrypted files. However, remember that encrypted files are binary files, so be careful to select the appropriate file-transfer method if you want to transfer the file over a modem to another computer. You cannot use ASCII transfer methods with a binary file; use XMODEM or YMODEM instead. Diskreet is also compatible with standard networks, but you must be careful not to leave decrypted files on the file server where others might find them. Copy the encrypted file to your local station and decrypt it there to maintain security.

Because encrypted files are binary files, you cannot use ASCII file-transfer methods to send these files over a modem. You should use XMODEM instead.

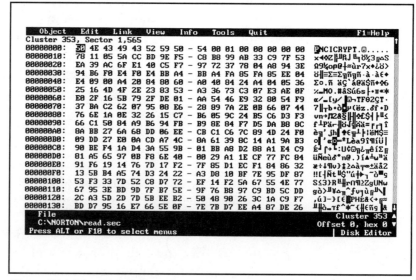

Figure 15.4: The Disk Editor shows the contents of READ.SEC after encryption

DECRYPTING YOUR FILES

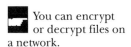 You can encrypt or decrypt files on a network.

Decrypting a file reverses the process of encryption. Diskreet restores a file to its original state, as long as you can provide the proper password.

To decrypt the READ.SEC file into the original READ.ME file, choose the Files selection from the Diskreet startup menu, and then choose Decrypt from the File pull-down menu. The Select Files to Decrypt window is shown in Figure 15.5.

Enter the name of the encrypted file into the File Name box, or enter the file specification to work with more than one file. Alternatively, you can choose a single file from the list of file names in the Files box. You can also change to another directory or to another disk using the Dirs or Drives boxes. Diskreet asks you to enter the same password you used when you first encrypted the file; if you make a mistake, Diskreet displays an error window and returns you to the Files menu again. No action is taken with the encrypted file; it is not decrypted. If the password is correct, during decryption an analog display

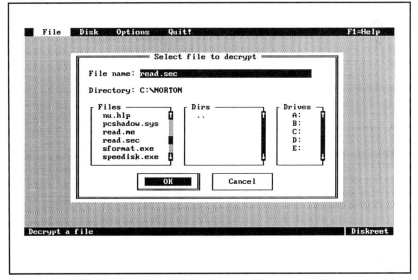

Figure 15.5: The Select Files to Decrypt window lets you choose the files you want to decrypt

window shows the progress of the operation. A final window reports that the file has been decrypted into its original state.

TRANSFERRING ENCRYPTED FILES BY MODEM

If you have encrypted a file or a group of files using Diskreet, you can send the files to another computer that is using the Norton Utilities for decryption. Remember that the recipient cannot decrypt the file without knowing the key, so you must arrange for a safe method of transferring the password before the file can be used. You should not give the password to the recipient over an ordinary phone line. Consider using a trusted courier or a scrambled phone to transfer the password, or use a prearranged password. After you have resolved this security issue, the transfer proceeds like any other binary file transfer.

1. Use Diskreet to encrypt the file using the agreed password.

2. Dial the number, establish a link, and transfer the file using the XMODEM (or a similar) file transfer protocol.

3. Decrypt the file using the password.

You can now use the file at both ends of the communications link.

MAKING AN NDISK

If you need more extensive security than encrypting a file or files can give, you can create an Ndisk. An Ndisk is an area of your disk that works like a regular disk, except that it is password protected. You must know the proper password to access the Ndisk.

You cannot create an Ndisk on a network drive.

To create an Ndisk, start Diskreet from the NORTON shell program or from the DOS prompt, and at the opening screen, choose the Disks option. If you have already created an Ndisk, it is displayed on the Diskreet Disks screen. If you are creating a new disk, you will see the screen shown in Figure 15.6.

 You can make an Ndisk on a RAM drive if you set the sector size to 512 bytes.

Choose Yes to define a new Ndisk, and at the next window, select a drive to use. After you have chosen the drive, the Make Ndisk window opens, as shown in Figure 15.7.

First, enter a name for the Ndisk, up to a maximum of 8 characters. This is the name that Diskreet assigns to a hidden directory in the root directory of the disk you chose.

 You can only have one Ndisk open on a drive at a time.

The name will appear on your list of Ndisks. You can then enter as many as 30 characters into the Description box as a text comment. This description might include a general heading that specifies the kind of information stored on the Ndisk, or it might distinguish one Ndisk from another. When you check the Show Audit Info When Opened selection, Diskreet lists all of the successful and unsuccessful attempts made to access your Ndisk. This serves to alert you if some unauthorized person is trying to access your data.

You must select the encryption method used for the Ndisk when you create it; you cannot change the method later. Choose

```
   File    Disk    Options    Quit!                          F1=Help




                        ═══ No NDisks Found ═══
                        No Diskreet Drives Defined
                   Do you wish to define a new Diskreet Drive?

                            ▐ Yes ▌      No




   Press Alt or F10 to activate menu                        Diskreet
```

Figure 15.6: The No Ndisk Found screen asks if you want to define a new Diskreet drive

either the relatively slow but extremely secure DES, or the less secure but faster Norton proprietary system. Remember you cannot change your mind at a later date.

There are four selections in the Password Prompting section of the Make Ndisk window. Diskreet provides three methods for opening an Ndisk automatically when an application needs access, or you can select to open the Ndisk manually every time.

- **Beep Only.** In automatic mode, a single beep prompts you to enter the Ndisk password. Choose this if you use programs that have a graphical interface, such as Windows.

- **Pop-up Prompt Only.** In automatic mode, a pop-up box prompts you for the password. This may be difficult to use if you run lots of graphics applications.

- **Choose Automatically.** This choice enables Diskreet to select the prompt it thinks is best for the current circumstances. This is the default setting, and it is usually the best setting to use.

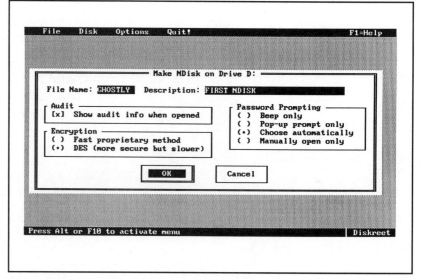

Figure 15.7: The Make Ndisk window lets you set up a new Ndisk

- **Manually Open Only.** This setting avoids any problems with automatic opening by making the Ndisks manual only. If you choose this option, you must open the Ndisk from the main Diskreet screen.

You cannot choose an automatic option from this list and also choose **Manual Open Only.** With this type of conflict, Diskreet uses the selection you made last.

The next window, the Select Ndisk Size window, is shown in Figure 15.8.

Diskreet calculates the amount of free space left on your disk and asks if you want to use all this free space for the Ndisk. You can also choose to use half of the available space, or you can specify the amount of space Diskreet can use in kilobytes. The size you choose will be determined by how you plan to use the Ndisk; however, remember that you can enlarge or reduce the Ndisk later.

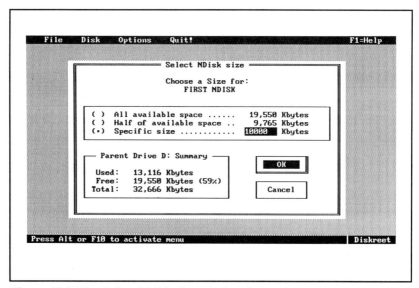

Figure 15.8: The Select Ndisk Size window helps you choose the size of your Ndisk

◉ Remember this password. If you forget it, you will never be able to decrypt the Ndisk again, not even with the Disk Editor.

Next, Diskreet asks for a password for the Ndisk. Choose a password of at least 6 characters; Diskreet will make you type it twice.

A warning window reminds you that if you forget this password, you will not be able to access the Ndisk again. If you must write down your password, do not keep it close to your computer; store it in another location or lock it in a drawer. Even the most powerful Norton Utilities, such as the Disk Editor, cannot help you if you lose this password, so be very careful.

The next window asks you to choose a drive letter to use with the Ndisk. Diskreet suggests the next unused drive letter in sequence for your computer.

Finally, the program displays audit information for the new Ndisk. This window lists three important items of information: the time and date the Ndisk was created or opened last, when the password was created or changed, and the number of successful and unsuccessful attempts at opening the Ndisk.

WORKING WITH YOUR NDISKS

When you first use Diskreet, only one drive letter is used. This means that you can only open one Ndisk at a time, because you must close one before you can open another. If you want to have two Ndisks open at the same time, you must specify more drive letters.

You access Ndisks the same way that you access other drives, by drive letter. For example, to copy the READ.ME file from the Norton directory on drive D to the Ndisk on drive G, type:

COPY READ.ME G:\

Accessing Ndisks takes slightly longer than with regular disks because the file must be encrypted or decrypted as it is written or read. If you work with small files, you might not notice the difference; however, you will definitely see a change if you use large files and opt for the complex DES encryption.

While the Ndisk is open, you (or anyone else) can access the files on the disk as usual, with DOS commands such as DIR or PRINT, or with Norton Utilities programs such as Disk Editor or FileFind. You can create and maintain the usual DOS hierarchical directory structure exactly as you would on any other disk. Diskreet makes the file that holds the Ndisk a hidden, read-only, system file, so you will not notice it in your usual directory listings. However, you can see this file if you use the Disk Editor; note the characteristic file name extension of .@#!. The fact that the file is hidden adds another layer of security, making it difficult to delete by accident. You should always close an Ndisk when you have finished using it to prevent other people from accessing your confidential files.

After you create an Ndisk, choosing the Disks option from the startup screen displays the main Diskreet Disks screen shown in Figure 15.9.

You can make four selections from this screen:

- **Open.** If you want to open your Ndisk manually,
  choose this option. Highlight the appropriate Ndisk,

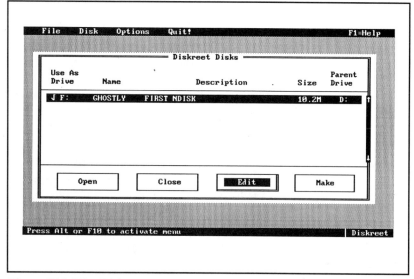

Figure 15.9: The Diskreet Disks screen lists all of your Ndisks

and select **Open**. A window opens and asks you to specify a drive letter for this disk. The window also displays the current status of the Ndisk and reminds you of the name and description you used when you first created it. If you choose **OK** to open the Ndisk, you must then enter the correct password for that specific Ndisk. Finally, the audit window opens and shows the time and date when you last accessed this Ndisk. A checkmark on the Diskreet Disks screen shows that the Ndisk is now open. You can now exit Diskreet and use your Ndisk as you would use any other normal disk.

- **Close**. Select this option to close an Ndisk manually. Highlight the appropriate Ndisk, and select **Close**. The open checkmark toggles off.

- **Edit**. If you want to change the Ndisk audit or the password prompting mechanism, choose **Edit**. You can also write-protect the Ndisk as an additional safety factor. In that case, you can write-enable the disk when you want to add files, and then write-protect the Ndisk again afterward. Although the encryption method is shown on this screen, you cannot change it.

- **Make**. This selection lets you create another Ndisk. Follow the sequence of steps you used to create an Ndisk in the previous section.

The selections in the Disk pull-down menu enable you to perform several basic Ndisk operations.

When you start Diskreet, the program lists all the Ndisks that it can find; it does not know about Ndisks that you have created on floppy disks, so you can use the Search Floppies (Alt-S) selection to locate them and add them to the list of available Ndisks. When you select the Search Floppies option from the Disk pull-down menu, a window opens to let you specify a floppy disk drive letter. Use the arrow keys to move the highlight to your choice, or simply type in the drive letter. Diskreet searches the drive; if it finds an Ndisk, it adds the disk to the list shown in the main Diskreet display.

To close all open Ndisks at the same time, select Close All from the Disk pull-down menu. Alternatively, you can press Alt-C at the main Diskreet screen as a shortcut.

If you want to change the size of an Ndisk, first close the Ndisk, then highlight the Ndisk in the main Diskreet Disks display, and choose Adjust Size from the Disk pull-down menu. After you enter the Ndisk password, Diskreet checks the current size of the Ndisk, and then opens the Adjust Ndisk Size window shown in Figure 15.10.

The window lists the name of Ndisk, the amount of used and free space, and the total size of the Ndisk. To make the Ndisk larger, choose **Expand**; to make it smaller, choose **Shrink**. A warning window reminds you to back up the Ndisk before altering its size, because if there is a power loss or system problem during the adjustment operation, your data may become

Back up the contents of your Ndisk before changing its size.

You must first close an Ndisk before you can adjust its size.

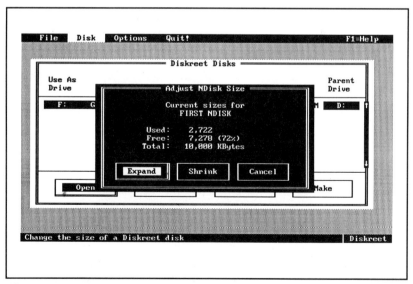

Figure 15.10: The Adjust Ndisk Size window lets you change the size of an Ndisk

inaccessible. If you choose Shrink, the Reduce Ndisk Size window opens, as shown in Figure 15.11.

The window summarizes the Ndisk and the parent disk, showing the amount of used and free space, as well as the total size. Choose the appropriate reduction from the following options:

- **Maximum Reduction** lets you shrink the Ndisk so that it is only large enough to hold your existing files.

- **Half Reduction** cuts the available space by half.

- **Quick Reduction** cuts the Ndisk space by approximately 5 percent.

- **Specific Size** lets you enter the size reduction in kilobytes.

After you choose an option from this list, select OK to implement the change.

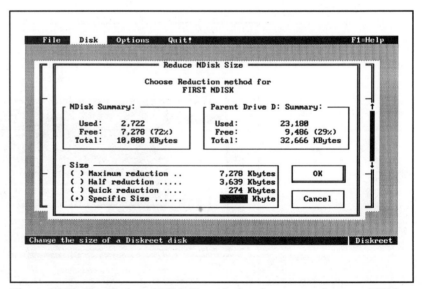

Figure 15.11: The Reduce Ndisk Size window lets you make your Ndisk smaller

If you want to expand your Ndisk, the sequence of steps is almost identical. Choose Expand, and the Expand Ndisk Size window lists the summary information for the Ndisk and the parent disk. This time the options add more free space to your Ndisk. You can choose from the following options:

- Maximum Expansion increases the size of the Ndisk so that it uses all of the remaining free space on the parent drive.

- Half Expansion increases the size of the Ndisk so that it uses half the remaining free space on the parent drive.

- Quick Expansion increases the Ndisk by approximately 10 percent of its original size.

- Specific Size lets you specify the increase in size in kilobytes.

After you make your selection, choose OK to implement the change.

To delete an Ndisk you no longer need, first close it if it is open. Then, choose Delete from the Disk pull-down menu. After you enter your password, Diskreet warns you that you are about to delete the Ndisk. When the Ndisk has been deleted, control returns to the main Diskreet screen.

If you think someone may have gained access to your password, or you want to change it as part of your normal operations, you can do so by using the Change Disk Password option from the Disk pull-down menu. If you need a high degree of security, change your password daily; otherwise, change it on a weekly or monthly basis. You must enter the current password for the Ndisk if you want to change to a new password. Remember that the password serves as the encryption key for all the files on your Ndisk. Changing it is not a trivial step because all of your files will have to be encrypted again based on this new password.

Diskreet lets you change a password without re-encrypting all the files on the Ndisk, but if someone knows the old password, or

If you want to re-encrypt your files based on the new password, back them up first, because a power outage or system problem during the encryption process could cause you to lose files.

you require the maximum level of security, you should always choose to re-encrypt your files too. In the Change the Ndisk Password window, choose Quick to change the password without re-encrypting all your files, or choose Full to ensure all your files are re-encrypted based on the new password. Re-encrypting a 25MB Ndisk after a password change can take as long as ten minutes.

CHOOSING NDISK OPTIONS

The Options pull-down menu contains several more selections to help you configure Diskreet to work with Ndisks.

The default Diskreet configuration allows for one drive letter, which is all you need if you only want to open one Ndisk at a time. To select more drive letters, choose System Settings from the Options pull-down menu. However, don't make too many available; your data will be more secure if you keep your Ndisks closed when you are not using them.

The System Settings window also contains a checkbox that prevents the loading of the Ndisk Manager. For proper Diskreet operation, your CONFIG.SYS file should contains a line similar to the following:

```
DEVICE=D:\NORTON\DISKREET.SYS
```

so that the Ndisk device driver is loaded from the NORTON directory each time you boot up your computer. This device driver occupies approximately 49K of DOS memory. It is not needed for single file encryption using the File pull-down menu; it is only used with Ndisks. If you use large applications programs and free memory is at a premium, check the box in this window to prevent the Ndisk device driver from loading the next time you boot up your computer. To make this option take effect now, you must reboot.

You can choose to open your Ndisk either when you first boot up your computer or when you first reference it with the Startup Disks selection from the Options pull-down menu. When the

Startup Ndisks window opens, select Edit to open the All Ndisks window. Highlight the Ndisk you want to use, and choose OK. The next window lets you choose when you will be prompted for the Ndisk password:

- **As soon as machine starts up** asks you for the Ndisk password during the bootup process.

- **The first time the drive letter is used** lets you wait until you need to use the Ndisk before asking for the password.

Make a choice and then select OK. Your data will be more secure if you wait until the drive is used before entering the password. Keep your Ndisks closed until you have to use them. Select OK in the next window to return to the main Diskreet screen.

You can also specify that an Ndisk closes automatically after a fixed period of time has elapsed without any Ndisk access. Choose Auto-Close Timeouts from the Options menu to open the Set Auto Close Timeouts window. Press the spacebar to toggle this setting on or off. When you select this option, Diskreet lets you enter the time period (in minutes) that you want to wait before closing the Ndisk. The maximum time period you can enter is a rather unrealistic 99 minutes; choose a shorter time interval, such as 2 minutes or 5 minutes.

An additional safety feature in Diskreet lets you lock your keyboard and blank the screen if you leave your computer unattended for a period of time. Select the Keyboard and Screen Lock item from the Options pull-down menu to display the window shown in Figure 15.12.

You can choose options from two checkboxes at the left side of this window:

- **Enable Quick-Close** lets you close all open Ndisks by pressing a hot-key combination. You must then use the main Diskreet menu to reopen your Ndisks.

- **Enable Locking** lets you press a hot-key to clear your monitor screen and lock the keyboard. Your system remains in this state until you enter the main password.

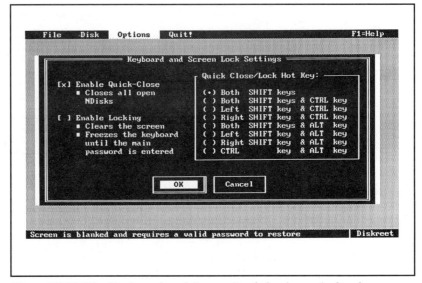

Figure 15.12: The Keyboard and Screen Lock Settings window lets you choose several important security configurations

Choose the hot-key combination from the list of keys shown at the right side of the window. Press the spacebar, or click on your selection with the mouse. This hot-key combination always clears the screen and closes all open Ndisks—even if you are at the DOS prompt or in another application program. If you use hot-keys with other TSR programs, be careful to choose a unique key combination; otherwise, you will create a conflict between Diskreet and your other TSR programs.

Diskreet keeps your Ndisk files encrypted while you use the Ndisk. However, what happens when you delete an Ndisk because you no longer need it, or you decide to shrink your Ndisk to a smaller size? Select Security Options from the Options pull-down menu to specify what happens. The Security Options window is shown in Figure 15.13.

This window lets you select from these three options:

- Quick Clear leaves the encrypted data intact on the disk.

- Overwrite writes a single pattern over the data before it is returned to the DOS pool of available disk space.

See Chapter 16 for more details about Department of Defense requirements for data removal.

• **Security Wipe** is the most secure of the three options because it overwrites your Ndisk several times using the Department of Defense approved technique.

Make your selection from this list, and then press OK to return to the main Diskreet screen.

Finally, if you want to change the main Diskreet password, use Change Main Password from the Options pull-down menu. Diskreet asks you to enter your new password twice to be sure that you entered it correctly. If you forget the main password, delete the DISKREET.INI file from your hard disk. This sets the main password to a null entry; when Diskreet asks for the password, press Enter. Remember, changing the main password does not affect the passwords you've used for encrypted files or Ndisks; they stay the same.

Use the Quit selection on the pull-down menu line to leave Diskreet. You will return to DOS or to the NORTON shell program, depending on how you originally started Diskreet.

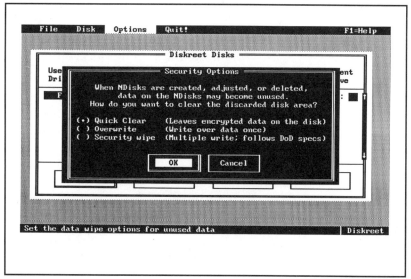

Figure 15.13: The Security Options window lets you choose what happens after you delete an Ndisk

BACKING UP ENCRYPTED FILES AND NDISKS

In several places in this chapter I have mentioned the need to back up files or Ndisks before starting a particular Diskreet process; this ensures that if an accident happens, you will have a copy of your data. If you back up one or more files encrypted using the File option in Diskreet, those files are backed up in encrypted form.

You can also use FileFind to manipulate the hidden bit of the attribute byte.

When you back up a file from an Ndisk, Diskreet decrypts the file so that the backup is in its native form. If you want to back up an entire Ndisk in encrypted form, use the Disk Editor to clear the hidden attribute of the file, and then back up the file using the Ndisk name and the .@#! extension. After the backup is complete, use the Disk Editor to hide the file again. Note that you can also hide or reveal an Ndisk by using Diskreet from the DOS prompt.

USING DISKREET FROM THE DOS PROMPT

There are several important ways you can use Diskreet directly from the DOS prompt, and one of the most useful Diskreet command line switches lets you "unhide" an Ndisk. Merely type:

DISKREET /SHOW *drive letter*

to reveal all of the Ndisks on a specific parent drive. You can now see the Ndisk files in directory listings, and you can use your backup program to make an archive copy. To hide the Ndisk when the backup is complete, type:

DISKREET /HIDE *drive letter*

To close all open Ndisks, type:

DISKREET /CLOSE

You can enable the DISKREET.SYS device driver by typing:

DISKREET /ON

and you can disable the device driver by typing:

DISKREET /OFF

See Chapter 23 for a complete list of all the Diskreet command line switches and their meanings.

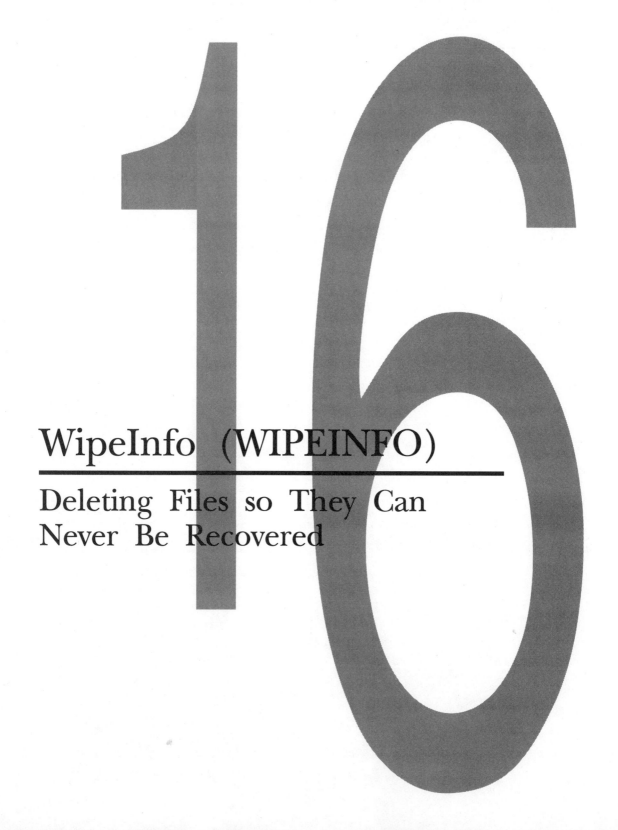

WipeInfo (WIPEINFO)

Deleting Files so They Can Never Be Recovered

CHAPTER *16*

IF YOUR JOB INVOLVES DEMONSTRATING A SOFTWARE
package on a client's computer, you will want to install the package on the hard disk to demonstrate the speed and efficiency of
the program. However, if the client does not want to buy the
package, simply deleting the files using DOS commands will
only remove the entries from the FAT. With a good utilities
package, your client could probably unerase the files quite easily. This is, of course, illegal.

Here's another example. Let's say you have just finished working on the documentation for a confidential project. You keep
backup copies of your files in a safe place, but you want to
remove all traces of the original files from your hard disk.

In both cases, your solution is the Norton Utilities WipeInfo
program. Using this utility ensures that the deleted files are
removed permanently. Not even the Norton Utilities' UnErase
program can recover files that have been overwritten by WipeInfo.

USING WIPEINFO

WipeInfo eradicates files from a disk completely; it does not
merely erase them. WipeInfo writes new data into each sector of
the file on your disk, overwriting any data that was already there.

To practice using the WipeInfo program, first make a small
test file on a blank floppy disk in drive A by typing:

```
COPY CON A:MYFILE.TXT
This is a short test
```

Press F6 to end the file, and then press Enter to return to the
DOS prompt. This small file now exists on the floppy in drive A.

Assuming that the disk is a newly formatted 360K floppy disk, sector 0 is the boot sector, sectors 1 to 4 contain the FAT, sectors 5 to 11 contain the root directory, and MYFILE.TXT should start in sector 12.

Now use WipeInfo to clear the disk's contents. To do this, choose WipeInfo from the menu in the NORTON shell program, or type:

WIPEINFO

from the DOS prompt. The WipeInfo opening screen is shown in Figure 16.1.

To set up WipeInfo before you use it, select Configure. This opens the Wipe Configuration window shown in Figure 16.2.

This window offers three main selections:

WipeInfo is a powerful and irreversible process, so proceed slowly and carefully.

- **Fast Wipe** writes the value you specify into each sector that the file occupied. The default value is zero; to change this value, enter the decimal equivalent of the

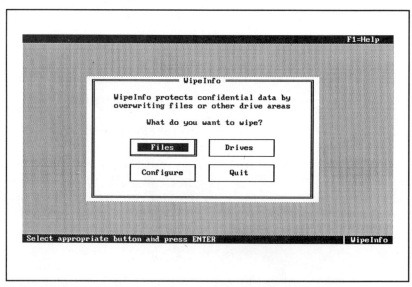

Figure 16.1: The WipeInfo opening screen offers four choices

character you want to use. For example, to write **E**, enter 69 in decimal.

- **Government Wipe** is much slower than **Fast Wipe**, but it meets the latest Department of Defense 5220.22-M 116b(2) standards for media protection. This specifies that a 0/1 pattern must be repeated three times, followed by a write of the characters F6H, followed by a verification of the last write.

- **Repeat Count** lets you specify the number of times you want to repeat the Fast Wipe or the Government Wipe. The default is 1.

Choose **Save Settings** so that WipeInfo will use your chosen selections every time you run the program. The settings are saved in the NU.INI file. To use these settings only for the current WipeInfo session, choose **OK**; otherwise, choose **Cancel**.

Next, choose **Files** from the main WipeInfo screen to display the window shown in Figure 16.3.

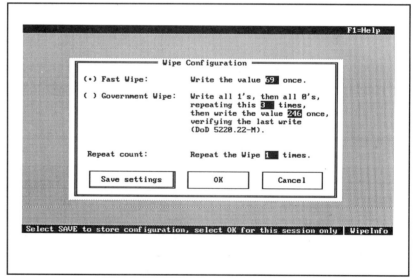

Figure 16.2: The Wipe Configuration window lets you set up WipeInfo

The current directory is shown in the File Name box; use the backspace key if you want to change or edit this entry. You can include details of the drive, path, and file name, and you can also use the DOS wildcard characters.

The top section of the screen displays the following four checkboxes:

- **Include Subdirs.** Choose this selection if you want to include all the subdirectories on the disk.

- **Confirm Each File.** This option forces the program to ask for permission before wiping a file. Use it if you are not sure of what is on the disk.

- **Hidden Files.** If you want to remove hidden files, check this box. The default setting leaves hidden files intact.

- **Read-Only Files.** To remove files with the read-only bit set in the attribute byte, check this box. Again, the default setting leaves these files untouched.

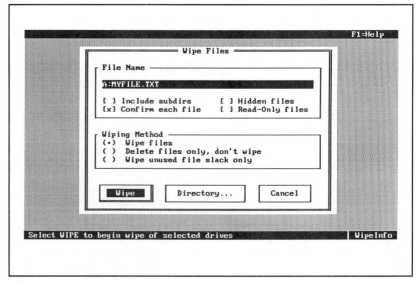

Figure 16.3: Choose the file you want to wipe and the Wiping Method in this window

Next, choose the wiping method that the program will use:

- Wipe Files. This selection deletes files and then writes the specified pattern into every location on the disk occupied by those files.

- Delete Files Only, Don't Wipe. This option deletes the specified files but does not wipe the space that they occupied. This is the same as using the DOS DEL or ERASE command, except that you can use it to remove complete directory trees from your hard disk if you check the Include Subdirs box.

- Wipe Unused File Slack Only. This selection wipes the unused slack area at the end of the file.

You can use the Directory box at the bottom of the screen to change to another directory or drive if you don't want to work with the current directory.

When you are ready to run WipeInfo, be sure the current drive is drive A and that MYFILE.TXT is shown as the File Name entry. Check the Confirm Each File box, select the Wipe Files radio button, and then click on the Wipe box to start the process. A warning window opens (see Figure 16.4) to remind you that you are about to wipe MYFILE.TXT and that the file will be lost forever if you proceed. Choose the Wipe box to continue. If the Confirm Each File option is turned on, you are given one more chance to change your mind; a window lists the file you want to wipe with a question mark at the end of the line. You have four options:

- Skip. This lets you cancel the operation for the file shown in the window. The next file that matches the file specification you entered is listed on the screen.

- Wipe (or Delete). The title of this box varies according to whether you selected Delete Files Only or Wipe Files in the Wipe Files window. When you choose Wipe, the highlighted file or the slack unused area at the end of the file is wiped.

- **Auto.** This option bypasses any further prompting on the screen and wipes all the files that match the file specification you entered. WipeInfo then acts as if you had not checked the Confirm Each File checkbox.

- **Stop** cancels the rest of the wipe list and returns you to the main WipeInfo screen.

When all the files that match the file specification have been wiped, control returns to the main WipeInfo menu.

If you now examine the floppy disk's second cluster with the Disk Editor, you will see that both of the sectors that comprise cluster two are filled with E characters, as shown in Figure 16.4. The original text message is gone, and if you use the DOS DIR command, it will report that the disk is empty.

You can also run WipeInfo to wipe only the erased or unused portion of a disk if you choose Drives from the main menu; in fact, this is probably one of its most frequent uses of the utility. The top part of the window lets you select the drives you want

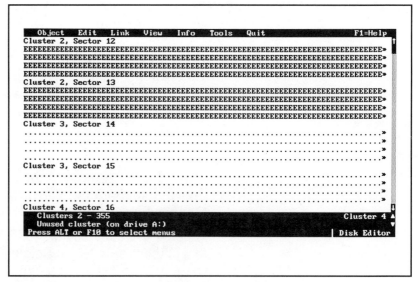

Figure 16.4: Displaying the wiped cluster

to wipe, and the lower portion lets you choose one of the two following wiping methods:

- Wipe Entire Drive obliterates everything on the drive, including the system area and any files. If you chose the Government Wipe method you will have to reformat the disk if you want to use it again.

- Wipe Unused Areas Only wipes the unused area of the disk, including the space occupied by any deleted files.

The wiping method you choose is applied to all the drives you specify at the top of this window.

Wiping an entire disk can be a lengthy procedure, depending on the options you choose. For example, performing a Government Wipe on a 1.44MB floppy disk can take as long as two hours to complete, and wiping a large hard disk can take all day.

USING WIPEINFO FROM THE COMMAND LINE

You don't have to use the full screen method with WipeInfo; you can run it from the DOS command line. The general form of the command is:

WIPEINFO *filespec file-switches common-switches*

For example, to remove all the *.BAK files from the floppy disk in drive A, type:

WIPEINFO A:*.BAK /S

This command wipes all the *.BAK files in all directories on drive A; the /S switch tells WipeInfo to include all subdirectories in the search for files matching the file specification.

As a final cautionary word, remember that WipeInfo actually writes over files and destroys the original data. After this treatment, the original files cannot be recovered by utility programs, not even by programs as powerful as the Norton Utilities.

Part V describes how to use several of the most important Norton Utilities programs to examine and control aspects of your computer's hardware, to find lost or misplaced files, and to navigate around your hard disk.

Chapter 17 provides a comprehensive introduction to batch file programming, including how to use the Batch Enhancer to improve the scope and functionality of your batch files. Chapter 19 explains how to use the Norton Control Center to configure your computer hardware. In Chapter 20 you learn how to use Norton Change Directory to access programs and files on your hard disk quickly and easily. Chapter 21 describes the Safe Format utility— the quick and safe alternative to the DOS FORMAT command. Finally, Chapter 22 lets you peer inside your computer and examine information that usually takes complex programming to reveal.

PART

V

Tools

17

Batch Enhancer (BE)

Automating Operations with Batch Files

CHAPTER *17* _____

BATCH-FILE PROGRAMMING, WHICH CAN AUTOMATE many of your daily computer tasks, is a powerful tool that you may find indispensable after you know how to use it. *Batch,* a term that originated with mainframe computers, signifies a series of commands contained in a file that are invoked by running the file. In a DOS batch file, you can include any of the DOS internal and external commands, exactly as you would if you were using them at the command prompt. Batch files can also accomplish more complex tasks if they include elements of the DOS batch-programming language. This limited language allows for looping, conditional branching, prompting the user for input, and pausing.

The Norton Utilities provide several extensions to the DOS batch-programming language. These extensions are grouped together into the BE (Batch Enhancer) program; they let you control the screen, open and close windows, position text anywhere on the screen, and add capabilities to make truly interactive batch files.

All DOS batch files are ASCII text files, with a carriage return and a line feed at the end of every line. You cannot include any word processor formatting commands in them. Every batch file must have a unique name and .BAT as its name extension, so that DOS knows to invoke the batch-file processor. However, you do not have to type the .BAT extension when you run the file.

Each command in a batch file must be on its own line.

When you run a batch file, the DOS batch-file processor executes each of the file's commands in order. After DOS has run all of the batch file's commands, you are returned to the DOS prompt. Batch files are useful for automating lengthy processes. For example, a batch file can set up your system automatically when you boot the computer, or it can simplify the procedure for backing up your hard disk.

HOW DO YOU MAKE A BATCH FILE?

There are several different ways to make a batch file. I do not describe how to make batch files with specific programs; instead I present the most general method for performing this task and explain the underlying principles. Then you can use whichever program you are comfortable with.

You can use DOS's EDLIN program to make a batch file, or you can use your word processor, provided it has a feature for making straight ASCII text files. If you use a word processor that automatically adds its own extension to files, you will have to change the file's extension to .BAT.

USING COPY CON

You can use the DOS COPY command to create short, simple batch files. Longer, more complex batch files usually require some degree of editing, which COPY doesn't provide.

When you use the COPY command, you actually copy characters from the console (which is the monitor and keyboard) directly to a file. If the file you are writing to already exists on your disk, it will be overwritten by this process, and the original contents will be lost.

To create a batch file with COPY, enter:

COPY CON MYFILE.BAT

The DOS system prompt will disappear, and you can now enter your text directly from the keyboard, pressing Enter at the end of each line. After you have typed in all the text, press F6 and then Enter. MYFILE.BAT is now ready for use as a batch file.

To check the contents of the file, reverse the items in the COPY command by typing:

COPY MYFILE.BAT CON

and pressing Enter. This displays the commands contained in MYFILE.BAT exactly as you entered them. (Of course, you can also use the DOS TYPE command to display the file.)

STARTING AND STOPPING A BATCH FILE .

To run a batch file, merely type the file name at the DOS prompt and press Enter. There is no need to specify its .BAT extension. Each command line in the batch file is executed exactly as if you had typed it at the DOS prompt. At the end of the batch file, execution stops, and the DOS prompt reappears.

To abort, or interrupt, a batch file while it is running, type Ctrl-C or Ctrl-Break. This sends a break character to DOS and usually results in the message:

Terminate batch job (Y/N)?

Typing Y stops the batch file completely and returns you to the DOS prompt. If you want to stop the current command's execution but continue with the next command in the batch file, type N. Some programs do not recognize the break character and will not stop when you press Break. Other programs may not be able to stop immediately.

USING A BATCH FILE TO RUN A PROGRAM

If you work primarily with your word processor, you can place its start-up commands at the end of your AUTOEXEC.BAT file so that the program is automatically loaded every time you boot up your computer.

One common use of a batch file is to start a program quickly. For example, if you have the word processor PFS:Write installed on your hard disk in a directory called PFS, you must enter several commands to start the program. You can place these commands in a batch file and give the file a meaningful, easy-to-remember name. Running the batch file will then execute the commands automatically. In this example, you could create a batch file called PFSTART.BAT and include in it the following commands:

CD \PFS
WRITE

When you run the batch file, the command CD \PFS makes the PFS directory current, and the command WRITE starts the word processor. You can even name the batch file after yourself, the primary user of the word processor; then all you have to do is type your name after booting the computer.

USING A BATCH FILE TO
AUTOMATE A COMMON PROCESS

Another common use of a batch file is to automate a complex procedure, simplifying it to an easy-to-remember name. For example, if you have an Epson- or IBM-compatible printer, you can create a batch file that puts the printer into 132-column (compressed) mode. Simply include the following line:

MODE LPT1: 132

In DOS 4 these MODE commands become MODE LPT1: COLS=132 and MODE LPT1: COLS=80.

in a batch file called COMPRESS.BAT. If you make another batch file called NORMAL.BAT that includes the line:

MODE LPT1: 80

you now have an easy way of setting and resetting your printer width. To choose compressed mode, type:

COMPRESS

Any output you then send to the printer will be printed in 132 columns across the page. To return the printer to the normal mode, type:

NORMAL

The printer will now print in the more usual 80-column width.

THE BATCH-PROGRAMMING LANGUAGE

In this section I introduce the DOS batch-programming language, describing briefly the main commands you might require.

Although batch files can only contain commands, you can add a descriptive line to your batch file by prefacing the line with a colon. DOS will then ignore the line, and you will have a reference that explains what the batch file does.

Keep in mind that you can only use these commands in batch files; you cannot use them from the DOS prompt.

USING ECHO

Normally, DOS displays batch-file commands as the batch file executes them. If you don't want the commands to be displayed, place the line:

ECHO OFF

at the beginning of the batch file. To turn on the display of commands again, include the following line:

ECHO ON

You can also use ECHO to display short text messages on the screen to help you or other users follow the batch file's processing. To send a message to the screen with ECHO, use the form:

ECHO *message*

The message will be displayed on the screen even if you included the ECHO OFF statement at the beginning of the batch file—the displayed message is the *result* of the command, not the command itself. For example, if ECHO is off and you run a batch file that contains the line:

ECHO This is a short message.

DOS will display:

This is a short message.

However, if ECHO is on, the resulting display is:

ECHO This is a short message.
This is a short message.

You see both the command and its output.

After you understand how ECHO works, it isn't so confusing; just be careful to turn ECHO on and off again in the appropriate places in the batch file.

In DOS 3.3 and later versions, there is another way to stop commands from being displayed. Simply add the @ character to the beginning of the batch-file command that you do not want displayed. Thus the statement:

@ECHO OFF

instructs DOS to execute this command without displaying it on the screen. (ECHO OFF, in turn, tells DOS to do the same for subsequent commands in the batch file.)

Another command that is often used in this way is the CLS (clear screen) command. If you use ECHO OFF followed by CLS, you will not see the ECHO OFF command because the screen will be cleared quickly by CLS. You can start your batch files with the sequence:

ECHO OFF
CLS

so that they start at the top of a clear screen.

INCLUDING REMARKS IN YOUR BATCH FILES

Use REM or a colon to create brief descriptions of the batch file's commands.

You can add comments or remarks to a batch file with the REM command. A REM statement is simply the word REM followed by any text. If ECHO is on, the REM statements are displayed, including the word REM. If you want to add comments to your batch file that are never displayed, regardless of whether ECHO is on or off, add a colon to the beginning of the comment line. Such comments help explain what the batch file is doing. Although this may be obvious to you when you write the batch file, you may forget some or all of the details in a year's time, particularly if the batch file executes complicated procedures.

PAUSING YOUR BATCH FILES

You can use the PAUSE command to halt a batch file's execution and give instructions to the user. For example, you can include the command:

PAUSE Position Paper!

in a batch file that sends output to the printer. However, you must also use ECHO ON in the batch file to display the instruction, but this displays the whole command. The following lines demonstrate a cleaner way of doing the same thing:

@ECHO OFF
ECHO Position Paper!
PAUSE

When the batch file pauses, DOS displays the message:

Strike a key when ready...

After following the displayed instruction, the user merely presses any key to continue executing the batch file.

RUNNING BATCH FILES
WITHIN BATCH FILES WITH CALL

Only DOS Versions 3.3 and later have the CALL command. In earlier versions of DOS you can mimic CALL by starting another shell with COMMAND /C.

In DOS 3.2 and earlier, this becomes COMMAND /C ADDRESS.

By using the CALL command, you can have a batch file execute another batch file as part of its process; the second batch file is treated as a subroutine. After the subroutine has been called and executed, the original batch file continues executing the rest of its commands. For example, if you want to write your name and your company address at the top of a page, you can call a batch file called ADDRESS.BAT from inside another batch file by including the following line:

CALL ADDRESS

in the batch file. When ADDRESS.BAT has written out your name and the company address, control returns to the original batch file, which then executes the command following the CALL command. Having ADDRESS.BAT as a separate file enables you to use it in different batch files, without having to retype it for each file. This way, if you change your address, you only have to modify ADDRESS.BAT, not all the other batch files.

STARTING ONE BATCH FILE FROM ANOTHER BATCH FILE

You can also run a batch file from another batch file by invoking the second file in the last line of the first one. However, if you invoke the second file before the last line of the first file, any remaining commands in the first file will not be executed because control passes to the second file and does not return to the first batch file.

TESTING RESULTS WITH ERRORLEVEL

ERRORLEVEL is a variable within DOS that can be set by a DOS command, an application program, or a batch file. Several DOS commands, including BACKUP, FORMAT, and RESTORE, return an ERRORLEVEL code when they finish running, indicating whether they completed successfully or encountered an error. ERRORLEVEL can contain a number between 0 and 255. When used with IF and GOTO, ERRORLEVEL can help your batch files make complex decisions.

CREATING ALTERNATIVE PROCEDURES WITH IF AND GOTO

IF allows conditional branching in a batch file. A *conditional branch* simply means: "If a certain thing is true, do this; otherwise, do that."

With this capability you can create batch files to run increasingly complicated procedures. For example, you can use IF and GOTO with ERRORLEVEL codes to test your program or batch-file commands. When ERRORLEVEL reports no error, the file's execution would continue as intended. However, if there is an error, the GOTO statement would send control to lines that would deal with it in some way. GOTO passes control to a point in the program indicated by a label, in effect bypassing a section of the batch file. A *label* is merely a name of up to eight characters, usually preceded by a colon (although the colon is optional in the GOTO statement), which identifies a section of code. The label indicates where execution should continue; it is not executable code. For example, when DOS encounters the line:

```
GOTO :END
```

in a batch file, it jumps to the line:

```
:END
```

(usually the last line in the file) and returns you to the DOS prompt.

USING REPLACEABLE PARAMETERS IN A BATCH FILE

You can set up placeholding variables in a batch file so that you can specify different parameters when you invoke the file. By doing so, you can run the batch file with different files, for example. You can specify as many as ten variables in a batch file, each identified by a percent sign followed by a number. Suppose you make a batch file called R.BAT that contains the statement:

```
RENAME %1 %2
```

To run it, you would type:

R FILE1 FILE2

DOS will replace the %1 with the first name, FILE1, and replace the %2 with the second name, FILE2. In other words, the DOS batch-file processor translates the sequence you typed to:

RENAME FILE1 FILE2

> The variable %0 always contains the name of the batch file.

The SHIFT command moves all the variables down one number; for example, %2 become %1, %3 becomes %2, and so on. The %1 variable is lost each time you use SHIFT. This lets you create batch files that can handle more than ten replaceable parameters at a time.

THE CONFIG.SYS FILE

The CONFIG.SYS file resembles a batch file in that you create it and it executes commands; however, it can only contain special DOS configuration commands. CONFIG.SYS is loaded only when you boot the computer, and its commands are restricted to those that set up your system for DOS; other commands cannot be included in the file. If DOS doesn't find this file in the root directory of the disk used to boot the system, it provides default values for the system's setup. The contents of a typical CONFIG.SYS file are shown in Figure 17.1.

The commands in your CONFIG.SYS file configure your computer's hardware, allowing you to set certain internal DOS variables and load special device drivers. These commands each have the general form:

COMMAND = *value*

Following is a discussion of the commands that you can use in your CONFIG.SYS file.

```
FILES = 20
BUFFERS = 20
DEVICE = C:\DOS\ANSI.SYS
DEVICE = C:\DOS\VDISK.SYS 64
```

Figure 17.1: A typical CONFIG.SYS file's contents

USING BREAK

Usually DOS operates with BREAK set to OFF, which means DOS will occasionally check for the Break key being pressed during standard input, output, or printing operations. If you include the command:

BREAK ON

in your CONFIG.SYS file, DOS will check for the break key more often, but because of this extra check, DOS runs up to 2% slower.

CREATING MEMORY BUFFERS

DOS creates several buffers in memory to store data that is read from or written to a disk temporarily. Each buffer uses 512 bytes of memory. You can specify the number of buffers in your system by using the BUFFERS command in your CONFIG.SYS file. The general format of the command is:

BUFFERS = *nn*

in which *nn* is the number of buffers you want to use. Most people use a setting somewhere between 10 and 25, but you must determine the ideal number for your system based on the requirements of the applications programs you use.

ESTABLISHING THE DATE AND TIME FORMAT

The COUNTRY command selects the format for the date and time commands, as well as currency symbols and decimal separators. You can also use it to select the character sets for various countries. The COUNTRY command codes are based on the international telephone dialing codes. Table 17.1 lists the COUNTRY codes.

ACCESSING MORE FILES WITH THE FCBS COMMAND

Many older applications programs use file control blocks (FCBS) instead of file handles when creating, opening, and closing files. If you use one of these programs on a network, you

Table 17.1: COUNTRY Codes for DOS 3.3 and Later Versions

CODE	COUNTRY
001	United States
031	The Netherlands
032	Belgium
033	France
034	Spain
039	Italy
041	Switzerland
044	Great Britain
045	Denmark
046	Sweden
047	Norway
049	West Germany
061	Australia

may have to increase the number of files that can be opened by FCBS from its default setting of 4.

ACCESSING MORE FILES WITH THE FILES COMMAND

The default setting of FILES allows 8 files to be open at one time. This number is often too small for modern applications programs. If you see the message:

Too many files open

you should increase the FILES specification in CONFIG.SYS. Use the line:

FILES = *nn*

in your CONFIG.SYS to increase the number of files open at the same time to *nn*.

DOS reserves an area of memory so that it can keep track of each open file; however, as with buffers, the more files you have open at once, the more memory you use. If you use database software you will need a larger FILES specification than if you only use a word processor.

USING MORE THAN FIVE DRIVES

By default, the highest drive letter that DOS can recognize is E. Therefore, if you have more than five drives on your system, you must add a LASTDRIVE specification to your CONFIG.SYS file. The general form is:

LASTDRIVE = *n*

in which *n* is a letter between A and Z.

LOADING SPECIAL DEVICE DRIVERS

DOS loads standard drivers for all devices—such as monitors, floppy disks, hard disks, and printers—during the bootup process. If, however, you need to install a nonstandard device driver (for a mouse, for example), you can do so with a DEVICE specification in the CONFIG.SYS file. Usually, the manufacturer of the special hardware supplies the device driver. DOS, however, includes several device drivers: DISPLAY.SYS, PRINTER.SYS, DRIVER.SYS, ANSI.SYS, and VDISK.SYS (or RAMDRIVE.SYS). In the next sections I discuss ANSI.SYS and VDISK.SYS in more detail.

ANSI.SYS   ANSI.SYS is a device driver that allows you to set screen colors and attributes, as well as special key assignments. ANSI stands for American National Standards Institute. To take advantage of these features, the driver must be installed on your system by the CONFIG.SYS file's DEVICE command. For example, if the ANSI.SYS file is in the DOS directory on drive C:, CONFIG.SYS should contain the line:

DEVICE = C:\DOS\ANSI.SYS

Because several Norton Utilities programs use the facilities extended by the ANSI.SYS driver, be sure your CONFIG.SYS file contains the command that loads ANSI.SYS.

For non-IBM computers the RAM disk device driver is often called RAMDRIVE.SYS.

VDISK.SYS   DOS also includes a device driver that creates a RAM disk. A RAM (random-access memory) disk is memory that is set aside to simulate the operation of a disk drive and, therefore, operates very quickly. Because files placed in a RAM disk are actually in memory, they will be lost if the computer's power is turned off before they are written to a real disk. To add a 64K RAM disk to your system, include the following line in your CONFIG.SYS file:

DEVICE = C:\DOS\VDISK.SYS 64

In this example, the VDISK.SYS file is located in the DOS directory of drive C. VDISK.SYS creates and maintains the directory structure, FAT, and program and data files for the RAM disk.

You can create several RAM disks if you have sufficient memory by including a separate statement for each disk in the CONFIG.SYS file, as follows:

```
DEVICE = C:\DOS\VDISK.SYS 64
DEVICE = C:\DOS\VDISK.SYS 128
```

You can also use the /E switch to place the RAM disk in extended memory—extra memory above the limit of conventional memory—if your system has this additional memory. To use extended memory for the two RAM disks in the previous example, simply change the DEVICE specifications to the following:

```
DEVICE = C:\DOS\VDISK.SYS 64 /E
DEVICE = C:\DOS\VDISK.SYS 128 /E
```

If your system has two floppy disk drives and one hard disk drive, DOS will name the two new RAM disks D and E, respectively.

If you copy the Norton Utilities programs you use most frequently to your RAM disk, they will be loaded at blistering speed, as DOS will load them from memory rather than from disk. You should use a batch file to copy the programs to the RAM disk because you need to reload them each time you reboot your system. Assuming you have created a RAM drive D, the batch file to initialize the RAM disk might contain the statements:

When you copy program files to a RAM disk, the original files remain on your hard disk.

```
:batch file to load files to the RAM disk
COPY C:\NORTON\NORTON.EXE D: > NUL
COPY C:\NORTON\NCD.EXE D: > NUL
COPY C:\NORTON\NCC.EXE D: > NUL
```

If you redirect the output from the COPY command to the device called NUL, you will not see any of COPY's messages written on the screen.

These lines will copy the Norton program, the Norton Change Directory, and the Norton Command Center programs to the RAM disk. Remember to alter the PATH command (for details, see the next section, "The AUTOEXEC.BAT File") to include this new drive, putting the drive D specification before any reference to drive C in the PATH. For example, your PATH statement might include the following:

PATH D:\;C:\;C:DOS;C:\NORTON;C:\BATCH

This way, DOS will find and load the programs on the RAM disk, rather than the slower disk-based programs. You can load programs into the RAM disk from a regular batch file that you run each time you want to use the RAM disk, or you can include the commands in the AUTOEXEC.BAT file, which runs automatically every time you start your system. You can even load the batch file for your RAM disk automatically by invoking it as the last command in AUTOEXEC.BAT.

THE AUTOEXEC.BAT FILE

AUTOEXEC.BAT is similar in concept to the CONFIG.SYS file, but there is an important difference between the two files. AUTOEXEC.BAT can contain *any* DOS command you want to use every time you start up your computer, unlike CONFIG.SYS, which can use only configuration commands. For example, it can load terminate-and-stay-resident (TSR) programs, such as the Norton Cache, or start an application program.

After DOS boots itself, it looks for AUTOEXEC.BAT in the root directory of the boot disk. If the file is present, DOS executes its contents line by line until they have all been processed, exactly like any other batch file. Figure 17.2 presents the contents of a typical AUTOEXEC.BAT file.

Let's examine these commands more closely. Remember that you do not necessarily have to include all of them in your AUTOEXEC.BAT file. On the other hand, your file may contain all these and more, according to your needs.

```
ECHO OFF
PROMPT = $e[37;44;1m$p$g
PATH = C:\;C:\DOS;C:\NORTON;C:\BATCH
DATE
TIME
```

Figure 17.2: A typical AUTOEXEC.BAT file

SETTING THE DATE AND TIME

You can use the DATE and TIME commands to set or look at the date and time. Setting the correct date is important, because many programs use your system's date and time to track activity. To set the date and the time, simply include the commands in your AUTOEXEC.BAT file individually, without any of the parameters. While DOS is running AUTOEXEC.BAT, you will be prompted to enter the date and time.

Date is specified as *mm-dd-yy*, in which *mm* is the month, numbered as 01 through 12; *dd* is the day, numbered as 01 through 31; and *yy* is the year, numbered as 80 through 99 or 1980 through 2079. You can use periods, dashes, or slashes to separate the date's elements. The order of the date's elements is determined by the settings of the COUNTRY command in your CONFIG.SYS file.

Time is specified as *hh:mm:ss.xx*, in which *hh* is the current hour in the 24-hour format, *mm* is the number of minutes, *ss* is the number of seconds, and *xx* is the number of hundredths of a second. You must use a colon to separate the TIME command's elements, except for hundredths of a second. Entering seconds and hundredths of a second is optional. The order of the time's elements is also determined by the COUNTRY command.

ESTABLISHING A PATH

If you do not set up a PATH statement, DOS can only check the current directory for files when you give a command. The

PATH command creates a list of directories through which DOS searches when it tries to locate a file. When you run a program or an external DOS command, DOS searches the PATH for the program file. Consider the PATH command in Figure 17.2:

PATH = C:\;C:\DOS;C:\NORTON;C:\BATCH

DOS first searches through the entries in the current directory for the file you have requested. If DOS doesn't find the file, it next searches the drive C root directory, DOS directory, NORTON directory, and BATCH directory, in that order. (It doesn't matter which directory is current when you request the file.) Note that the directory names listed in the PATH specification must be separated by semicolons.

By including in the PATH the names of the directories that contain the files you use most often, you can work more efficiently; you won't have to specify long path names with each command, and DOS will find your files quickly.

To display your current PATH, type:

PATH

at the DOS prompt. DOS will list the current PATH if one has already been set up. If no PATH has been established, DOS will reply with the message:

No Path

To cancel a previously defined PATH, type:

PATH;

If you have already included the PATH statement in your AUTOEXEC.BAT file, running the file again will reset the PATH to its original setting.

USING THE PROMPT COMMAND

You can set or change the DOS prompt with a command that uses the following format:

PROMPT *string*

in which *string* can be a simple or complex expression. It can contain both straightforward text or metasymbols. *Metasymbols* are special IBM codes that represent elements to be included in the prompt. For example, if you type:

PROMPT $p

the DOS prompt will be the name of the current directory. On the other hand, if you type:

PROMPT pg

the prompt will be the name of the current directory and the > symbol. Table 17.2 lists all of the metasymbols that can be used with the PROMPT command.

You can also add special display characters to the prompt by in-cluding a control sequence in the command statement or by using the Alt key with the numeric keypad. You can use these methods to display most of the ASCII characters from 0 to 31 and 128 to 255. For example, to make your DOS prompt a "happy face" using the control sequence, type PROMPT, press Ctrl-A, and then press Enter. You can get the same result by typing PROMPT, pressing Alt-1 (using the numeric keypad), and pressing Enter. The prompt setting will stay in effect until you change it by typing another PROMPT sequence, or until you reboot your system and DOS loads the AUTOEXEC.BAT file, which resets it.

SETTING THE SCREEN'S COLORS AND ATTRIBUTES
WITH PROMPT If you include the ANSI.SYS driver in your CONFIG.SYS file, you can use the PROMPT command to

Table 17.2: The PROMPT Command's Metasymbols

SYMBOL	MEANING
$b	Vertical bar character (|)
$d	Current date
$e	Escape character for an ANSI sequence
$g	> character
$h	Backspace one character
$l	< character
$n	Default drive specifier
$p	Current drive and path name
$q	= character
$s	Space character
$t	Current time
$v	DOS version number
$_	Inserts carriage return/line feed sequence

manipulate the default colors on your color monitor. If you have a monochrome screen that can display different shades of its color, you can still use PROMPT to reset the screen. To use the PROMPT command to define screen attributes, use the following general format:

PROMPT $e[*nnnn*m

in which *nnnn* defines the screen attributes or colors. The metasymbol $e represents the Esc character. There is no limit to the number of attributes you can enter between the left bracket, [, and the terminating character, m. Note that the starting character, e, and the terminating character, m, must be lowercase. See Table 17.3 for a list of the colors that you can use and Table 17.4 for a list of the screen attributes you can use.

Table 17.3: Codes for Changing the Screen Colors

COLORS	FOREGROUND	BACKGROUND
Black	30	40
Red	31	41
Green	32	42
Yellow	33	43
Blue	34	44
Magenta	35	45
Cyan	36	46
White	37	47

Table 17.4: Codes for Changing the Screen Attributes

ATTRIBUTE CODES	EFFECTS
0	Turns all attributes off
1	Boldfacing
4	Underlining (on IBM-compatible monochrome monitors)
5	Blinking
7	Reverse video

To change your display to black characters on a white screen (in other words, to generate "reverse video"), type:

PROMPT $e[7m

To reset the screen and turn off all special attributes, type:

PROMPT $e[0m

You can combine attributes and colors in a command line by separating the settings with semicolons. For example, to make your screen a blinking, reverse video display, enter:

PROMPT $e[7;5m

The reverse attribute is set with code 7, and blinking is set with code 5.

You can also combine screen attributes with metasymbols to produce eye-catching DOS prompts. For example, type:

PROMPT $e[5m COMMAND $e[0m$p$g

The $e[5m sequence turns on the blinking screen attribute. COMMAND will be blinking text in the prompt because it is sandwiched between the commands that set and reset the blinking attribute. (The $e[0m sequence resets it.) The metasymbol $p displays the name of the current directory, and the metasymbol $g displays the > symbol.

Research has shown that white text on a blue background is the easiest to read. You can set your screen to this color combination by typing:

PROMPT $e[37;44m

You may want to add the metasymbols for the name of the current directory, $p, and the > symbol, $g, to this PROMPT command:

PROMPT $e[37;44m$p$g

Including these metasymbols helps you to identify the current directory.

After you have decided which prompt and screen setup you prefer, you should include its PROMPT command in your AUTOEXEC.BAT file.

You don't have to worry about running out of keys because you can reprogram up to 40 keys by using the function, Shift-function, Ctrl-function, and Alt-function keys.

REDEFINING KEYS WITH PROMPT AND ANSI.SYS By using ANSI.SYS you can also program virtually any of the keys on the keyboard to type DOS commands. Like setting the screen attributes, assigning a new meaning to a key requires the use of an Esc sequence. In this case, the sequence starts with $e[and continues with the ASCII value of the key you want to use (if the key is a standard letter key), followed by a **p** character. The lowercase **p** character terminates key assignment sequences, exactly as **m** terminates screen attributes sequences. If you want to assign a command to one of the function keys or function key combinations, you must use a zero followed by a special code that indicates the key. These special codes are listed in Table 17.5.

Suppose you want to assign the FORMAT command to a function key because you use this command frequently. To make the F5 key automatically type the command:

FORMAT A:

enter the following line:

PROMPT $e[0;63;"FORMAT A:";13p

A semicolon separates each command.

The $e alerts the ANSI driver that an ANSI escape sequence is starting, and the 0 indicates that the key to be redefined is a key on the extended keyboard. Code 63 stands for F5, and "FORMAT A:" is the command to be assigned to the F5 key. Remember to include any text in quotes. Code 13 represents a carriage return character, and p is the terminating character for the whole sequence.

SPECIFYING THE MODE

The MODE command selects the mode of operation for the parallel printers, modems, and display units. It can also redirect output and specify different character sets that you can use with your printer.

Table 17.5: Function Key Redefinition Codes

FUNCTION KEY	REDEFINITION CODE
F1	59
F2	60
F3	61
F4	62
F5	63
F6	64
F7	65
F8	66
F9	67
F10	68
Shift-F1	84
Shift-F2	85
Shift-F3	86
Shift-F4	87
Shift-F5	88
Shift-F6	89
Shift-F7	90
Shift-F8	91
Shift-F9	92
Shift-F10	93
Ctrl-F1	94
Ctrl-F2	95
Ctrl-F3	96
Ctrl-F4	97
Ctrl-F5	98

Table 17.5: Function Key Redefinition Codes (continued)

FUNCTION KEY	REDEFINITION CODE
Ctrl-F6	99
Ctrl-F7	100
Ctrl-F8	101
Ctrl-F9	102
Ctrl-F10	103
Alt-F1	104
Alt-F2	105
Alt-F3	106
Alt-F4	107
Alt-F5	108
Alt-F6	109
Alt-F7	110
Alt-F8	111
Alt-F9	112
Alt-F10	113

VERIFYING COMMAND SETTINGS WITH SET

You can use the SET command to redefine operating parameters in the DOS environment that batch files or applications programs can use.

If you type:

```
SET
```

at the DOS prompt, DOS will display the name and location of the command processor and the current settings of the PATH and PROMPT commands, as follows:

```
COMSPEC = C:\COMMAND.COM
```

```
PATH = C:\;C:\DOS;C:\NORTON
PROMPT = $e[37;44m$p$g
```

If a LASTDRIVE specification is in effect, it too will appear in the list of predefined reserved names. DOS's environment space is limited, so it is a good idea to remove any commands that you no longer need. You remove these by typing:

SET *Name* =

in which *Name* represents the command name.

AUTOMATICALLY LOADING TERMINATE-AND-STAY-RESIDENT PROGRAMS

Your AUTOEXEC.BAT file can load the TSR programs that you use routinely. After TSR programs are loaded into memory, they stay there, remaining inactive until you use a particular key sequence to activate them. *SideKick* waits for you to press Ctrl-Alt, and *Keyworks* presents its menu when you press the large plus (+) key on the right side of the keyboard. You can activate them from within other programs, and when you are finished with them, you are returned to your original program.

Memory-resident utilities are extremely fast; however, you pay for their speed dearly—you must relinquish a section of memory to them. This reduces the amount of memory available for your other applications.

Some TSR programs are extremely sensitive to the order in which they are loaded, and you should consult the documentation accompanying your TSR programs to determine the best sequence. As always, it is good practice to have a recent complete backup of your hard disk, just in case something should go wrong.

USING THE BATCH ENHANCER UTILITY IN YOUR BATCH FILES

The Norton Utilities BE (Batch Enhancer) program includes several older Norton Utilities programs, such as ASK, BEEP, and SA (Screen Attributes), that you can use to extend the scope of your batch programming. The BE utility provides more control over the screen colors and attributes than the DOS ANSI.SYS driver does. You can also use its subprograms' routines to clear the screen, draw a box on the screen, open exploding windows, position the cursor at a particular location on the screen, and write a character on the screen.

BE SA (SCREEN ATTRIBUTES)

■ BE SA requires that the ANSI.SYS device driver is loaded. Remember, you must include the DEVICE command in your CONFIG.SYS file to do this.

BE SA lets you set the screen colors and attributes either from the DOS prompt or from inside a batch file. You can specify the color names as BE SA's parameters, although when you become more familiar with them, you can abbreviate them to their first three letters. Table 17.6 shows the list of settings you can use with BE SA.

Applications programs often set their own colors and attributes when they start running, and some programs are so well-behaved that they reset the screen when they finish running. Because other programs do not do this, however, you can make a batch file called RESET.BAT that contains the following BE SA command:

BE SA BRIGHT WHITE ON BLUE

■ This command creates my favorite screen setup. You can substitute other parameters if you find another setup that you prefer.

To reset the screen quickly, all you have to do is invoke this file.

You can also include BE SA in a batch file to change the screen and draw attention to whatever the batch file next executes. For example, the following BE SA command will get your attention no matter what you are doing:

BE SA REVERSE

Table 17.6: BE SA's Attributes

SCREEN SETTING	COLOR
Color (background and foreground)	Black
	Red
	Green
	Yellow
	Blue
	Magenta
	Cyan
	White
Intensity	Bright (Bold)
	Blinking
Text on screen	Normal
	Reverse
	Underline

BE SA settings will produce different results on different systems. Some monochrome screens can produce gradations of their color to correspond to the colors set by BE SA, while others cannot. You will have to experiment with BE SA to discover which settings you find the most appealing.

The brackets around SINGLE or DOUBLE indicate that these are optional parameters. If you don't enter either one, BE will draw a single outline, which is its default. (Specify SINGLE to reset it after using DOUBLE.)

BE BOX

BE BOX draws a box on the screen of a specified size at a specified location. The command uses the following general format:

BE BOX *top left bottom right* [SINGLE or DOUBLE] *color*

in which *top* and *left* are the pair of screen coordinates defining the row and column position of the top-left corner of the box, and *bottom* and *right* similarly define the position of the bottom-right corner of the box on the screen. SINGLE or DOUBLE makes the box outline either a single line or a double line, and *color* specifies the color of the box's outline. In fact, you can even specify two colors for it. For example, if you enter:

BE BOX *top left bottom right* GREEN ON BLUE

your box will have an attractive two-toned frame. See Table 17.6 for the list of colors you can use.

BE BOX draws a box anywhere on the screen. The following example:

BE BOX 10 10 20 20 DOUBLE RED

draws a red double-lined box from row 10, column 10 to row 20, column 20.

BE CLS

BE CLS clears the screen and positions the cursor at the top-left corner, which is called the *home* position.

Using BE CLS is simple. To include it in a batch file, merely add the line:

BE CLS

Place this command in batch files that draw windows or boxes; preceding the drawing command with BE CLS ensures that you start with a fresh screen.

BE GOTO

BE GOTO transfers the flow of the batch file to another place in the file by referencing a label. A label is a string of up to eight characters preceded by a colon. For example, to skip a section of code in a batch file, you might add the following lines to your batch file:

```
BE GOTO LAST
more code here...
:LAST
```

BE WINDOW

BE WINDOW is similar to BE BOX, except that two more parameters can be defined. SHADOW draws a drop shadow below and to the right of the window, and EXPLODE makes the window zoom to its full size. When you omit SHADOW, the window does not have a drop shadow; when you omit EXPLODE, the full-sized window appears immediately, and you will not see it enlarge on the screen.

Although BE WINDOW's *color* parameter uses the same format as *color* in BE BOX, it operates differently. When you specify two colors, the first color becomes the window's outline and the second fills in as the background color.

BE WINDOW uses the following general format:

BE WINDOW *top left bottom right color* SHADOW EXPLODE

For example, try the following WINDOW sequence directly from the DOS command line:

BE WINDOW 5 20 20 60 RED ON CYAN SHADOW EXPLODE

just to see what happens. If you specify coordinates that position one window on top of another, the second window will overlay the first one, displaying the uncovered portion of the first window.

BE PRINTCHAR

BE PRINTCHAR can display a character a specified number

of times at the cursor's current location. This command uses the following general format:

BE PRINTCHAR *character repetitions* [*color*]

in which *character* is any character that you type, and *repetitions* specifies how many times the character is to be repeated. The optional *color* parameter lets you specify the character's color.

Try this PRINTCHAR sequence just to see what happens:

BE PRINTCHAR 1 20 RED

BE ROWCOL

BE ROWCOL positions the cursor at a particular row and column location on the screen, displaying the specified text in the requested color. It uses the following general format:

BE ROWCOL *row column* [*"text"*] [*color*]

If you use ROWCOL with WINDOW, you can place text in windows. For example, the following batch file creates three windows, labeling them WINDOW 1, WINDOW 2, and WINDOW 3:

```
@ECHO OFF
BE CLS
BE SA BRIGHT WHITE ON BLUE
BE WINDOW 4 4 14 64 SHADOW
BE ROWCOL 9 25 "WINDOW 1" YELLOW ON BLUE
BE WINDOW 8 8 18 68 SHADOW
BE ROWCOL 13 29 "WINDOW 2" YELLOW ON BLUE
BE WINDOW 12 12 22 72 SHADOW
BE ROWCOL 17 33 "WINDOW 3" YELLOW ON BLUE
```

Each window overlays part of the previous window.

Now that you have set up overlapping windows, you can reverse the order by having window 2 cover part of window 3 and window 1 cover part of window 2. To do this, add the following commands to the end of the batch file:

```
BE WINDOW 8 8 18 68 SHADOW
BE ROWCOL 13 29 "WINDOW 2" YELLOW ON BLUE
BE WINDOW 4 4 14 64 SHADOW
BE ROWCOL 9 25 "WINDOW 1" YELLOW ON BLUE
BE ROWCOL 24 0
:EXIT
```

This redraws the second and first windows in that order. The last ROWCOL command sends the cursor to the last position on the screen and returns you to DOS.

By using this batch-file example as your guide, you can construct a windowed menu system for loading applications programs or other batch files.

BE ASK

BE ASK provides an easy way to add conditional branching to a DOS batch file. It pauses the batch file during its execution and prompts the user to choose the branch that the batch file should then take. When you include a BE ASK command in a batch file, you need to specify which keystrokes are associated with the possible branches. You can also instruct BE ASK how long it should await a keystroke before returning a default value that you specify.

The general format of BE ASK is as follows:

BE ASK *"prompt" key-list* DEFAULT=*key* TIMEOUT=*n* ADJUST=*m color*

in which

- *"prompt"* is a text string, often a question, that gives two or more choices.

- *key-list* lists the valid keystrokes as responses to *"prompt"*. If no *key-list* is given, any key from the keyboard is accepted.

- DEFAULT=*key* specifies the key BE ASK will use if no key is pressed within the TIMEOUT period.
- TIMEOUT=*n* specifies a wait period in seconds. If you set TIMEOUT to zero or don't specify any value, BE ASK waits forever.
- ADJUST=*m* adjusts the return value by the value of *m*.
- *color* sets the color of the prompt text.

After you type a key at the prompt, BE ASK transfers control back to the batch file, passing along the ERRORLEVEL value that corresponds to the key you pressed. This is ASK's method of setting the value for the keystroke. For example, if you type the first key in the list, ASK generates an ERRORLEVEL value of 1. The IF statement then evaluates the value returned in ER-RORLEVEL, and the GOTO command passes control to the branch of the batch file that is indicated by that value.

Let's examine a branching batch file that contains two IF statements as an example. This file could be used to make a simple yes/no decision because it offers two branching choices. So that the batch file can evaluate these choices correctly, you need to list them in reverse order in the file; that is, the statement IF ERRORLEVEL 2 must precede IF ERRORLEVEL 1. The entire batch file might resemble this sequence:

```
@ECHO OFF
BE CLS
BE ASK "Yes or No ? ( Press Y or N ) ", YN TIMEOUT=30 DEFAULT=2
IF ERRORLEVEL 2 GOTO NO
IF ERRORLEVEL 1 GOTO YES

:YES
ECHO YES
GOTO END

:NO
ECHO NO
GOTO END
:END
```

When you run this batch file, it turns ECHO off, clears the screen, and prompts:

Yes or No ? (Press Y or N)

BE ASK is not case sensitive; it treats the uppercase Y and the lowercase y as the same character.

If you answer Y for yes, BE ASK sets ERRORLEVEL to 1, which is then tested by the IF statement. Control passes to the subroutine labeled :YES, which echoes the word YES to the screen. The GOTO END statement ends the batch file.

If you answer N for no, BE ASK sets ERRORLEVEL to 2, which is then tested by the IF statement. Control passes to the subroutine called :NO, which echoes the word NO to the screen. Control is passed to the label :END and the batch file terminates.

Set DEFAULT to the value for "no"; it is usually the safest response to any yes or no prompt.

If you do not press a key in 30 seconds, BE ASK returns the default ERRORLEVEL value, which is 2 in this example.

BE BEEP

You can use BE BEEP to play a single note from the DOS prompt or play a series of notes loaded from an ASCII text file. You can specify the frequency and the duration of a note, the number of times a note is repeated, and the length of the wait period between notes.

BEEP uses the ticks of your system clock as its timer. Because the system clock ticks about 18.2 times a second, BEEP requires that you enter values in eighteenths of a second for notes' durations and wait periods.

The general format of BE BEEP is:

BE BEEP *switches*

or

BE BEEP *filename* /E

To specify durations and wait periods, you can include the following switches in your BEEP command:

- /D*n* specifies the duration of the note in $\frac{1}{18}$ths of a second.

- /F*n* specifies the frequency of the note in Hertz, or cycles per second.

- /R*n* tells BEEP how many times a note is to be repeated.

- /W*n* establishes the length of the wait period between notes in $\frac{1}{18}$ths of a second.

- /E echoes any text in quotation marks following the notes.

Remember that you replace *n* with the number you want.

To practice working with BEEP, enter:

```
BE BEEP
```

at the DOS prompt. This produces a single short tone. Entering the following:

```
BE BEEP /F50/D18/R5/W18
```

plays five low notes a second apart. Each note is one second long. The following example:

```
BE BEEP /F3000/D1/R5/W9
```

plays five short-duration high notes at half-second intervals.

When you specify a file name as input for BE BEEP, you can specify its path; however, you cannot include wildcards in the file name.

Let's assume you want to create a file called BEEPTEST. Remember to include a comment line prefaced with a colon to describe what the file does. For example, BEEPTEST might contain the following:

```
:This generates three low, medium, and high notes
/F100/D9/R3/W18
/F500/D18/R3/W18
/F1000/D36/R3/W18
```

This file plays three low notes that are each half a second long, three middle notes that are one second long, and three high notes that are two seconds long. To invoke this file from the DOS prompt, type:

```
BE BEEP BEEPTEST
```

By providing a file as input, you enabled BE BEEP to play a simple tune.

Although you can use BE BEEP in a variety of ways, it is most convenient for signaling the completion of a process in a batch file.

BE DELAY

BE DELAY lets you specify the delay period in a batch file that must elapse before the batch file can continue executing. To include BE DELAY in your batch file, use the general format:

```
BE DELAY time
```

in which *time* is specified in $\frac{1}{18}$ths of a second, as in BE BEEP. For example, when the batch-file processor encounters a delay of $\frac{9}{18}$ths of a second, which is the command:

```
BE DELAY 9
```

it waits a $\frac{1}{2}$-second before continuing with the next command in the file.

COMBINING NORTON AND DOS COMMANDS IN A MENU BATCH FILE

Now that you know what BE's subprograms can do, you can use them to create more complex batch files. For example, you could make one that produces a menu system, calling it MENU.BAT. This file could display a menu and let you choose an application program to load from the selections presented. The batch file would then run the program of your choice, and when your selection stopped running, it would return you to the menu to await your next selection. Let's create an example batch file that loads a word processor, a spreadsheet, or a database program. After you understand how this batch file works, you can extrapolate the rules of selection and branching to create more elaborate menus.

This example batch file will use the BE CLS, GOTO, WINDOW, ROWCOL, ASK, SA, and PRINTCHAR commands from the Norton Utilities, along with the IF, ECHO OFF, and ERRORLEVEL commands from DOS. Comments are included in the batch file to make things clearer; remember that a comment line must always begin with either a colon character or the REM statement.

The first few commands in the file set up the screen:

```
:BE startup menu file

@ECHO OFF
BE CLS

:set the screen colors

BE SA BRIGHT WHITE ON BLUE
```

@ECHO OFF instructs DOS not to display the batch file's commands as they are executed, BE CLS clears the screen, and BE SA BRIGHT WHITE ON BLUE sets the screen colors and attributes to bold white text on a blue background.

When using batch files to create screen displays, be careful to use spaces to position text properly.

To draw the menu window, enter the following lines to the MENU.BAT file:

```
:draw the menu window

BE WINDOW 05 10 17 30 BRIGHT WHITE ON BLUE SHADOW EXPLODE
BE ROWCOL 07 12 "  --- MENU ---"

BE ROWCOL 09 12 "1:" BRIGHT WHITE ON MAGENTA
BE ROWCOL 09 14 "   Lotus 1-2-3" BRIGHT WHITE ON BLUE
```

The BE WINDOW command opens a window at the left side of the screen (row 5, column 10 to row 17, column 30). Its outline is bright white, with a black shadow, and it is filled in blue. The first BE ROWCOL command writes the text " — Menu —" at the top of the window using the default colors, bright white on blue. The next BE ROWCOL command moves the cursor two rows down and writes the bright white text "1:" into the window using a magenta background. This highlights the number in a different color, so that it will later be obvious that this number is what you enter to choose the menu selection. The last BE ROWCOL command moves the cursor two columns over on the same row and adds the bright white text " Lotus 1-2-3" on a blue background. This sequence creates the first menu item.

Of course, you can substitute other program names for the menu entries if you want to use this batch file on your system.

Now repeat the last two BE ROWCOL commands for three more menu choices: WordStar, dBASE IV, and Exit to DOS. Space them two rows apart by changing the first parameter (09) to 11, 13, and 15, respectively. Figure 17.3 shows what the MENU.BAT screen looks like so far.

Run your MENU.BAT file and compare the results with Figure 17.3. After you are sure that your batch file is working correctly, add the following lines to it:

```
:draw the dialog box

BE WINDOW 19 10 21 30 BRIGHT WHITE ON BLUE SHADOW
BE ROWCOL 20 12 "Enter a Number    "
BE ROWCOL 20 28
```

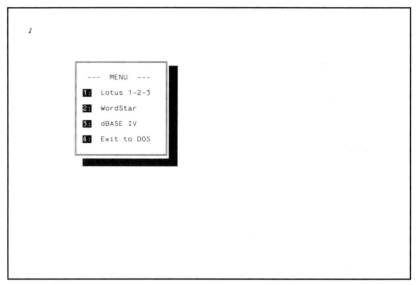

Figure 17.3: MENU.BAT's startup window

```
BE PRINTCHAR " " 1 ON BLACK
BE ROWCOL 20 28
```

This creates a dialog box that prompts you to choose a menu item. The window opens below the menu and is also blue with a bright white outline. It contains the text "Enter a Number   ". The BE ROWCOL 20 28 command backspaces the cursor one space, and the BE PRINTCHAR " " 1 ON BLACK line prints a space character there. By printing a space with a black background, the batch file creates a box to display the character that you type to choose a menu item. Figure 17.4 shows you the results of running the current version of MENU.BAT.

So that the batch file can evaluate your response, enter the following BE ASK sequence:

```
:evaluates menu selection
:if no key pressed in 30 secs, exit to DOS

BE ASK "", 1234 TIMEOUT=30 DEFAULT=4
   IF ERRORLEVEL 4 BE GOTO FOUR
   IF ERRORLEVEL 3 BE GOTO THREE
```

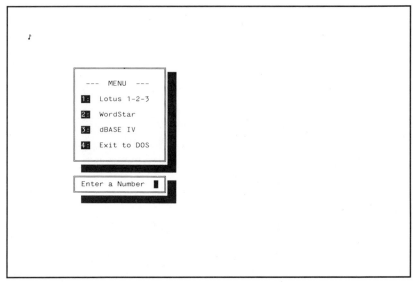

Figure 17.4: MENU.BAT now displays two windows

```
IF ERRORLEVEL 2 BE GOTO TWO
IF ERRORLEVEL 1 BE GOTO ONE
```

Because the prompt is already displayed in the dialog box, the
BE ASK command requires no prompt string. The legal entries
for BE ASK are 1, 2, 3, and 4. TIMEOUT is set to 30 seconds;
if this time elapses before a key is pressed, the DEFAULT
parameter instructs the batch file to choose 4, the Exit to DOS
menu item. If a key is pressed, one of the four IF statements passes control to one of four branches, depending on which key
you press when the batch file prompts you.

At the moment, however, there aren't any branching sequences to go to; you need to add them. Each sequence must
start with the label specified in its corresponding BE GOTO
command. For example, the branch for the Exit to DOS menu
option begins with the label:

```
:FOUR
```

Because you need to list the IF statements in reverse order,
order the branches the same way. Thus, to continue with the

fourth menu item's branch, enter the following:

```
BE ROWCOL 20 28 "4" BRIGHT WHITE ON MAGENTA
GOTO EXIT
```

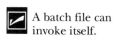 Use this technique of echoing a character back to the screen for all data-entry processes; it confirms that the computer has accepted a person's input and is processing that information.

The BE ROWCOL statement displays the key pressed in response to the prompt as a bright white on magenta character, indicating that the batch file has accepted the key you entered. The GOTO statement sends the batch-file processor to the end of the file and exits to DOS.

The remaining three branches share essentially the same sequence. Let's look at the WordStar menu item's branch as an example:

```
:TWO
BE ROWCOL 20 28 "2" BRIGHT WHITE ON MAGENTA
BE WINDOW 19 35 21 75 BRIGHT WHITE ON BLUE SHADOW
BE ROWCOL 20 37 "Loading WordStar, Please Be Patient"
CD \WS4
WS
CD \BATCH
MENU
```

The selection is again echoed to the screen and another window opens to tell you which application program is being loaded. (The actual loading of WordStar is done by the two command lines following the ROWCOL command.) Figure 17.5 displays the MENU.BAT screen that you should see at this point.

The last two commands of the label :TWO branch:

```
CD \BATCH
MENU
```

A batch file can invoke itself.

make the BATCH directory current and run MENU.BAT again. With this setup, you are always returned to the menu screen when you exit an application.

Use this example for your remaining applications. When you finish, compare your batch file to Figure 17.6, which shows a complete listing of MENU.BAT.

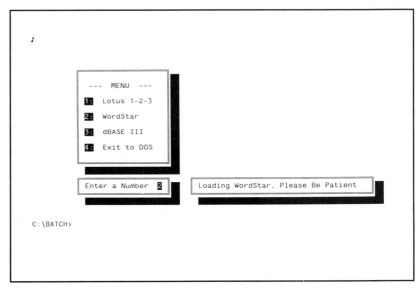

Figure 17.5: The MENU.BAT screen with all three windows open

If you add MENU.BAT to your AUTOEXEC.BAT file, you can make your system completely menu-driven. If the DOS programs are in a directory called DOS, the Norton Utilities are in a directory called NORTON, and your batch files are in a directory called BATCH, your PATH setting might look like this:

PATH = C:\;C:\DOS;C:\NORTON;C:\BATCH

If you then add the line:

MENU

to the end of your AUTOEXEC.BAT file, the MENU.BAT file will be loaded automatically each time you boot up your computer. Now, you or other users won't have to work in DOS to run your application programs. Including the Exit to DOS option in the menu, however, lets you return to DOS to perform other important tasks necessary for managing and backing up your disks.

```
:BE startup menu file

ECHO OFF
BE CLS

:set the screen colors

BE SA BRIGHT WHITE ON BLUE

:draw the window

BE WINDOW 05 10 17 30 BRIGHT WHITE ON BLUE SHADOW EXPLODE
BE ROWCOL 07 12 " ---  MENU  --- "

BE ROWCOL 09 12 "1:" BRIGHT WHITE ON MAGENTA
BE ROWCOL 09 14 "  Lotus 1-2-3" BRIGHT WHITE ON BLUE

BE ROWCOL 11 12 "2:" BRIGHT WHITE ON MAGENTA
BE ROWCOL 11 14 "  WordStar" BRIGHT WHITE ON BLUE

BE ROWCOL 13 12 "3:" BRIGHT WHITE ON MAGENTA
BE ROWCOL 13 14 "  dBASE IV" BRIGHT WHITE ON BLUE

BE ROWCOL 15 12 "4:" BRIGHT WHITE ON MAGENTA
BE ROWCOL 15 14 "  Exit to DOS" BRIGHT WHITE ON BLUE

:draw the dialog box

BE WINDOW 19 10 21 30 BRIGHT WHITE ON BLUE SHADOW
BE ROWCOL 20 12 "Enter a Number  "
BE ROWCOL 20 28
BE PRINTCHAR " " 1 ON BLACK
BE ROWCOL 20 28

:evaluates menu selection
:if no key pressed in 30 secs, exit to DOS

BE ASK "", 1234 TIMEOUT=30 DEFAULT=4
      IF ERRORLEVEL  4 GOTO FOUR
      IF ERRORLEVEL  3 GOTO THREE
      IF ERRORLEVEL  2 GOTO TWO
      IF ERRORLEVEL  1 GOTO ONE

:FOUR
BE ROWCOL 20 28 "4" BRIGHT WHITE ON MAGENTA
GOTO EXIT

:THREE
BE ROWCOL 20 28 "3" BRIGHT WHITE ON MAGENTA
BE WINDOW 19 35 21 75 BRIGHT WHITE ON BLUE SHADOW
BE ROWCOL 20 37 "Loading dBASE, Please Be Patient"
CD \DB4
DBASE
CD \BATCH
MENU

:TWO
BE ROWCOL 20 28 "2" BRIGHT WHITE ON MAGENTA
BE WINDOW 19 35 21 75 BRIGHT WHITE ON BLUE SHADOW
BE ROWCOL 20 37 "Loading WordStar, Please Be Patient"
CD \WS4
WS
CD \BATCH
MENU
```

Figure 17.6: The completed MENU.BAT file

```
:ONE
BE ROWCOL 20 28 "1" BRIGHT WHITE ON MAGENTA
BE WINDOW 19 35 21 75 BRIGHT WHITE ON BLUE SHADOW
BE ROWCOL 20 37 "Loading Lotus 1-2-3, Please Be Patient"
CD \123
CD \BATCH
MENU

:EXIT
BE WINDOW 19 35 21 75 BRIGHT WHITE ON BLUE SHADOW
BE ROWCOL 20 37 "Returning to DOS"
BE CLS

:reset screen colors for DOS

BE SA BRIGHT WHITE ON BLUE
```

Figure 17.6: The completed MENU.BAT file (continued)

If you find that MENU.BAT runs too slowly, you can speed it up considerably by using two files instead of just one. To do this, place all the commands for drawing the menu window and the dialog box in a separate batch file called MENU.TXT. This file will then be loaded by MENU.BAT at the appropriate point. The revised MENU.BAT file is shown in Figure 17.7, and MENU.TXT is shown in Figure 17.8. Note that in MENU.TXT, the BE statements at the start of each line have been removed because they are no longer necessary. They have been replaced by the single command:

BE MENU.TXT

in MENU.BAT. Because the MENU.TXT file is sent to BE all at once, the number of separate calls made to BE are reduced. As a result the new MENU.BAT file executes about ten times faster than the original batch file.

If you plan to use the BE utility extensively, copy the BE.EXE program to your RAM disk by including another COPY command in the batch file that initializes your RAM disk. BE is then copied to the RAM disk automatically when you (or AUTO-EXEC.BAT) invoke this batch file, and all the BE programs will run more quickly because they will be executing from memory.

```
:BE startup menu file

ECHO OFF
BE CLS

:set the screen colors

BE SA BRIGHT WHITE ON BLUE

:creates menu window and dialog box
:system runs faster when separated into two files; less calls to BE

BE MENU.TXT

:evaluates menu selection
:if no key pressed in 30 secs, exit to DOS

BE ASK "", 1234 TIMEOUT=30 DEFAULT=4
     IF ERRORLEVEL  4 GOTO FOUR
     IF ERRORLEVEL  3 GOTO THREE
     IF ERRORLEVEL  2 GOTO TWO
     IF ERRORLEVEL  1 GOTO ONE

:FOUR
BE ROWCOL 20 28 "4" BRIGHT WHITE ON MAGENTA
GOTO EXIT

:THREE
BE ROWCOL 29 28 "3" BRIGHT WHITE ON MAGENTA
BE WINDOW 19 35 21 75 BRIGHT WHITE ON BLUE SHADOW
BE ROWCOL 20 37 "Loading dBASE, Please Be Patient"
CD \DB4
DBASE
CD \BATCH
MENU

:TWO
BE ROWCOL 20 28 "2" BRIGHT WHITE ON MAGENTA
BE WINDOW 19 35 21 75 BRIGHT WHITE ON BLUE SHADOW
BE ROWCOL 20 37 "Loading WordStar, Please Be Patient"
CD \WS4
WS
CD \BATCH
MENU

:ONE
BE ROWCOL 20 28 "1" BRIGHT WHITE ON MAGENTA
BE WINDOW 19 35 21 75 BRIGHT WHITE ON BLUE SHADOW
BE ROWCOL 20 37 "Loading Lotus 1-2-3, Please Be Patient"
CD \123
123
CD \BATCH
MENU

:EXIT
BE WINDOW 19 35 21 75 BRIGHT WHITE ON BLUE SHADOW
BE ROWCOL 20 37 "Returning to DOS"
BE CLS

:reset screen colors

BE SA BRIGHT WHITE ON BLUE
```

Figure 17.7: The MENU.TXT file's contents

```
:file for accessing BE all at once

WINDOW 05 10 17 30 BRIGHT WHITE ON BLUE SHADOW EXPLODE
ROWCOL 07 12 " ---  MENU  --- "

ROWCOL 09 12 "1:" BRIGHT WHITE ON MAGENTA
ROWCOL 09 14 "  Lotus 1-2-3" BRIGHT WHITE ON BLUE

ROWCOL 11 12 "2:" BRIGHT WHITE ON MAGENTA
ROWCOL 11 14 "  WordStar" BRIGHT WHITE ON BLUE

ROWCOL 13 13 "3:" BRIGHT WHITE ON MAGENTA
ROWCOL 13 14 "  dBASE IV" BRIGHT WHITE ON BLUE

ROWCOL 15 12 "4:" BRIGHT WHITE ON MAGENTA
ROWCOL 15 14 "  Exit to DOS" BRIGHT WHITE ON BLUE

WINDOW 19 10 21 30 BRIGHT WHITE ON BLUE SHADOW
ROWCOL 20 12 "Enter a Number   "
ROWCOL 20 28
PRINTCHAR " " 1 ON BLACK
ROWCOL 20 28
```

Figure 17.8: The MENU.TXT file's contents

Using batch files can make tedious, repetitive, or complex DOS operations much more straightforward. BE's subprograms are an important addition to the batch-programming language: they let you create interactive conditional branching in a batch file and make complex screen handling and windowing easy to do.

UPDATING ASK, BEEP, AND SA

If you are using batch files that you made with an earlier version of the Norton Utilities, you can modify them by inserting the name BE before each occurrence of ASK, BEEP, and SA. This lets you continue to use them. For example, the line:

BEEP MARY

must now become:

BE BEEP MARY

Similarly, the following example:

ASK "Option A or Option B", AB

must now become:

BE ASK "Option A or Option B", AB

This simple change to existing batch files is all that is needed to update them.

Norton Control Center (NCC)

Controlling Your Computer's Hardware

CHAPTER *18* _____

THE NORTON CONTROL CENTER LETS YOU CHANGE
many of the computer's hardware configuration settings by
using simple menu selections that don't require you to have any
knowledge of programming or of the DOS MODE command.

From the main NORTON program screen, select Control
Center from the Tools sub-heading, or from the DOS prompt,
type:

NCC

to run NCC and display the Norton Command Center startup
screen (see Figure 18.1). The ten options in the Select Item list
at the left side of the screen let you perform the following
operations:

- Alter the cursor size
- Change the DOS colors
- Select the palette colors
- Choose the video mode
- Control the keyboard speed and repeat rate
- Alter the mouse speed
- Configure your serial ports
- Set and reset from one to four stopwatches
- Select the country information
- Set the system time and data

Some of these options might not work on your computer. To
use Palette Colors, your computer must have an EGA or VGA

display adapter. To use Keyboard Speed, you need an IBM PC/AT or compatible with the 80286 processor, or an 80386-based PC. To set the country information, you must first install the COUNTRY.SYS device driver in your CONFIG.SYS file. All other menu choices in the Norton Control Center window will run on most PCs and compatibles.

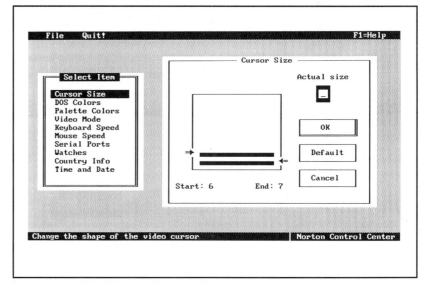

Figure 18.1: The Norton Control Center startup screen

To choose an option from the Select Item list, use the cursor-control keys to move the highlight up or down the list and then press Enter, or click on your selection with the mouse. You can also choose an option by typing the first letter of the menu choice. (Note, however, that you must press I for Country Info.)The area at the right side of the screen is where you will work with your choice from the Select Item menu.

CURSOR SIZE

The Cursor Size option lets you change the size of the cursor on your display screen. Enlarging the cursor size is useful if you

The rate of the cursor blink is built into the computer hardware and cannot be changed.

have a laptop computer whose cursor is difficult to see.

The configurations that you can use for the cursor vary according to your video display adapter:

- A CGA cursor can be configured to seven sizes in a single block

- An EGA cursor can be configured to thirteen sizes in a single block or a block that consists of two separate sections

- A VGA cursor can have up to fourteen sizes in a single block

The **Start** number at the lower-left of the Cursor Size box shows the starting position of the cursor, and the **End** number at the lower-right shows the ending position. The center box shows an enlargement of the cursor, and the cursor itself appears in the box beneath the "Actual size" label. To reconfigure the cursor, use the arrow keys to add or remove lines from the cursor character. The changes you make will register in the box in the center of the screen and in the "Actual size" box.

If you have a VGA, the default cursor is a thin horizontal line starting at position 6 and ending at position 7. With the left indicator arrow highlighted, use the up arrow key to add lines to the top of the cursor. You now have a cursor that looks like a large vertical rectangle. Tab to the **OK** box to accept this cursor if you like it. Alternatively, you can Tab to the other indicator arrow, and use the up arrow to take lines away from the bottom of the cursor until it is a single line at position 0. Press Tab again to move to the **OK** box, and press Enter to accept the new cursor.

When you have completed your changes, choose **OK** to save your changes and return to the main Select Item list. Your new cursor will remain in effect until you turn off your computer at the end of the session. To return to the Select Item list without making changes to the cursor, press Esc or click on **Cancel**. If you want to return the cursor to its original configuration, select **Default**.

DOS COLORS

The DOS Colors option lets you change the colors of the screen's foreground, background, and border. NCC refers to the color of any character drawn on the screen (text, lines, or symbols) as the *text color*. The *background color* is the color behind the text characters—usually the main screen color. The screen *border color* refers to the color of the border (if any) around a CGA or VGA screen. Because the EGA video display has no borders, the border color setting has no effect with an EGA. Figure 18.2 shows the DOS Colors selection screen.

At the top of the screen there are two color charts—one showing the current *text color* and one showing the current *border color*. Below the border color chart is another window, the *text box*, which lets you see exactly how your color selections will look on the screen. The text in the box is set to the foreground color selection, the background behind these characters is set to the background color selection, and the border around the box is set to the border color selection. Many of the color combinations

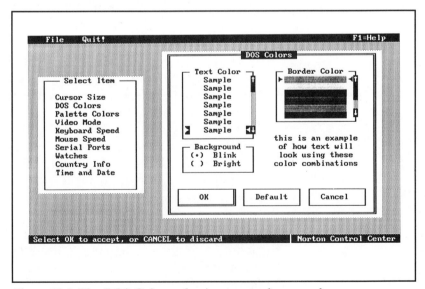

Figure 18.2: The DOS Colors selection screen lets you choose newscreen colors.

that you can create on your hardware are impossible to read or very difficult to work with at best. The display boxes will help you find the most effective color combinations for your system. Some monochrome screens can display different shades of their foreground color (usually gray, green, or amber) that correspond to color settings.

To move from one color chart to another, press the Tab key. You'll know you have selected a chart when the indicator arrows are highlighted. Use the up and down arrow keys to change the color selection inside each chart. As you press the arrow keys, the colors in the text box will change so that you can preview a different color combination. Press Enter or click on OK when you've completed your changes, or press Esc or click on Cancel to exit without making any changes. To return to the original settings, select Default.

On an EGA video display, you can choose the foreground and background colors from the selections listed in Table 18.1. You wouldn't want to select any of the second set of eight background colors because they make the text on the screen blink. Note that you can use all sixteen border colors with a VGA video display.

Table 18.1: DOS Color Settings Available for EGA Monitors

FOREGROUND COLORS	
Black	Dark Gray
Blue	Light Blue
Green	Light Green
Cyan	Light Cyan
Red	Light Red
Magenta	Light Magenta
Brown	Yellow
Light Gray	Bright White

Table 18.1: DOS Color Settings Available for EGA Monitors
(continued)

BACKGROUND COLORS
Light Blue
Light Green
Light Cyan
Light Red
Light Magenta
Yellow
Bright White

PALETTE COLORS

The Palette Colors option works only on computers with EGA (Enhanced Graphics Adapter) or VGA (Video Graphics Array) boards installed. It is not available with monochrome or CGA (Color Graphics Adapter) computers. If you try to run Palette Colors without the proper hardware, the program merely displays a message informing you that this option is not available on your hardware. Figure 18.3 shows the Palette Colors screen.

If you have an EGA or a VGA adapter, your computer can display 16 colors derived from a total selection (or *palette*) of 64 colors. The Palette Colors option lets you choose which 16 colors you want to display on the screen. With 64 colors to choose from, you can create some exotic color combinations for your daily use.

The names and numbers of the 16 base colors are shown in the working window. Use the up arrow and down arrow keys to move from color to color. When the arrows point to the color you want to change, select the Change box. Another window opens so that you can choose the replacement color from the rest of the colors in the palette. Color changes are displayed on the screen as you make them.

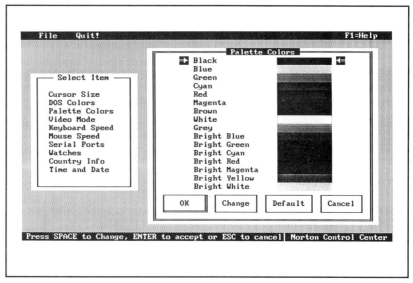

Figure 18.3: The Palette Colors screen

Press Enter or click on OK to accept the changes and return to the Select Item menu. Press Esc or Cancel to exit without making any changes.

VIDEO MODE

If you have a CGA, you can only choose between Black and White or Color.

The Video Mode options let you select the number of lines that your screen displays, and they let you choose between color and black-and-white display modes. The work area in the Video Mode screen shows the possible selections for your system, and filled-in radio buttons show the current settings. Figure 18.4 shows the settings for a VGA video display.

The number of display lines that you can select varies with different video adapters:

- The CGA supports only 25 screen lines.
- The EGA supports 25, 35, or 43 lines.
- The VGA supports 25, 40, or 50 lines.

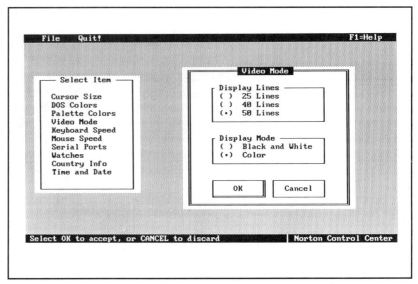

Figure 18.4: The Video Mode screen for a VGA monitor

You will find the EGA and VGA condensed modes very useful when you are viewing a file with Disk Editor. Press Enter or click on OK to accept your new choice, or press Esc or click on Cancel to return to the NCC main menu. Select Default if you want to return the display to its original settings.

KEYBOARD SPEED

Be careful not to set the keyboard speed parameters at too short an interval— it may cause you to make typing errors.

The Keyboard Speed option works only on computers equipped with 80286, 80386, or 80486 microprocessors. This selection specifies in keystrokes per second the rate at which "keystrokes" repeat if you simply hold down one key. Figure 18.5 shows the Keyboard Speed screen.

At the bottom of the work area is a small window ("Keyboard Test Pad") in which you can type text to evaluate your changes. It is surprising what a difference a subtle change in these parameters can make to your typing. If you set the repeat rate at too short an interval, you will type more characters than you

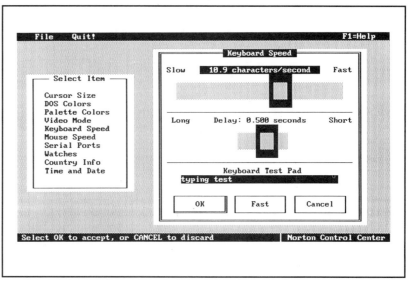

Figure 18.5: Keyboard Speed screen

intend to, and you will probably see a lot of "Bad command or file name" messages as a result.

The keyboard speed can be set anywhere from 2 characters per second, the slowest rate, to 30 characters per second, the fastest rate. The "delay" rate (the time it takes for one character to automatically repeat itself) can be set at a quarter of a second, a half a second, three quarters of a second, or one second.

MOUSE SPEED

The Mouse Speed option lets you set the responsiveness of your mouse on a scale from 0 to 100. The nearer your setting is to 0, the more unresponsive the mouse is; the nearer your setting is to 100, the more sensitive the mouse is. Figure 18.6 shows the Mouse Speed screen.

Again, select OK to accept the new mouse setting, press Esc or click on Cancel to return to the main NCC menu, or select Default to reset the mouse speed to its original configuration.

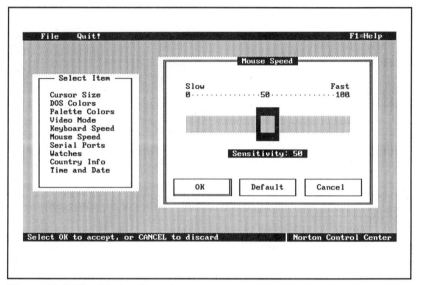

Figure 18.6: The Mouse Speed screen

SERIAL PORTS

The Serial Ports option lets you configure the serial ports attached to your computer. The ports and their current settings are shown in the work area of the Serial Ports screen (see Figure 18.7). A filled-in radio button indicates the current setting for each of the serial port parameters, and a short summary of these settings is shown at the top of the screen.

If you have more than one serial port, use the up and down arrows to choose the port you want to examine. The settings on the rest of the screen change as you switch serial ports.

Use the Tab key to move between the different boxes on the screen, and use the up and down arrow keys to move around inside the boxes themselves. To change a radio button setting, move the cursor to the new setting and press the spacebar, or click on the new setting with the mouse.

Tab to the OK box to accept your changes or the Cancel box to ignore the changes.

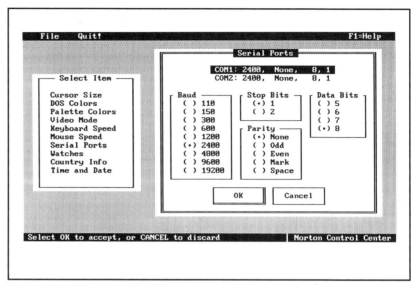

Figure 18.7: The Serial Ports screen

You can set the baud rate, the number of stop bits at the end of the data word, the number of data bits in a data word, and the parity type for each of your serial ports.

BAUD RATE

Baud rate refers to the speed, measured in bits per second, at which data bits are transmitted through the serial port to another device. The baud rate can be selected at the computer end of a communications link, or it can be selected on the peripheral device itself, often by a hardware switch. The settings at both the computer and the peripheral must match for communications to work. For example, if data is sent at 2400 baud, it must also be received at 2400 baud. The most common communications errors are caused by mismatched baud rates.

Baud rates on computer serial boards can be set to 110, 150, 300, 600, 1200, 2400, 4800, 9600, in all versions of DOS, and to 19,200 in DOS 3.3 or later. An acoustic coupler might run at 150 or 300 baud; a modern modem at 300, 1200, 2400, or 9600; a

Mismatched baud rates are a common cause of communication errors.

printer at 4800 or 9600; and a direct computer-to-computer link at 9600 or 19,200 baud.

STOP BITS

Stop bits indicate the end of each group of bits, or *frame.* They follow the parity bit at the end of the data word, and they signal the receiving device that there are no more data bits in this frame. There is usually only one stop bit.

DATA BITS

The actual information that you send through a serial port (for example, the file you are transmitting to another computer) is encoded in seven or eight *data bits* (collectively called a *data word*). A seven-bit data word is sufficient if you are sending nothing but standard ASCII characters. However, you must use an eight-bit data word if you want to send anything else (for example, a file containing any of the mathematical, Greek, foreign-language, or other special characters in the extended ASCII set). Most systems use eight data bits.

PARITY

Parity is a simple form of error checking. In communications, *parity* can be set to ODD, EVEN, MARK, SPACE, or NONE. ODD indicates that the sum of all the 1 bits in the byte plus the parity bit must be odd. If the total is already odd, the parity bit is set to zero; if it is even, the parity bit is set to 1. In EVEN parity, if the sum of all the 1 bits is even, the parity bit must be set to 0. If it is odd, the parity bit must be set to 1. ODD and EVEN are the most common settings. In MARK parity, the parity bit is always set to 1 and used as the eighth bit. In SPACE parity, the parity bit is set to 0 and used as the eighth bit. If parity is set to NONE, there is no parity bit, and parity checking is not performed. The parity setting on your computer must match the parity setting on the remote computer for successful communications.

Consult your communications software documentation for the appropriate serial port settings. If any of the settings is wrong—if you set the wrong baud rate, parity setting, or so on—communications will be scrambled because the data bits will be misinterpreted. Use the left and right arrow keys to move from parameter to parameter, and the up and down arrow keys to change the settings of the parameters. Press Enter or select OK to confirm your selections, or choose Esc or Cancel to exit without saving your changes.

WATCHES

The Watches option lets you start, stop, or reset one of four stopwatch timers using full-screen entry techniques. The Watches screen is shown in Figure 18.8.

Use the up and down arrows to select the timer you want to use; then press Enter to start the stopwatch running. You will see the current time displayed in the Start Time column, and you will see the stopwatch counting the time in the Elapsed Time

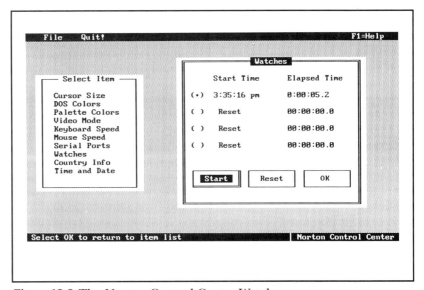

Figure 18.8: The Norton Control Center Watches screen

column. Tab to the **Pause** box, or click on it with the mouse to stop the watch for a moment. The **Pause** box is now renamed **Start**; choose it again to restart the watch. Press Esc to return to the Select Item list.

COUNTRY INFO

The Country Info option lets you alter the way your computer displays the time, date, currency and other selectable items. To use Country Info you must have a statement similar to the following:

NLSFUNC C:\DOS\COUNTRY.SYS

in your AUTOEXEC.BAT file. You can also type this statement from the DOS command line. If you do not use NLSFUNC, you will see the following message:

Country support not loaded
(Unable to change country code)

at the bottom of your screen, and you will not be able to access the Country Info selection boxes.

The NLSFUNC (National Language Support Function) lets you examine the many items that differ from country to country—time and date formats, list separators, decimal separators, and currency symbols. For example, the U.S.A. uses a 12-hour clock divided into AM and PM, but most other countries use a 24-hour clock; most countries use two decimal places in currency displays, but Italy uses no decimal places for lira.

The Country Info screen is shown in Figure 18.9.

Use the up and down arrow keys to change from one country to the next. The End key moves to the last entry in the table, the Home key moves to the first. The PgUp and PgDn keys move four entries at a time. As you change from the U.S.A., to Arabic Speaking, to Australian, and so on down the list, notice that the

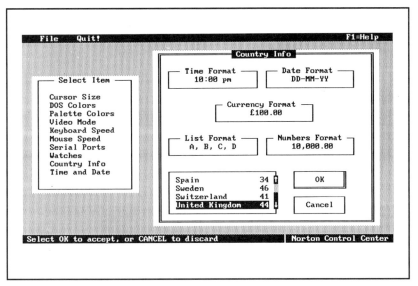

Figure 18.9: The Country Info screen

displays in the Time, Date, Currency, List, and Numbers Format boxes all change to show how that information is presented in each country. The code number next to each country is the international dialing code for that country: the U.S.A. is 001, the United Kingdom 044, and so on.

As an example of how to make changes with Country Info, position the cursor over Germany, Tab to the OK box and press Enter to accept this change; then press the Esc key to return to DOS. Now use the DOS DIR command to list a directory, and you will see a listing such as the one shown in Figure 18.10. Note that the file dates are in DD.MM.YY format with a period as the separator character rather than the hyphen, and also note that the file creation times are shown in the 24-hour clock format without AM or PM labels.

To reset the format, run Country Info again; this time select U.S.A., Tab to the OK box, and press Enter or click on the box with the mouse. You have now restored all the Country Info settings back to their U.S.A. equivalents.

```
Volume in drive C has no label
Directory of  C:\NORTON

     .          <DIR>      29.07.90   1.43
     ..         <DIR>      29.07.90   1.43
DISKREET SYS     52886     17.07.90  17.00
PCSHADOW SYS       848     17.07.90  17.00
NORTON   OVL     87068     17.07.90  17.00
FILESAVE EXE     86248     17.07.90  17.00
READ     ME      23552     17.07.90  17.00
NDD      EXE    187344     17.07.90  17.00
UNERASE  EXE    171447     17.07.90  17.00
FILEFIX  EXE    137082     17.07.90  17.00
UNFORMAT EXE     74084     17.07.90  17.00
CALIBRAT EXE    124566     17.07.90  17.00
IMAGE    EXE     11894     17.07.90  17.00
DISKEDIT EXE    216730     17.07.90  17.00
DISKTOOL EXE    122712     17.07.90  17.00
BE       EXE     24304     17.07.90  17.00
SFORMAT  EXE     91256     17.07.90  17.00
SPEEDISK EXE    115664     17.07.90  17.00
SYSINFO  EXE    135652     17.07.90  17.00
FILEFIND EXE    104708     17.07.90  17.00
-- More --
```

Figure 18.10: A DIR listing with the country code set to Germany

TIME AND DATE

The Time and Date option lets you set or reset the system time and date. The top box in the work area of the screen (see Figure 18.11) controls the date, and the bottom box controls the time.

Press the up arrow, down arrow, or Tab key to select the Time box or the Date box. After you've chosen one of these options, the numbers in the appropriate box are highlighted. You can use the left arrow or right arrow key to select hours, minutes, seconds, or meridian in the Time box, and month, day, or year in the Date box. When you're ready, press Enter or click on OK to confirm your entries, or press Esc to return to the NCC main menu. Select Default to reset the original values.

On some PC/AT and most PC/XT computers, the DOS TIME and DATE commands do not actually change the setting of the clock connected to the internal battery. You must use a special program (usually named SETUP) to change that clock's setting. However, because NCC is usually on the disk that contains

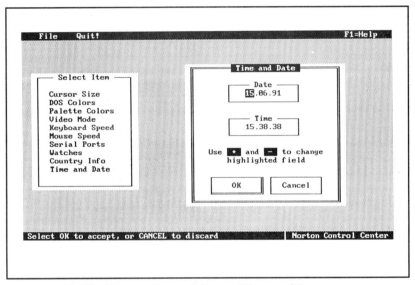

Figure 18.11: The Norton Control Center Time and Date screen

the hardware diagnostic programs, this program will usually change the internal clock. If it doesn't change the clock setting, you will have to use the program on your diagnostic program disk to perform the operation.

LOADING AND SAVING THE NCC CONFIGURATION

When you've finished making changes in NCC, use the Save Settings selection from the File pull-down menu to save your changes. Alternatively, you can press F2. Figure 18.12 shows the Save Settings screen.

Tab to the Settings box, and click on the individual selections you want to save. Alternatively, you can use the spacebar or the X key to choose the options you want to save.

NCC asks you to specify the file name to use and then saves your changes in this file.

You can also use Load Settings from the File pull-down menu to load a configuration you've saved previously.

Figure 18.12: NCC Save Settings screen

LOADING NCC CHANGES FROM THE COMMAND LINE

After you've saved the NCC settings in a file, you can load one or all of them back into your computer by using NCC from the command prompt. To load all the NCC settings from a file called NCC.DAT, type:

NCC NCC.DAT /SET

If you include this command in your AUTOEXEC.BAT file, you can load all of your favorite settings every time you start your computer.

To load only one setting from the file, add the appropriate switch to this command-line sequence. (All of the file-loading switches are listed in Chapter 23.) To set the Video Mode or Keyboard Speed, you can also use a group of quick switches from the command line. For example, to set the Video Mode to color and 80 columns by 25 lines, enter:

NCC /CO80

USING NCC FROM THE DOS COMMAND LINE

You can also use NCC from the DOS command line to start, stop, or reset any of the four stopwatch timers. To start the first of the four stop watches, enter the following command:

NCC /START:1

This displays the system's current time and date at the right side of the screen. If you type:

NCC /START:1 /L

the display will appear at the left side of the display. To stop the timer, type:

NCC /STOP:1

In this example, not only are the time and date displayed on the screen, but also the elapsed time between the START and STOP commands (see Figure 18.13).

You can specify that you want to use one of the other three stopwatches with the /START:n switch, in which n is the number of the stopwatch you want to start.

If you use the /C: switch, you can add comments to the time display. For example, if you enter:

NCC /START:1 /C:"Start Time"

you will see the words "Start Time" displayed on the screen to the left of the stopwatch display.

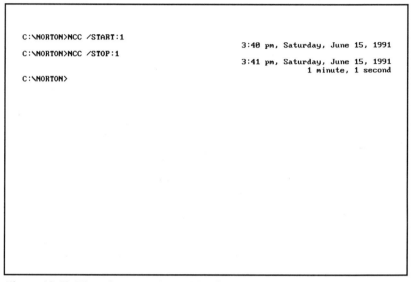

Figure 18.13: Timed output from Watches

FileFind (FILEFIND)

Locating Files and Changing File Attributes

CHAPTER **19** _____

FILEFIND IS MORE THAN A SIMPLE FILE LOCATION UTILITY; in fact, you can use it to perform the following complex tasks:

■ If you have used previous versions of the Norton Utilities, you will see that File-Find combines the capabilities of several of the early utilities, including FileFind (FF), Text Search (TS), File Size (FS), File Attribute (FA), and File Date (FD).

- Finding files anywhere in your directory structure.

- Locating specific occurrences of text inside those files.

- Testing to see if a specific file will fit when you copy it to another disk.

- Inspecting and modifying file attributes.

- Changing a file's creation time and date.

_____ *LOCATING FILES WITH FILEFIND* _____

Sometimes you know the name of a file that you want to work with, but you can't remember its location. Occasionally you can't even remember the complete name of the file. The DOS DIR command is of little use in this situation. However, you can use FileFind to locate lost or misplaced files.

To start FileFind, select it from the program menu shown in the main screen of the NORTON program, or run it from the DOS command line by typing:

FILEFIND

The FileFind opening screen is shown in Figure 19.1. The main menu selections are available as pull-down menus along the top of the screen. However, you can use FileFind in its simplest mode—to locate one or more files on your disk—without using any of the pull-down menus.

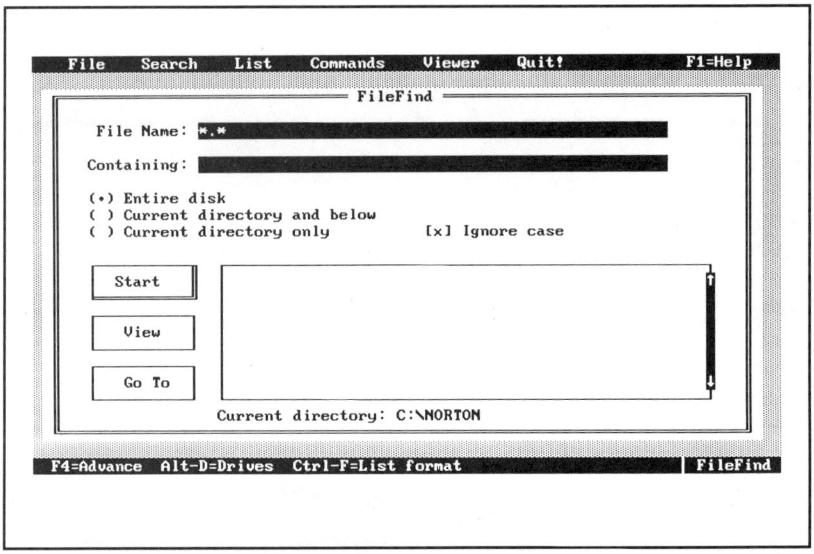

Figure 19.1: FileFind opening screen

You can use the DOS wildcard characters * and ? when searching for a file, or you can merely enter as much of the file name
as you can remember. For example, to find all the copies of the
file AUTOEXEC on the current drive, type AUTOEXEC.* into
the File Name box, press the down arrow key to move past the
Containing box (I'll describe this option in a moment), and
select the Entire Disk radio button. Press Enter to start the
search. The program immediately displays a list of all the occurrences of AUTOEXEC.* in the box at the lower right of
the screen. Figure 19.2 shows that FileFind located two files:
AUTOEXEC.BAT and AUTOEXEC.BAK. Notice that the bottom line of the main FileFind screen shows the number of files
found in the search and the name of the current directory.

If you want to find a specific piece of text that you think is in
one of your files, enter that text in the Containing box. FileFind
now searches through your files for the text you entered as the
search text, or *search string*. My AUTOEXEC.BAT file contains
the command @ECHO OFF to prevent commands from being
displayed on the screen every time AUTOEXEC.BAT runs. To

You cannot use
wildcards in the
search text because File-
Find will look for those
specific characters.

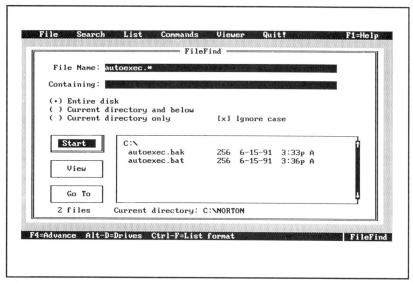

Figure 19.2: FileFind has located two files: AUTOEXEC.BAT and
AUTOEXEC.BAK

search for this command in the AUTOEXEC.* files, type:

@ECHO OFF

into the **Containing** box, and then press Enter to begin the
search. This time FileFind is looking for files with the name
AUTOEXEC.* that also contain the search string @ECHO OFF.
The file names found are shown in the list box, and the number
of files found is shown at the lower left of the screen.

To help you to find exactly the right file, FileFind provides
several other options at the left side of your screen.

Searching an en-
tire disk can take a
long time. Be sure you
really want this option
before you start the
search.

- Use **Entire Disk** when you want to extend the search
  through all of the files on your disk.

- Use **Current directory and below** when you want to
  restrict the search to the current directory and its
  subdirectories.

- Use Current directory only to search the current directory and ignore all other directories.

- Use Ignore case to make the FileFind text search independent of upper- and lowercase letters. For example, @ECHO OFF, @Echo Off, and @echo off will all match the search text @ECHO OFF. Alternatively, you can make a search more specific by turning off Ignore case. Move the cursor to the box and press the spacebar or the X character, or click on the box with the mouse, to toggle Ignore case off or on.

- Use Start to begin the search for a file or group of files.

- Use View to examine the contents of a file you have found. When you select View, the screen changes and displays the contents of the file as ASCII characters. The search text will be highlighted. Use commands from the Viewer pull-down menu to make selections here. Use Next Match or F6 to go to the next occurrence of the search text in the file, or use Previous Match or F5 to return to the last occurrence. Next File or F8 loads the next file into the viewer, and Previous File or F7 reloads the last file into the viewer. To return to the main FileFind screen, press the Esc key or select the Main! option from the menu bar. Alternatively, click on Main! with the mouse.

- Use Go To to change directly to the directory that contains the found file or files. This works like a fast Norton Change Directory command.

CHANGING DRIVES

To change to a different drive, select the Drive option from the File pull-down menu, or press Ctrl-D when you are in the main FileFind screen. The Change Drive window opens in the center of the screen and lists all the drives on your computer. Use the up and down arrow keys to select the new drive; then select or click on the OK box. Choose Cancel to ignore this change.

SEARCHING DRIVES

Choose Search Drive from the Search pull-down menu, or press Alt-D from the main FileFind screen to select the drives you want to include in the search. The Drives To Search window is shown in Figure 19.3.

You can select one of three options from this window:

- **Default drive.** Choose this to restrict the search to the current drive.

- **All drives.** Select this option to extend the search through all of the drives on your computer.

- **The following drives.** Specify the drive or drives you want to search from the list of the drives available on your computer. Move the highlight and press the spacebar, or click on the boxes with the mouse to make your selection.

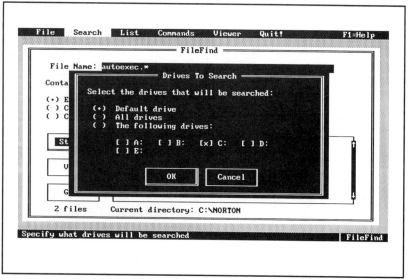

Figure 19.3: Select the drives to be searched with Search Drive or Alt-D

CHANGING DIRECTORIES

To change to another directory, select the Directory option from the File pull-down menu, or press Ctrl-R from the main FileFind screen. When the Change Directory window opens, it lists the name of the current directory in the Current Directory box and all its subdirectories in the Subdirectories box, as shown in Figure 19.4. Use the Tab key to move from the Current Directory box to the Subdirectories box; then use the down arrow key to select a new directory. Select OK or Cancel when you have made your choice or double click the mouse. You can also change to another drive in this window.

MAKING ADVANCED SEARCHES

To localize a search even more, you can use the Advanced Search options. Choose Advanced Search from the Search pull-down menu, or press F4 from the main FileFind screen; this displays the window shown in Figure 19.5.

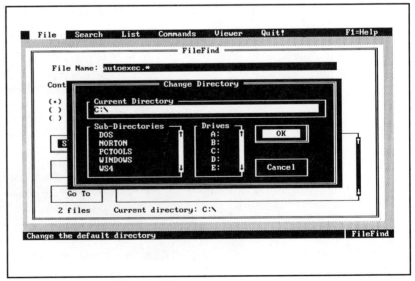

Figure 19.4: The Change Directory window lets you change to another directory or to another drive

You can use the selections in this window to speed operations by defining your search with greater precision. The search will be limited to those files that meet the new criteria you specify. You can choose from the following settings:

- **Date is After.** The file date must be later than this date.

- **Date is Before.** The file date must be earlier than this date.

- **Size is Greater Than.** The file size must be greater than this size in bytes.

- **Size is Less Than.** The file size must be less than this size in bytes.

- **Owner Is.** If you are working on a network, you can limit the search to files that belong to a particular owner. (This is the name the user typed during the log-on procedure.)

- **File is Hidden.** The file is a hidden file.

Figure 19.5: Advanced Search from the Search menu lets you customize a search

For a more detailed description of file attributes, see the section "Looking at File Attributes with FileFind" later in this chapter.

- **File is System File.** The file is a system file.

- **Include Directories.** Include directories in the search.

- **File is Read-Only.** The file is a read-only file.

- **Archive Bit is Set.** The archive bit of the attribute byte is set.

When you have completed your selections, choose **OK** to proceed with the search or **Cancel** to return to the main File-Find screen. You can also select **Clear All** to remove all of the settings in this window so that you can enter new ones. Note that the message "Advanced Search ON" appears on the main File-Find display directly above the **Ignore Case** when you select options from the Advanced Search screen.

CHANGING THE LIST DISPLAY

Select Set List Display from the List pull-down menu, or press Ctrl-F to change the way FileFind lists files in the main display area. The List Display window is shown in Figure 19.6.

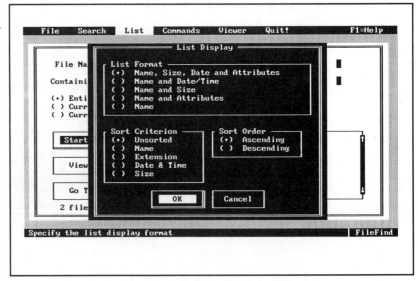

Figure 19.6: The List Display window offers several ways to customize the main FileFind display

You can choose the amount of information displayed for each file in the List Format box, the file sorting options in the Sort Criterion box, and the type of sort in the Sort Order box.

- List Format. Display files with almost any combination of file name, file size, date, date and time, and file attributes.

- Sort Criterion. Sort the list of files by file name, extension, or date and time. You can also choose to leave the list unsorted.

- Sort Order. Force FileFind to perform an ascending sort or a descending sort.

PRINTING THE LIST

You can also use Print List (Ctrl-P) from the List pull-down menu to list files according to your search criteria. The Print List display is shown in Figure 19.7. You can send the list directly to

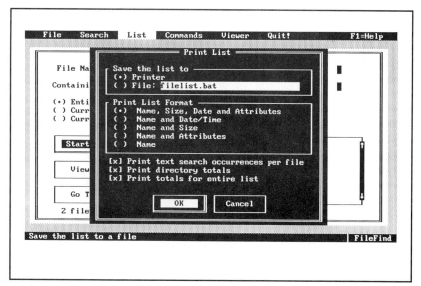

Figure 19.7: The Print List window lets you customize the listing

your printer, or you can save the list as a file so that you can print it later. Print List lets you format the list and choose to print the file name, size, attributes, and date and time.

You can also indicate the number of occurrences of the search text that there are in the list, and you can print size totals for subdirectories and totals for the entire list. Using these selections, you can determine the size of a group of files without having to use a calculator to generate file size totals.

CREATING A BATCH FILE

You can also create a batch file that will run on each of the files the FileFind program locates. Select Create Batch File from the List pull-down menu, or press Ctrl-B from the main display to see the screen shown in Figure 19.8.

First, enter the name of your batch file; then, enter any commands you want to have executed before or after the file names

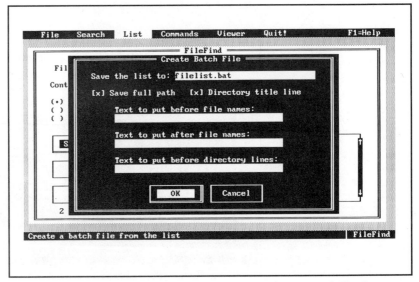

Figure 19.8: Creating a batch file to operate on the located files is easy with FileFind

that the search locates. For example, you could create a batch file that copies all files meeting a search criteria from their current directory to another directory or even to another disk.

If a batch file with the specified name already exists, a window opens to ask if you want to overwrite the existing file or to append the new file to the end of the existing file.

USING FILEFIND TO LOOK AT FILE SIZES

If you need to refresh your memory about clusters, see the section entitled "Clusters" in Chapter 2.

When a file is copied between a hard disk and a floppy disk, the number of clusters it occupies will change because cluster size varies according to the capacity of the disk. (However, the file data itself will not change.) This differing cluster size can sometimes lead to unexpected results when you try to copy a file from one disk to another; for example, DOS might report that the target disk has enough room, but you find that you cannot copy the file because the disk does not have enough available clusters. To circumvent this problem entirely, use the Target Fit selection from the Commands pull-down menu. This presents information about the located file's size and its percentage of slack, and then determines if that file will fit onto a specified disk.

The DOS DIR command, on the other hand, reports the actual file size in bytes rather than the number of occupied clusters; it also reports the space remaining on the disk in bytes. Therefore, when you use DIR, numbers might not add up to the expected total.

DETERMINING WHETHER A FILE WILL FIT ON A DISK

Target Fit determines whether a file or files will fit on a disk. For example, let's see if our two AUTOEXEC files will fit on a 720K floppy disk in drive A (see Figure 19.9).

In Figure 19.9, each of the two AUTOEXEC files is 256 bytes in length. However, these files occupy 4,096 bytes of disk space

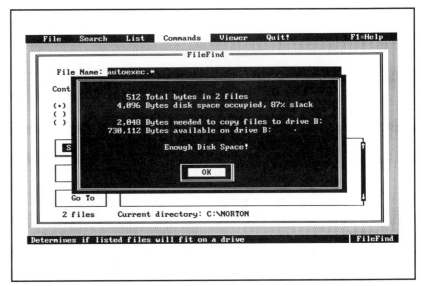

Figure 19.9: FileFind reports that there is sufficient space on drive A for the two AUTOEXEC files

on the hard disk, with 87 percent of this space unused, or *slack.* Note that this hard disk has a cluster size of 2,048 bytes (four 512-byte sectors) and that the AUTOEXEC files occupy one cluster each.

The 720K floppy disk, on the other hand, has 1024-byte clusters. Although the two AUTOEXEC files still require 2 clusters, they occupy less space on the disk. As you can see in Figure 19.9, there is plenty of space on the floppy disk for the files. Target Fit reports the total available disk space, which in the case of this 720K floppy disk is 730,112 bytes.

LOOKING AT FILE ATTRIBUTES WITH FILEFIND

There are many reasons why you might want to protect a file from being changed or deleted; you might even want to hide a file so other people are not aware that it exists. If you are working with other users on a local area network, you may want to restrict access to files containing sensitive data, such as payroll information or personnel records. You also may want to make important program files *read-only* so that no one—including yourself—can erase them accidentally.

You can provide some file protection by using the DOS ATTRIB command, but FileFind offers a much more complete and powerful set of capabilities.

WHAT ARE FILE ATTRIBUTES?

File attributes are characteristics that you can assign to your files. Following is a complete list of those attributes:

- A *read-only* file cannot be written to or erased by the normal DOS commands. However, you can use read-only files with other DOS commands. For example, you can print them or display them in listings made by DIR. Very few commercial software packages set the read-only bit.

- *Hidden* files do not appear in listings made by DIR and can't be used with most DOS commands. However, you *can* copy hidden files by using the DISKCOPY command, which makes a sector-by-sector duplicate of the original disk. Without Norton Utilities, you cannot erase them from a floppy disk unless you reformat the disk, which may not always be desirable.

- A *system* file is a hidden, read-only file that DOS uses and cannot be written to or erased. This attribute is probably a remnant from the CP/M operating system.

- The *volume label* identifies the disk and is an entry in the root directory.

- A *subdirectory entry* has an attribute that differentiates it from files, indicating that its entry points to another directory.

RESTORE, XCOPY, and some third-party backup programs also use the archive bit.

• The *archive bit* indicates whether a file has been changed since it was last backed up. If the file has been changed or has just been created, the archive bit is set. However, if you use the BACKUP command to copy the file, the archive bit is turned off. In this way, BACKUP keeps track of the files it has already copied and those it has not.

THE ATTRIBUTE BYTE

Bits are like toggles—they are either on (equal to 1) or off (equal to 0). You can also think of them as being *set* (1) or *reset* (0). Another term for reset is *cleared*.

A file's attributes are recorded in its attribute byte. The attribute byte is part of the file's directory entry, but unlike the other entries, the attribute byte settings are not displayed in the usual DIR listing. Each attribute corresponds to a single bit in the attribute byte. An attribute is turned on, or set, if the value of its bit equals 1. Each bit in the byte can be set or reset individually without affecting the other bits. For example, a read-only file may also be archived.

The numbers of the bits for each attribute are shown in Table 19.1. If none of the bits in the attribute byte is set, the program or data file can be read, written to, or erased. This is also true if only the archive bit is set. Almost all the files you will encounter are of these types.

Table 19.1: The Attribute Bit Values

ATTRIBUTE	BIT NUMBER
Read-only file	0
Hidden file	1
System file	2
Volume label	3
Subdirectory	4
Archive bit	5
Unused	6
Unused	7

USING THE DOS ATTRIB COMMAND

 The ATTRIB command is only available in DOS 3.*x* and later versions.

To display the status of a file's read-only and archive attributes with the DOS ATTRIB command, enter:

ATTRIB MYFILE.TXT

If MYFILE.TXT is a newly created file, DOS will display the following current setting:

A   C:\MYFILE.TXT

The A shows that the archive bit is set, indicating that the file will be backed up the next time you execute the BACKUP command. The read-only bit is not set, which means the file can be read, updated, or deleted.

You can use the ATTRIB command to set or reset a file's read-only and archive bits. However, ATTRIB cannot access any of the other bits in the attribute byte.

To manipulate the attribute bits using ATTRIB, you can specify the following parameters:

- +R makes the file read-only
- −R enables you to read, write to, or delete the file
- +A sets the archive bit
- −A resets the bit

For example, you would type the following command:

ATTRIB +R −A MYFILE.TXT

to set the read-only attribute bit (turn it on) and reset the archive bit (turn it off). If you now use ATTRIB to display the attribute settings by typing:

ATTRIB MYFILE.TXT

the command will report the following information:

R C:\MYFILE.TXT

As you can see, the read-only bit is set, but the archive bit is not.

USING FILEFIND WITH FILE ATTRIBUTES

Select Set Attributes from the Commands pull-down menu to work with the archive, read-only, hidden, and system attribute bits of a file. The Change Attributes window is shown in Figure 19.10. First, choose if you want to set the attributes for one file or for all the files in the list. Then press X or the spacebar to set or clear an attribute. You can also click on the attribute box with the mouse. When you have set or cleared the appropriate attributes, highlight the OK box, and click on it or press Enter. Another window opens to confirm that the attributes have indeed been changed to your settings.

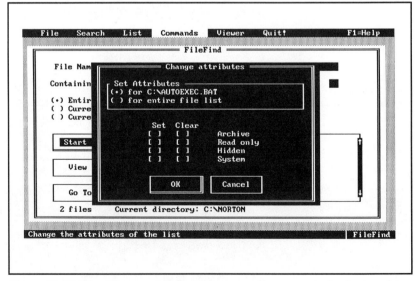

Figure 19.10: The Change Attributes screen allows you to look at and to change file attributes

SPECIAL CONCERNS WITH READ-ONLY FILES

Beware of making too many files read-only; many commercial software installation programs configure files to match your system's hardware. These programs write the details of your hardware system back into their own files. If you alter these files to read-only and then reconfigure the program with new information, the program will attempt to update its files, find that they are now read-only, and report an error. Some programs are friendly enough to display a meaningful error message. For example, if you try to use EDLIN to alter a read-only file, the program tells you: "File is READ-ONLY." dBASE III Plus, on the other hand, may display the more obscure message: "File cannot be accessed."

SPECIAL CONCERNS WITH HIDDEN FILES

Some applications programs differ in their response to hidden files: WordStar will load a hidden text file, whereas WordPerfect will not. To edit a hidden file in WordPerfect, you first have to reset the hidden bit to make the file visible.

Some commercial software packages use the hidden-file attribute as a part of their copy-protection scheme. If you do not remove the software properly, these hidden files may remain on your disk, occupying valuable space.

If you don't resist the temptation to make files hidden, the meaning of the saying "out of sight, out of mind" will become painfully evident. For example, there is no point in hiding batch files or program files because you will soon forget their names; when that happens, you will be unable to use them. If a directory is getting cluttered with files you do not use often, do not hide them by setting their hidden bits; instead, copy the files to another directory and add the directory's name to your PATH statement so that they will be available when you need them. Alternatively, you can copy the files to a floppy disk.

USING FILEFIND
TO CHANGE THE FILES' TIME AND DATE

You can use the Set Date/Time selection from the Commands pull-down menu to alter the creation time and date of a file. This can be useful if you are a software developer and you want all the files of a new program release to have the same date and time, or if you work in a finance department and you want all the Lotus 1-2-3 spreadsheets for a particular budget to reflect the date and time the budget was finalized. Choosing Set Date/Time displays the screen shown in Figure 19.11. The Set Date/Time window is similar to the Change Attributes window, and it works in the same way. Choose to work with a single file or with all of the files in the list. The current time and date are shown in the center of the window; use these settings, move the highlight to the **OK** box and press Enter, or click on **OK** with the mouse. If you don't want to use the current time and date, you can enter your own. Use the arrow keys to access the time display, and then

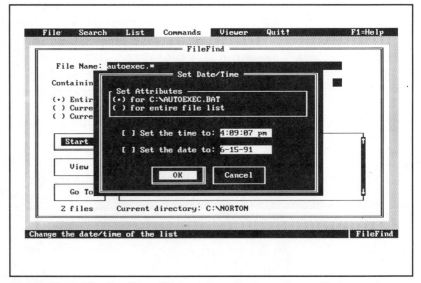

Figure 19.11: The Set Date/Time screen lets you alter a file's creation time and date

enter a new time. Similarly, enter a new date, and then highlight the OK box. Press Enter or click on the box with the mouse.

USING FILEFIND FROM THE DOS COMMAND LINE

If you are in a hurry, you can use FileFind directly from the DOS command line, rather than running the NORTON shell first. The general form for using FileFind from the command line is as follows:

FILEFIND *filename search-string switches*

For a complete list of all the command line options, see the FileFind entry in Chapter 23.

FINDING FILES

To find all of your AUTOEXEC files using FileFind from the command line, type:

FILEFIND C:\AUTOEXEC.*

The FileFind program starts running and locates the file or files. To extend the search to the subdirectories, add the /S switch to form the following sequence:

FILEFIND C:\AUTOEXEC.*/S

FINDING TEXT

To find a string of text in a text file, include the search-string after the file name on the command line. To look for the text @ECHO OFF in your AUTOEXEC files, type:

FILEFIND C:\AUTOEXEC.* "@ECHO OFF"

Remember, if the search-string includes any spaces, you must enclose the entire search-string in quotation marks.

WORKING OUT FILE SIZES

To see if your AUTOEXEC files will fit on a 720K floppy disk, use the /TARGET switch and the target drive letter as follows:

FILEFIND C:\AUTOEXEC.* /TARGET:A

EXAMINING FILE ATTRIBUTES

There are five switches you can use with FileFind when you are working with file attributes from the command line. Use the /CLEAR switch to remove all the attributes from the files you specify. There are four other switches available, one for each attribute type:

- /A sets or resets the archive bit.
- /HID sets or resets the hidden bit.
- /R sets or resets the read-only bit.
- /SYS sets or resets the system bit.

Specify a + after the switch to set the attribute; specify a − after the switch to reset the attribute.

CHANGING THE DATE AND TIME ON A FILE

FileFind lets you set or clear the date or time for an individual file or a group of files. For example, to reset the date for the MYFILE.TXT file, type:

FILEFIND MYFILE.TXT /D*mm-dd-yy*

in which *mm-dd-yy* represents the date format. If you don't specify a date, FileFind sets it to the current system date. Therefore, not specifying a date is a quick way to reset the date. If you

Both the date and time formats are determined by the COUNTRY code in your CONFIG.SYS file. The formats listed here are the defaults.

do this, be sure you change all the files that should have the system date.

To use FileFind to set the time for the previous example file, type:

FILEFIND MYFILE.TXT /T*hh:mm*

in which *hh:mm* represents the time format. If you don't specify a time in the command line, the time entry for the file is set to the current system time.

To reset the date and time for an entire directory at once, use the wildcard *.* specification in place of a file name. The following example:

FILEFIND A:*.* D/10-30-91/T00:00

sets the dates and times of all the files in the drive A root directory to October 30, 1991, 00:00 hours. To set the time and date to the current time and date, use the /NOW switch.

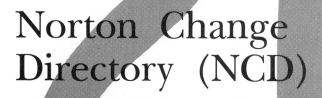

Norton Change
Directory (NCD)

Managing the Directory Structure
of Your Disks

CHAPTER **20** _____

ONE OF MOST CONFUSING TASKS IN THE MANAGEMENT of your hard disk is deciding how to organize your files into directories. You should implement a system that enables you and others to find files easily.

The Norton Change Directory (NCD) program contains several features that help you organize and work with your files. Before I present them in this chapter, however, let's examine how the DOS file system works.

THE DOS DIRECTORY STRUCTURE

The most useful feature of the DOS file system is its ability to organize directories hierarchically. This means that directories can contain subdirectories as well as files; in fact, you can consider a subdirectory to be another type of file.

THE ROOT DIRECTORY

Don't clutter up your root directory with files; isolate them in subdirectories, and reserve the root for directories.

The concepts of the root and ordered hierarchical directories originated in UNIX, which is another computer operating system. All disks start with the root directory, so called because, like the roots of a tree, it is the lowest level of the hierarchy, from which all other directories branch.

Because there is a limit to the number of entries that the root directory can hold, be careful to install as few files as possible in the root directory, AUTOEXEC.BAT, CONFIG.SYS, and COMMAND.COM being the three main exceptions to this rule. Other than the three files that *must* be in the root directory, all other entries should be subdirectories. For example, one subdirectory might contain your word processor, another your spreadsheet, another the DOS files, another your batch files, another the Norton Utilities, and so on. This will enable you to find your way around the disk quickly and easily, and DOS will run more efficiently.

ORGANIZING YOUR HARD DISK

The key to using your hard disk efficiently is organization. You should always group related programs and files together in their own subdirectories, rather than putting all files in the root directory. Placing all your files in the same directory defeats the purpose of DOS's hierarchical file system, which enables you to find files quickly.

Each software package that you install on your system (the program files, the device drivers, the help files, and so on) should go in one directory. For example, if you want to use Lotus 1-2-3, create a directory called 123 in the root directory, and install all of the Lotus 1-2-3 files into it. If necessary, you can create additional subdirectories below the 123 directory. Suppose you want to separate your quarterly budget files from the rest of your files. You could place them in a subdirectory of 123 called BUDGETS. Note, however, that you should only create separate subdirectories for easily identifiable groups of files. Otherwise, your files will quickly become so spread out that you will forget where many of them are.

By the same token, you don't want to create too many levels of subdirectories. I recommend that you limit yourself to three levels (root, subdirectories, and subdirectories of those subdirectories); with any more levels you will find it too time-consuming to move through your directory structure.

When you want to use a file or directory, you tell DOS where it is in the hierarchy. In other words, you give DOS the file or directory's *path*. For example, to move to your newly created BUDGETS directory from the root, you would type:

CD \123\BUDGETS

at the DOS prompt.

To learn more about the PATH command, see Judd Robbins' *Encyclopedia DOS* (SYBEX, 1990).

As you organize your directory structure, you must be sure that you install all the DOS files, except for COMMAND.COM, AUTOEXEC.BAT, and CONFIG.SYS, in a directory under the root directory. You should not install them in the root directory itself. Use the PATH command in your AUTOEXEC.BAT file to tell DOS where to look for those files.

For example, your PATH statement might contain the following entries:

PATH = C:\;C:\DOS;C:\123

This PATH statement tells DOS to look for a file in the root directory first, then to look in the \DOS directory, and, if it doesn't find the file there, then to look in the \123 directory. See Chapter 17 for a complete description of the PATH command.

LISTING DIRECTORIES

Perhaps the first step in organizing your hard disk is to take a look at the directory structure that already exists. I'll briefly discuss the DOS commands that allow you to do this, and then I'll show you how to use Norton Change Directory to do the same operations with less effort. Finally, I'll show you how Norton CD lets you perform operations that you simply can't do with DOS at all.

USING THE DOS DIR COMMAND

The DOS DIR command lists the names of all the files and subdirectories in a directory. In addition to the names, DIR displays the file size in bytes, the date and time of the file's creation or last modification, and the number of bytes remaining on the disk. DIR does not list hidden files. If the disk has a volume label, DIR will show the label text in the first line of the listing; otherwise DIR reports

Volume in drive *n*: has no label

To use DIR to display a listing of the DOS directory on drive C, type:

DIR \DOS

from the root directory.

You can compare the results on your screen with Figure 20.1, which shows a typical listing generated by the DIR command.

If your listing scrolls off the screen before you have time to read the first entries, you can press the Ctrl-S key combination to stop the listing. Press any key to continue the listing. Another alternative for pausing a long list is to force DOS to present only one screenful of information at a time. When you enter the command:

DIR /P

the display pauses at the end of each screenful of information. Pressing any key displays the next screenful. To generate a "wide" listing that shows only file and directory names, use the /W switch after the DIR command. Directories in this display

> If you want to print the DIR listing, rather than display it on the screen, type:
> DIR > PRN

```
         .           <DIR>      7-05-90   1:33p
         ..          <DIR>      7-05-90   1:33p
COMMAND  COM         25307      3-17-87  12:00p
ANSI     SYS          1678      3-17-87  12:00p
APPEND   EXE          5825      3-17-87  12:00p
ASSIGN   COM          1561      3-17-87  12:00p
ATTRIB   EXE          9529      3-17-87  12:00p
BACKUP   COM         31913      3-18-87  12:00p
BASIC    COM          1063      3-17-87  12:00p
BASICA   COM         36403      3-17-87  12:00p
CHKDSK   COM          9850      3-18-87  12:00p
COMP     COM          4214      3-17-87  12:00p
COUNTRY  SYS         11285      3-17-87  12:00p
DEBUG    COM         15897      3-17-87  12:00p
DISKCOMP COM          5879      3-17-87  12:00p
DISKCOPY COM          6295      3-17-87  12:00p
DISPLAY  SYS         11290      3-17-87  12:00p
DRIVER   SYS          1196      3-17-87  12:00p
EDLIN    COM          7526      3-17-87  12:00p
FASTOPEN EXE          3919      3-17-87  12:00p
FDISK    COM         48216      3-18-87  12:00p
FIND     EXE          6434      3-17-87  12:00p
XXFORMAT COM         11616      3-18-87  12:00p
Strike a key when ready . . .
```

Figure 20.1: A typical listing made by the DIR /P command

format, however, do not have the usual <DIR> notation, so you may easily confuse them with files, as you can see in Figure 20.2.

USING THE DOS TREE COMMAND

The DOS TREE command summarizes the directory information for all the directories on a disk and presents this data in an outline form. To make a TREE listing of your disk, type:

TREE

Add the /F switch to make TREE list all the files in each directory and subdirectory. This listing will be too long to fit on the screen. However, you can send the listing to your printer instead; merely type:

TREE > PRN

The output produced by this command will not be broken into neat pages; it will be an exact copy of what would have appeared on the screen.

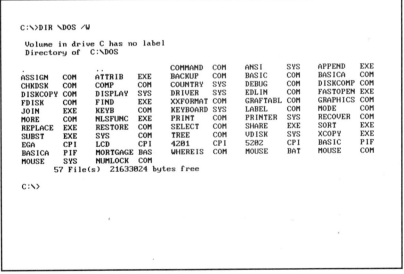

```
C:\>DIR \DOS /W

   Volume in drive C has no label
   Directory of  C:\DOS

                  .              ..          COMMAND  COM   ANSI     SYS   APPEND   EXE
ASSIGN   COM   ATTRIB   EXE   BACKUP   COM   BASIC    COM   BASICA   COM
CHKDSK   COM   COMP     COM   COUNTRY  SYS   DEBUG    COM   DISKCOMP COM
DISKCOPY COM   DISPLAY  SYS   DRIVER   SYS   EDLIN    COM   FASTOPEN EXE
FDISK    COM   FIND     EXE   XXFORMAT COM   GRAFTABL COM   GRAPHICS COM
JOIN     EXE   KEYB     COM   KEYBOARD SYS   LABEL    COM   MODE     COM
MORE     COM   NLSFUNC  EXE   PRINT    COM   PRINTER  SYS   RECOVER  COM
REPLACE  EXE   RESTORE  COM   SELECT   COM   SHARE    EXE   SORT     EXE
SUBST    EXE   SYS      COM   TREE     COM   VDISK    SYS   XCOPY    EXE
EGA      CPI   LCD      CPI   4201     CPI   5202     CPI   BASIC    PIF
BASICA   PIF   MORTGAGE BAS   WHEREIS  COM   MOUSE    BAT   MOUSE    COM
MOUSE    SYS   NUMLOCK  COM
        57 File(s)  21633024 bytes free

C:\>
```

Figure 20.2: A wide listing made with DIR /W

MAKING, CHANGING, AND REMOVING DIRECTORIES

Creating and deleting directories and moving between directories are essential tasks for hard-disk users. You can accomplish these common operations faster with Norton Change Directory than you can with DOS, and you can use the utility's graphic display of the directory structure to instantly view the results of your changes. I'll quickly explain the DOS commands for these operations and then show you the more powerful Norton CD alternatives.

USING DOS COMMANDS

To create a directory called 123 from the root for your Lotus files, type:

MKDIR 123

You can also abbreviate this command as follows:

MD 123

DOS creates the new 123 directory and assigns it a creation time and date. If you make a DIR listing now, you will see an entry whose format differs slightly from that of the file entries. The 123 directory has a creation time and date, but no file size. Instead, the designation <DIR> appears in the middle of the listing. This confirms that 123 is not a file but a directory. To make this new directory the current directory, type:

CHDIR 123

for change directory. You can also abbreviate this command as the following:

CD 123

The 123 directory is now the current, or default, directory. To make the root directory the default directory again, type:

CD \

When you create a directory, DOS automatically places two special entries in it. These entries (known as . and ..) are short-hand notations for the full path name of the new directory (.) and the path name of the parent directory (..). Thus, for your new 123 directory, . is equivalent to \123, and .. is equivalent to the root directory (\). Although you can change to the root directory by typing:

CD \

you can also change to the root from the 123 directory by typing:

CD ..

because the root is its parent directory.

If a directory contains only the . and .. entries, DOS considers it empty, and you can delete it. If the directory is not empty when you try to remove it, DOS responds with this message:

Invalid path, not directory,
or directory not empty

Use the DOS DEL or ERASE command to delete the files from the directory. For example, to remove all the files from the current directory simultaneously, type:

DEL *.*

Because this is a potentially calamitous command, DOS has a safety net built into it. When you press Enter, DOS displays the prompt:

Are you sure? (Y or N)

so that you have to confirm that you really want to erase all the files. If you press **N**, DOS cancels the operation.

If the directory contains subdirectories, you will also need to delete all their files and then remove them individually before you can erase the directory. For example, to remove the BUDGETS subdirectory from the 123 directory, you must first delete all of the files in BUDGETS, then change to the 123 directory, and type:

RMDIR BUDGETS

When the 123 directory is empty of all files and subdirectories, you can remove it by changing to the root directory and typing

RD 123

(RD is short for RMDIR).

If you no longer use a directory, you really should remove it; you will find it easier to work with your hierarchical structure if it is not cluttered with old, unused entries. Removing unused directories and files also conserves disk space.

USING NORTON CHANGE DIRECTORY

The Norton Change Directory utility includes all the functions of the DOS MD, CD, and RD commands. NCD also lets you change to another directory without specifying its complete path.

USING NCD IN FULL-SCREEN MODE

From the NORTON program, choose Norton CD from the command list, or NCD in full-screen mode by entering:

NCD

from the command line. The display you see will be similar to that shown in Figure 20.3, but it will show your own directories.

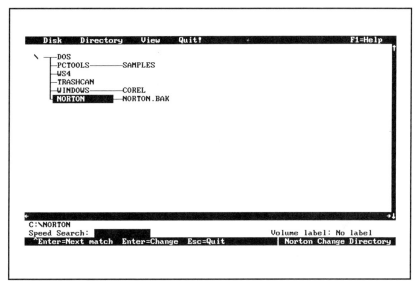

Figure 20.3: NCD's full-screen display

NCD shows the directory structure in graphical form, using lines to link directories and subdirectories together. With NCD you can change, create, remove, and rename directories.

NCD lets you use pull-down menus or function keys to issue its available commands. To run a command, choose or click on the item in the pull-down menu, or press the appropriate function key. Table 20.1 lists the function keys and the menu selections and explains their uses.

Your system must be using DOS 3.0 or later for you to be able to rename directories in NCD.

When you start NCD, the highlight is on the name of the current directory (that is, the directory you were in when you started NCD). You can move the highlighted selection bar with the up and down arrow keys. Pressing the PgUp and PgDn keys scrolls the display up and down one page at a time. The Home key returns you to the top of the directory listing, and the End key takes you to the end of the listing. With the mouse, first click on the directory you want to change to, or use the scroll bar on the right side of the screen to display the rest of the directory structure.

To change to another directory, highlight it and press Enter. NCD will make it the new current directory, end the program,

Table 20.1: NCD Function Keys and Their Uses

KEY	MENU SELECTION	USE
F1	Help	Displays a help screen
F2	Rescan Disk	Makes NCD re-read the disk's directory structure
F3	Change Drive	Lets you change to another drive by choosing another drive letter
F6	Rename	Lets you rename a directory
F7	Make	Lets you create a new directory
F8	Delete	Lets you delete a directory
F9	View	Lets you display more than 25 lines on the screen
F10	Quit	Ends NCD and returns control to DOS or the NORTON main menu
Alt-P	Print Tree	Prints a graphic representation of your disk's directory tree
Alt-V	Volume Label	Lets you add or change the volume label on a disk

Press the F1 key to get help information, and press the Esc key or the F10 key to quit NCD and return to DOS.

Rescanning the disk is the same as running NCD /R from the command prompt.

and return you to the DOS command prompt or to the Norton program. Alternatively, you can use the **Speed Search** box at the bottom of the screen to specify the directory you want. As soon as you type enough letters to identify the directory uniquely, NCD moves the highlight to that directory. Press Enter to confirm your choice and return to DOS. If you have several directories with similar names, Speed Search will move to the first one when you start typing. To move to the next one, hold down the Ctrl key and press Enter or click on **Next Match**. Each time you press Ctrl-Enter, you move to the next directory name that matches the letters you typed in the **Speed Search** box.

If the directory structure shown by NCD is not up-to-date, because you have added or deleted directories, use the Rescan

Disk selection from the Disk pull-down menu or press the F2 key to make NCD reread the directories on the disk. After NCD updates the TREEINFO.NCD file with the new data, it displays the new structure. If you make changes to the directory structure from within NCD by using the function keys, the program will automatically update TREEINFO.NCD when you exit NCD.

You can use the Change Disk option from the Disk pull-down menu or the F3 key to change to another drive. When you use Change Disk, a dialog box appears on the screen showing the drives on your system. Highlight or type the drive letter you want to change to, and press Enter, or press the Esc key for no change. If you do not change the current drive but press Enter instead of Esc, the selection bar will return to the directory that was current when you invoked NCD.

To rename a directory, position the selection bar on it and choose Rename from the Directory pull-down menu, or press F6. A dialog box opens with the cursor under the first letter of that directory's name, and you can type the new name over the original. You must press Enter before you can continue.

To create a new subdirectory, move the highlight to what will be its parent directory in the directory structure and select Make from the Directory pull-down menu, or press F7. NCD then displays a blank highlighted box into which you enter the new directory's name, as shown in Figure 20.4. Type the new name, and press Enter. To add another subdirectory simply repeat the process.

To delete a directory, highlight the appropriate name and select Delete from the Directory pull-down menu or press F8. As with the DOS RD command, NCD requires that the directory be empty before it can be deleted, and you cannot delete the root directory.

If your computer has an EGA or VGA adapter, you can use the selections in the View pull-down menu or use the F9 key to change the number of lines NCD displays on the screen. (If you do not have one of these adapters, NCD does not use the F9 key, and the key's label on the screen will be blank.) With an EGA adapter you can choose to display 25, 35, or 43 lines on the

If you want to change the number of screen lines for an entire session, see the discussion of the Norton Control Center in Chapter 18.

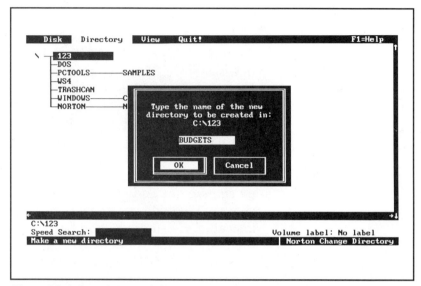

Figure 20.4: Creating a subdirectory under the 123 directory in NCD

screen; with a VGA adapter you can choose to display 25, 40, or 50 lines. The screen will revert to its normal settings when you exit the NCD program.

You can use the Print Tree option from the Directory pull-down menu to make a printout of your directory structure. When you select Print Tree or press Alt-P, NCD displays the Print Tree screen shown in Figure 20.5.

You can choose from three formats for the printout:

- Tree, Graphic Characters makes a neat printout of the tree using characters from the IBM extended-character set to join the entries.

- Tree, Non-graphic Characters makes a similar printout, but it uses standard ASCII characters rather than the line drawing set. The advantage of this selection is that it will print on almost any printer.

- List makes a simple listing of your directory structure.

Figure 20.6 shows an example printout made using the Tree, Graphics Characters selection.

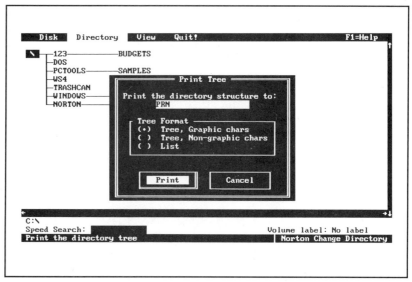

Figure 20.5: The Print Tree screen offers three print options

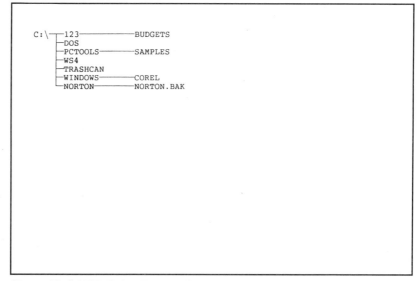

Figure 20.6: NCD Print Tree makes a compact printout of your
directory structure

IDENTIFYING YOUR DISKS WITH VOLUME LABELS

Each disk has a special entry in the root directory called the *volume label*. The DOS DIR command displays the volume label at the start of every file listing, and the label is often used as a title that describes the contents of the entire disk. For example, you might label a floppy disk containing word processing documents "MEMOS," or a disk containing Lotus 1-2-3 data files "BUDGETS."

CREATING AND VIEWING VOLUME LABELS IN DOS

The volume label can have as many as 11 characters, which DOS always displays in uppercase. To create a volume label on a disk, use the LABEL command. For example, enter:

LABEL A: BUDGETS

to add the volume label BUDGETS to the floppy disk in drive A. You can check a volume label by typing:

LABEL A:

DOS will respond with a message similar to the following:

Volume in drive A is BUDGETS

Volume label (11 characters, ENTER for none)?

The exact wording of this message varies according to the version of DOS you are using.

If you use the /V switch with the FORMAT command, DOS lets you add a volume label to the floppy disk immediately after you finish formatting it. For example, if you use the following command:

FORMAT A:/V

In DOS 4, the /V switch is built into the FORMAT command.

when the formatting process is finished, the following prompt appears:

Format complete
Volume label (11 characters, ENTER for none)?

which lets you enter the volume label for the disk.

You can use the DOS VOL command to display the volume label on a disk. When you type:

VOL

DOS will display the message:

Volume in drive A has no label

if a volume label has not been specified for the disk, or it will report:

Volume in drive A is BUDGETS

if the disk contains the label BUDGETS.

CREATING BETTER VOLUME LABELS WITH NCD

If a disk has a volume label, you will see it displayed in the lower right corner of the NCD screen. You can use the Volume Label command from the Disk pull-down menu, or you can press Alt-V to change the volume label. The Volume Label screen displays the current volume label (if one exists) and gives you the opportunity to enter another label. NCD lets you use both upper- and lowercase letters in the label; you are not restricted to only uppercase characters. You can also use a space character if you wish. Enter your new volume label into the box on the screen, and choose or click on OK to accept the new label. Otherwise, choose Delete to remove the volume label, or select Cancel to ignore any changes you have made.

USING NCD FROM THE DOS COMMAND PROMPT

The DOS CD command requires that you specify the entire DOS path name every time you use it. With a large hard disk and a complex structure, path names can be difficult to remember and typing them repeatedly can be time-consuming.

CHANGING DIRECTORIES

When using NCD, you do not need to enter the path of a directory. You sometimes don't even need to enter the directory's complete name.

You can use NCD with a directory name to change from any directory to another on the disk without having to type the new directory's path. For example, suppose you are in the root directory and want to change to C:\WS4\BOOK\TEXT. Instead of typing CD with the complete path name, merely type:

NCD TEXT

NCD will search the disk's directory structure, find the requested directory, and change to it. In fact, you only need to type the first few letters of the name—enough letters so that NCD can locate the correct directory. If your disk includes directory names that have the same initial letters (TEST and TEXT, for example), you will have to type more characters to make the entry unique.

UPDATING TREEINFO.NCD

If your disk contains less than five directories, it is actually faster for NCD to read the structure each time rather than read TREEINFO.NCD.

When you run NCD for the first time on your disk, it reads the complete directory structure from the disk and saves the data in a small file called TREEINFO.NCD, which is stored in the root directory. The next time you run NCD, the program reads the data from the TREEINFO.NCD file rather than the directory structure; this enables NCD to find the specified directory more quickly. However, if you make changes to the directory structure using DOS commands, NCD will not know about it until you explicitly specify that NCD must read the disk's directory structure again. To do this, type:

NCD /R

NCD then updates the TREEINFO.NCD file with the new information. If for some reason you don't want NCD to store any information in the TREEINFO.NCD file, type:

NCD /N

to prevent the program from writing the file.

MAKING AND REMOVING DIRECTORIES

To practice making and removing directories with NCD, let's work with a new 123 directory as an example. To make this directory, type:

NCD MD 123

from the root directory. You can also create a subdirectory in another directory using NCD MD. If you are not in the directory where you want the new subdirectory to be, you must give the new directory's full path when you create it. For example, if you are in your TEXT directory and want to create a BUDGETS subdirectory in the 123 directory, you must type:

NCD MD \123\BUDGETS

If you encounter any difficulties running NCD in full-screen mode, update the TREEINFO.NCD file.

Usually you don't have to update the TREEINFO.NCD file after making changes to your directory structure with NCD; however, you may find that NCD's full-screen mode doesn't work if you run it after using NCD MD from the root. For example, if trying to change directories ends NCD and returns you to the root, simply rescan your directory structure from NCD's full-screen mode, or run NCD /R at the DOS prompt.

To remove the BUDGETS subdirectory using NCD, type:

NCD RD BUDGETS

from the 123 directory. A directory must be empty of files and subdirectories before you can remove it. You can use either the DOS command DEL or ERASE to remove the files from a directory. If you are not in the parent directory of the directory you want to remove, specify the full path of the directory. For example, if you are in the TEXT directory, you can remove the 123 directory by typing:

NCD RD \123

USING NCD ON A NETWORKED DRIVE

NCD works in a slightly different way on a networked drive. First, it creates a new directory called NCDTREE, and then it writes the TREEINFO.NCD file into this directory. This helps ease the network supervisor's task of allocating users read and write privileges on files. If you work on a network and you want to use NCD, talk to your network supervisor first.

Safe Format (SFORMAT)

Formatting Disks without Overwriting Data

CHAPTER **21** _____

The Safe Format program is initially configured to format floppy disk drives only; this prevents you from accidentally formatting hard disks. You must change this configuration if you want to format a hard disk.

THE SAFE FORMAT UTILITY PROVIDES AN EASIER-TO-USE, faster alternative to the DOS FORMAT command. It also adds many useful safety features, including the ability to store information about the disk's original contents so that you can recover the original data on the disk even after the formatting process is complete. When you use Norton's INSTALL program to load the Norton Utilities onto your hard disk, you can substitute Safe Format (SFORMAT.EXE) for the DOS FORMAT command. The installation program automatically renames FORMAT.COM to XXFORMAT.COM and SFORMAT.EXE to FORMAT.EXE; therefore, when you type FORMAT, Safe Format runs instead.

RUNNING SAFE FORMAT IN FULL-SCREEN MODE

The Safe Format program always lets you change your mind before it executes your instructions.

From the main NORTON program screen, select Safe Format from the Tools subheading, or from the DOS prompt, type:

SFORMAT

and press Enter. Safe Format does not immediately begin formatting; you have to configure the program first. This two-step formatting procedure provides a safety net of sorts—it gives you time to change your mind.

The program displays the main Safe Format setup screen, as shown in Figure 21.1.

This screen is divided up into several smaller boxes, each relating to a specific part of the formatting process.

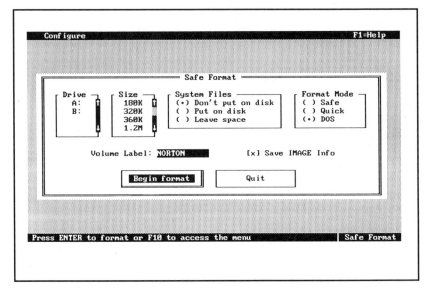

Figure 21.1: The Main Safe Format screen

Use the Tab key to move from box to box on the screen; then position the cursor on the selection you want with the up and down arrow keys. Finally, make your choice by pressing the spacebar to turn on the highlighted radio button. With a mouse, merely click on the radio button next to your selection.

DRIVE

This choice lets you change the current drive setting to another drive. Use the arrow keys to highlight the drive letter you want, and press Enter to confirm your choice.

SIZE

This selection lets you specify different formatting schemes for the disk, each of which store varying amounts of data on the disk. In this box, Safe Format displays a range of sizes that the current drive can support. Your choices here are limited to common disk sizes. With a 5¼-inch 360K drive, you can format a floppy disk as 180K, 320K, or 360K. With a 5¼-inch 1.2MB disk, you can format the disk as 180K, 320K, 360K, or as 1.2MB. If you have a 3½-inch 720K disk, this is the only format you can use, but if your 3½-inch disk is a 1.44MB disk, then you can format at 720K or at 1.44MB. Use the arrow keys to highlight your choice and press Enter.

SYSTEM FILES

This choice lets you create a bootable disk by installing the DOS system files on the formatted disk; it also lets you reserve space for these files so that you can add them later. Choose one of the following:

- **Don't put on disk** does not add the DOS system files, creating the maximum data space on the disk.

- **Put on disk** adds the DOS system files to the disk.

- **Leave space** reserves sections of the disk so that you can add the system files later. Remember that the DOS system files must go in a specific location on the disk unlike other files, which can go anywhere.

FORMAT MODE

This choice lets you select the format mode you want to use. You can choose one of the following:

- **Safe** formats a disk without erasing its existing data. This means that the UnErase and UnFormat options can both recover data from the disk.

- **Quick** is extremely fast because it only creates a new system area on the disk and does not overwrite the data area. (You cannot use **Quick** on a blank disk that has not been formatted before.)

- **DOS** invokes the regular DOS formatting procedure by which everything on the floppy disk is overwritten.

VOLUME LABEL

This choice lets you create or change the disk's 11-character volume label.

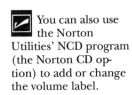
You can also use the Norton Utilities' NCD program (the Norton CD option) to add or change the volume label.

SAVE IMAGE INFO

The Image program stores a copy of the disk's system area in a file called IMAGE.DAT. If you accidentally format the disk, UnFormat uses the system information in the IMAGE.DAT file to recover the data on the disk. (See Chapter 8 for a complete description of the Image program.)

Use the Tab key, or the left and right arrow keys to move the cursor to the Save IMAGE Info box; then press X or the space-bar, or click on the box with the mouse to turn on the check-mark in the box.

BEGIN FORMAT

This choice actually starts the formatting process. If the disk contains data, Safe Format opens a window on the screen (see Figure 21.2) and displays the files found on the disk. Safe Format then asks if you want to continue with the formatting. This safety feature lets you remove an important disk that you inserted by accident. Next, the program checks the disk for errors; if one occurs, Safe Format displays the screen shown in Figure 21.3.

As the disk is being formatted, the Formatting screen shown in Figure 21.4 displays all of the pertinent information about the current operation, including the progress made and the amount of work that remains.

The screen also shows the estimated time it will take to format the disk and the actual elapsed time. Finally, the program shows (and updates, if necessary) the total disk space, system space, bad sector space, and usable disk space in bytes.

Select the Stop box if you want to interrupt the formatting operation.

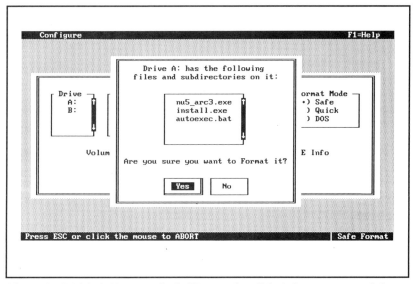

Figure 21.2: If Safe Format finds files on the disk, it lets you cancel the formatting operation

Figure 21.3: If Safe Format detects an error during the format, it displays the Unrecoverable Error screen

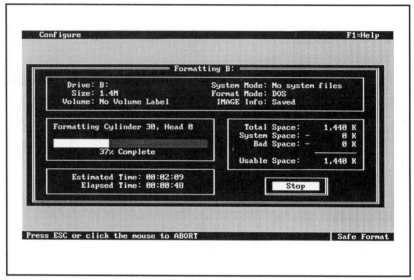

Figure 21.4: The Formatting screen shows pertinent information and updates progress

USING THE CONFIGURE MENU

You can use the selections in the Configure pull-down menu to customize Safe Format to your needs. From this menu, you can turn on the hard disk format, select your floppy disk types, and save your settings.

HARD DISKS

The Safe Format program is initially configured to work only with floppy disks, thus preventing you from accidentally formatting your hard disk. This is a useful safety feature, and you should retain this configuration until you actually need to format a hard disk. Then you can use the Hard disks selection from the Configure pull-down menu to change the configuration. Press Alt-H or click on Hard disks in the Configure menu to see the screen shown in Figure 21.5.

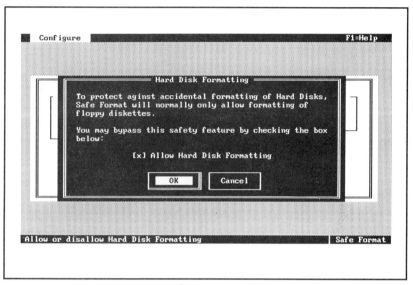

Figure 21.5: The Safe Format Hard Disk Formatting screen

To turn on hard disk formatting press an **X** character from the keyboard, press the spacebar, or click on the **Allow Hard Disk Formatting** box with the mouse. A check mark appears in the box to show that hard disk formatting is turned on, and when you return to the main Safe Format display you will see your hard disks listed below the floppy disk drives. A maximum of four drive letters can be shown at a time; use the up and down arrow keys to display the other drive letters if you have more than four drives.

FLOPPY TYPES

Use the Floppy types selection from the Configure pull-down menu to define your disk types. Safe Format automatically determines your drive types and sets the drive capacity to the highest capacity available. Figure 21.6 shows the details of this screen.

Use the arrow keys or click on a new selection with the mouse if you want to change any of these settings.

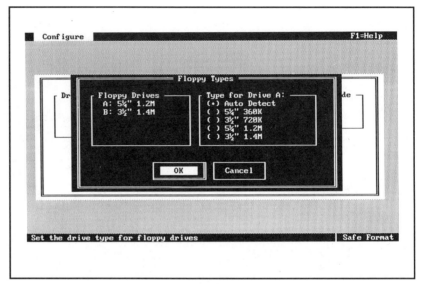

Figure 21.6: The Floppy Types screen from the Configure pull-down menu

SAVE SETTINGS

When you have configured Safe Format to your needs, save the new settings by selecting Save Settings in the Configure menu. The program automatically stores this information in a file called NU.INI, so that they will be loaded the next time you start the Safe Format program.

RUNNING SAFE FORMAT DIRECTLY FROM THE DOS COMMAND LINE

You can also run Safe Format from the DOS command prompt using one or more switches. For example, to put the system files on a disk, use the /S switch:

SFORMAT A: /S

To leave space for the system files without copying them, use the /B switch:

SFORMAT A: /B

For a complete list of all the Safe Format switches, see "Safe Format" in Chapter 23.

System Information (SYSINFO)

Peering inside Your Computer

CHAPTER **22**

NORTON UTILITIES 5 PROVIDES SEVERAL METHODS BY which you can examine and quantify your computer system's performance. System Information lets you inspect a great deal of internal computer information that you normally do not see; it also compares the performance of your computer with three industry-standard computers.

USING SYSTEM INFORMATION

The System Information program provides a wealth of information about your computer's hardware, including disk specifications, and memory layout and usage. It calculates performance indices and can even print a detailed report of its findings. If your job entails installing, demonstrating, or troubleshooting hardware or software products on unfamiliar computers, this is the program for you. System Information can also save the average computer user a lot of time and frustration. Many applications programs require users to supply hardware information during installation; however, most people do not know the details of their computer's hardware, particularly if they did not actually install it themselves. Also, some hardware can be used in different modes, which can further confuse the issue. Running System Information is a quick, efficient way to gather this information. You can run System Information from the DOS prompt or by selecting System Info from within the NORTON shell program. To run System Information from the DOS prompt, type:

SYSINFO

Across the top of the opening screen you will see several pull-down menu selections. You can specify one of these options directly by selecting it from the menu or by clicking on it with your mouse; you can also use the Next and Previous buttons at the bottom of the screen to cycle through all of the menu options in System Information in sequence. Use the Print button to print the information from a particular screen or store the information in a file. Use the Cancel button to return to the main System Information screen. I will describe all of the options in System Information in the sequence you will see them if you select the Next button, starting with the System Summary screen.

SYSTEM SUMMARY

The System Summary screen, shown in Figure 22.1, details the basic configuration of your computer: it lists information about your disks, memory, and other hardware systems. Several of the other display screens in System Information expand on

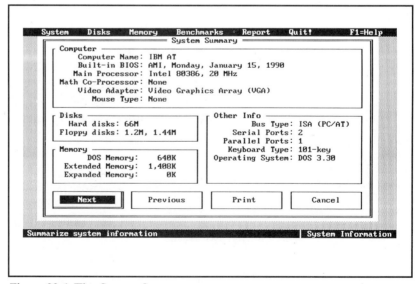

Figure 22.1: The System Summary screen

the basic information shown in this screen. This screen contains important information that is useful to all computer users; therefore, I will describe each of the elements in detail.

- Computer Name: System Information retrieves the name of the computer from the system's read-only memory (ROM). For many IBM compatibles, System Information displays only a copyright notice or a general computer type rather than the actual computer name.

- Built-in BIOS: This is the name of the read-only memory basic input/output system (ROM BIOS) and the date it was made. The BIOS is a layer of software that loads from ROM and lets DOS communicate with the computer's hardware. The BIOS handles the basic input and output functions in the computer.

- Main Processor: This is the name of the microprocessor used in your computer. The microprocessor is the computer's engine: It translates information from RAM, ROM, or the files on a disk into instructions that it can execute, and it executes them very quickly. The IBM PC, IBM PC/XT, and most compatibles use the Intel 8086 or 8088 microprocessor. The PC/AT computer and compatibles use the Intel 80286 chip. More recent machines use the Intel 80386 or the 80486 chip. The clock speed in MHz is also shown on the same line.

The Intel 80486 has an on-chip floating point unit as part of its circuitry. Software written for the 80387 math coprocessor will run on the 80486 on-chip floating-point unit without any modifications.

- Math Coprocessor: The Intel microprocessors used in PCs are designed so that other chips can be linked to them, thus increasing their power. One such additional chip is a math, or floating point, coprocessor, and the IBM PC and most compatibles include a socket on the main motherboard for it. Each Intel chip has a matching math coprocessor. The For example, the 8087 is used with the 8086, the 80287 is used with the 80286, and the 80387 is used with the 80386. These

'87s perform some of the number-crunching operations that the main microprocessors normally execute; in doing so, the coprocessors greatly increase the speed and accuracy of numeric calculations. In addition to simple add/subtract/multiply/divide operations, math coprocessors can do trigonometric calculations such as sine, cosine, and tangent. CAD applications and scientific or statistical programs usually benefit from the use of a coprocessor, whereas word processors generally do not. The speed gained by using a math coprocessor varies widely from application to application, but generally a math coprocessor performs calculations five to fifty times faster than a regular processor.

- Video Adapter: This is the name of the current video display adapter. Five types of video adapter boards are available: the monochrome display adapter (MDA); the color graphics adapter (CGA); the Hercules graphics adapter, which is also known as the monochrome graphics display adapter (MGDA); the enhanced graphics adapter (EGA); and the video graphics array (VGA), which was introduced with the IBM PS/2 computer in April 1987.

- Mouse Type: This is the name of the mouse (if one is in use) that is connected to your computer. In Figure 22.1, the example system includes a Microsoft mouse.

- Hard disks: This field lists the size of your hard disks in megabytes.

- Floppy disks: This entry provides details about your floppy disks.

- DOS Memory: This is the amount of main memory present in your computer.

- Extended Memory and Expanded Memory: These fields show the amount of additional memory you have installed in your computer.

These coprocessors are not the same as the add-in accelerator boards that occupy a slot in the computer chassis and actually take over the original microprocessor's work by replacing it with a faster processor.

IBM introduced the professional graphics adapter (PGA) at the same time as it introduced the EGA. However, the PGA needed a high-resolution monitor that was incompatible with existing standards, so it was discontinued.

- Bus Type: This describes the type of data bus your computer uses. ISA (Industry Standard Architecture) is found in PC/XT and PC/AT computers; EISA (Extended Industry Standard Architecture) is a new type of bus that supports 32-bit operations but retains compatibility with the original ISA; and MCA (Micro Channel Architecture) is IBM's proprietary bus for PS/2 computers.

- Serial Ports and Parallel Ports: These entries report the number of installed parallel and serial interface ports. DOS 3.2 and earlier supported only two serial ports, but beginning with DOS 3.3, the number increased to four. The parallel port is normally used to connect the system printer; the serial ports can connect a variety of serial devices, including a modem, a mouse, a serial printer, or a digitizer. As their names imply, the serial port can handle data one bit at a time, and the parallel port handles eight data bits at once; consequently, the data transfer rate of a parallel port is usually higher than that of a serial port. The serial port, however, is more flexible and can be configured to work with a variety of devices. See Chapter 18 for details about how to use Norton Control Center to configure your serial ports.

- Keyboard Type: This lists either a standard 84-key or an extended 101-key keyboard.

- Operating System: This is the version of DOS being run on the computer.

VIDEO SUMMARY

Choose Video Summary from the System pull-down menu, or click on the **Next** button to display the Video Summary screen, as shown in Figure 22.2.

All video systems except the MDA can be programmed with different parameters. This enables you to select from several

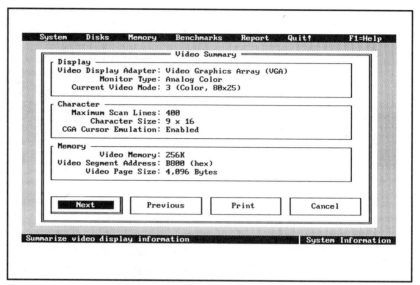

Figure 22.2: The Video Summary screen

different video modes. Each video mode is characterized by the resolution (the number of pixels displayed horizontally and vertically) and by the number of different colors that can be displayed at the same time. CGA video modes include 80-column-by-25-line mode and 40-column-by-25-line mode. The EGA can support as many as 43 lines of text; the VGA can support as many as 50 lines of text. The amount of video memory needed to support these different display adapters varies in each case.

HARDWARE INTERRUPTS

Before I discuss the information in the next two screens, Hardware Interrupts and Software Interrupts, let's briefly examine what interrupts are and how they work.

Often, after you have given the computer a task to perform, you will need it to respond quickly to a new request; for example, to begin a new task at the press of a key or the click of a mouse. The mechanism that accomplishes this is known as an *interrupt*. An interrupt is an "event" that causes the processor to suspend its current activity, save its place, and look up an *interrupt vector* in the *interrupt vector table*. The interrupt vector tells the processor the address of the *interrupt handler,* or service routine, that it should branch to. After the service routine performs its task, control is returned to the suspended process. DOS interrupts are often divided into three types: internal hardware, external hardware, and software interrupts. The Intel 80*x*86 family of processors supports 256 prioritized interrupts, of which the first 64 are reserved for use by the system hardware or by DOS itself.

In the PC, the main processor does not accept interrupts from hardware devices directly; instead interrupts are routed to an Intel 8259A Programmable Interrupt Controller (PIC) chip. This chip responds to each hardware interrupt, assigns a priority, and forwards it to the main processor. Each hardware device is hardwired, or "jumpered," into inputs known as IRQs or *interrupt requests,* and this is why you see an IRQ assigned to an interrupt.

A hardware interrupt is generated by a device such as the keyboard, the computer clock, or one of the parallel or serial ports on the computer. To see a list of the IRQs on your computer, select Hardware Interrupts from the System pull-down menu. Your display will look similar to Figure 22.3.

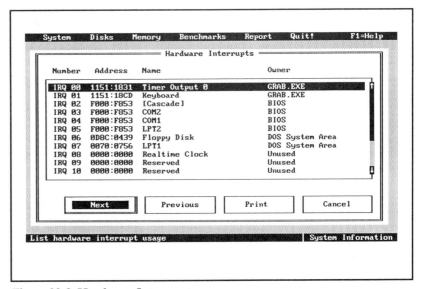

Figure 22.3: Hardware Interrupts screen

At the left of the screen is the list of IRQs, followed by their hex addresses. The hardware devices that need the most attention have lower IRQs, so the system timer has IRQ 0, the keyboard has IRQ 01, and so on up the list. The name and address of each interrupt is displayed at the center of the screen, and the name of the owner of the interrupt is displayed at the right.

If you have a PC or a PC/XT (or clone) computer, you have one 8259A chip, and you will see eight IRQs in the display, numbered from zero to seven.

If you have a PC/AT (or clone) or a Micro Channel PS/2 computer, you have two programmable interrupt controllers tied together. That is, interrupt two on one of the interrupt controllers accepts its input from the other 8259A chip. This generates a total of 15 interrupts, with interrupt two usually described as the *cascade*.

The Model 25 and 30, like the PC and the PC/XT have a total of eight interrupts, but they are shared. Interrupt one, assigned to the keyboard in PC-type computers, is shared by the keyboard, the mouse, and the time-of-day clock on the Model 25 and 30.

SOFTWARE INTERRUPTS

All interrupts on the PC are channeled through a common internal vector table called the *interrupt vector table,* regardless of whether the interrupt is generated as an external or an internal hardware interrupt, or as a software interrupt. The entry into this table for hardware devices is directly related to the IRQ number. To find the address of the interrupt handling routine for a hardware interrupt in the interrupt vector table, add eight to the IRQ number.

Select Software Interrupts from the System pull-down menu to see a list of all the entries in the interrupt vector table on your computer. Figure 22.4 shows a sample display for an 80386 computer.

Many of the software interrupts perform more than one single service. For example, interrupt 21H is the main entry point for

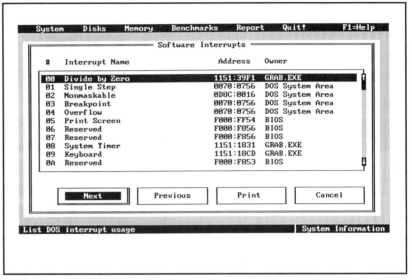

Figure 22.4: The Software Interrupts screen lists the entries in the interrupt vector table

DOS services and offers the programmer more than 100 different *function calls,* including character input and output, file creation, file reading and writing, and file deletion.

CMOS VALUES

Remember to print out the CMOS values; then, if your computer battery fails and loses the current settings, you can simply reenter the values.

Computers made after the PC/AT use a portion of Complementary Metal Oxide Semiconductor memory (usually abbreviated as CMOS) to hold basic configuration information for the computer. This CMOS memory requires such low power levels that it can be maintained by a small battery; therefore, this information is not lost when you turn off the power at the end of your session. To examine the information held in CMOS, select CMOS Status from the System pull-down menu in System Information. Figure 22.5 shows a typical example from an 80386 computer.

One of the most crucial pieces of information on this screen is the hard disk type number shown in the **Hard Disks** box at the upper left of the screen. In Figure 22.5 the disk type number for the first, or primary, hard disk drive is 1. The BIOS in your computer can read many types of hard disk from different manufacturers; this hard disk type number is the code that tells the BIOS how many heads and cylinders your specific disk drive has. If your computer's battery loses power, the contents of CMOS memory will be lost, and you will not be able to boot up your computer from the hard disk until you replace the battery and reset this number. With some computers you must use the "setup" disk that came with your computer to reset the number; other computers have the setup routines built into the ROM BIOS itself.

The rest of this screen displays details about your floppy disk types and installed memory, and includes additional information contained in CMOS. Select the Print button to make a hard copy of the CMOS Status screen. Keep the report in a safe place so that you can reenter these values if your computer battery fails.

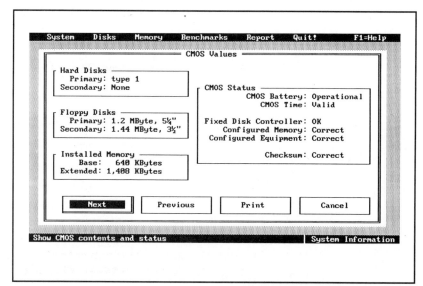

Figure 22.5: Typical CMOS values from an 80386 computer

DISK SUMMARY

Select Disk Summary from the Disks pull-down menu to see a single-screen listing of all the disks on your computer. An example screen is shown in Figure 22.6.

In Figure 22.6, drive A is a 5¼-inch floppy disk. This computer doesn't have a drive B, so it is labeled as a "phantom" drive. Drives C, D, and E are three partitions on a 65MB drive. Drive F is a RAM disk of 128K; notice that it is described as Device Driven in the **Type** column. The remaining drive letters are shown to be available.

DISK CHARACTERISTICS

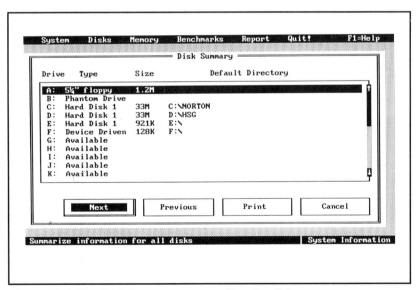

See Chapter 2 for detailed information about disk structure.

Choose Disk Characteristics from the Disks pull-down menu to see more detailed information about the disk drives on your computer. Figure 22.7 shows the Disk Characteristics screen for the same system depicted in the previous figure.

Figure 22.6: The Disk Summary screen lists the disks on your computer

Use the selection bar at the right side of the screen to choose the drive you want to examine. Figure 22.7 shows information for drive C, a 33MB partition on a 65MB disk. The display is divided into two main sections: Logical Characteristics and Physical Characteristics.

The Logical Characteristics box contains information about the layout of the disk from the DOS viewpoint, including the number of bytes per sector, the number of sectors per cluster, the total number of clusters, the number and type of the FAT, and the media descriptor byte. It also includes details of the starting location and size of the FAT, root directory, and the data area. If you are using a RAM disk, notice that it contains only one copy of the FAT.

The Physical Characteristics box provides details about the actual disk hardware, including the number of disk sides and tracks, and the number of sectors per track. If you examine a RAM disk with this option, the Physical Characteristics box contains the message "No physical information."

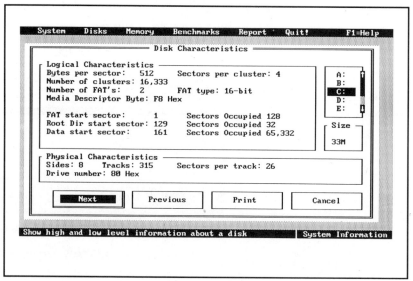

Figure 22.7: Disk Characteristics screen gives more detailed disk information

PARTITION TABLES

Select Partition Tables from the Disks pull-down menu to display the partition table information for your computer, as shown in Figure 22.8.

Figure 22.8 provides details about all three partitions on the example 65MB hard disk, including starting and ending side, track, and sector numbers. Note that partition number 1 is the partition from which the disk boots up. Individual partition details are given at the bottom of the screen. In this example, the first partition is located on hard disk number 1, which has 8 sides, or heads, and 639 tracks configured with 26 sectors per track.

If you reconfigure your system after a hard disk repair or replacement, you can use the values from this screen to rebuild your disk system.

MEMORY SUMMARY

To see a one-screen synopsis of the memory available in your computer, select Memory Usage Summary from the Memory

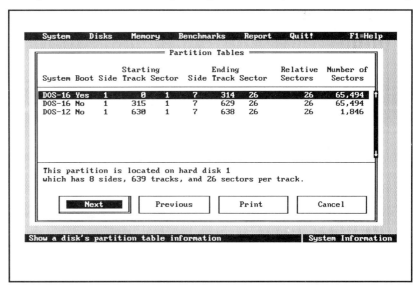

Figure 22.8: The Partition Tables display screen gives details of all three partitions on this 65MB hard disk

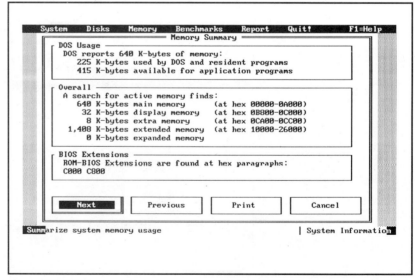

See the next section for more details about TSRs.

pull-down menu. Your display will be similar to the one shown in Figure 22.9.

DOS reports how much memory it can access (in this example, 640K), the amount of memory being used by DOS and any terminate-and-stay-resident (TSR) programs you have loaded, and the remaining memory available for use by your applications program(s). System Information doesn't merely take DOS's word for the amount of memory present in the computer; it goes out and checks for itself. The second part of the screen, titled Overall, lists the memory that System Information actually found in your computer. Some computers might lock up and report a memory parity error when System Information makes its memory check. This does not harm your computer, although you must reboot to recover. You can bypass this memory test if you start System Information from the DOS command line by typing:

SYSINFO /N

```
┌──────────────────────────────────────────────────────────────────────┐
│ System   Disks   Memory   Benchmarks   Report   Quit!      F1=Help     │
│ ┌───────────────────────── Memory Summary ──────────────────────────┐ │
│ │ ┌ DOS Usage ──────────────────────────────────────────────────┐   │ │
│ │ │  DOS reports 640 K-bytes of memory:                          │   │ │
│ │ │       225 K-bytes used by DOS and resident programs          │   │ │
│ │ │       415 K-bytes available for application programs         │   │ │
│ │ └──────────────────────────────────────────────────────────────┘  │ │
│ │ ┌ Overall ────────────────────────────────────────────────────┐   │ │
│ │ │  A search for active memory finds:                           │   │ │
│ │ │       640 K-bytes main memory      (at hex 00000-0A000)      │   │ │
│ │ │        32 K-bytes display memory   (at hex 0B800-0C000)      │   │ │
│ │ │         8 K-bytes extra memory     (at hex 0CA00-0CC00)      │   │ │
│ │ │     1,408 K-bytes extended memory  (at hex 10000-26000)      │   │ │
│ │ │         0 K-bytes expanded memory                            │   │ │
│ │ └──────────────────────────────────────────────────────────────┘  │ │
│ │ ┌ BIOS Extensions ────────────────────────────────────────────┐   │ │
│ │ │  ROM-BIOS Extensions are found at hex paragraphs:            │   │ │
│ │ │  C000 C800                                                   │   │ │
│ │ └──────────────────────────────────────────────────────────────┘  │ │
│ │                                                                    │ │
│ │    ┌─────────┐   ┌──────────┐   ┌─────────┐   ┌──────────┐         │ │
│ │    │  Next   │   │ Previous │   │  Print  │   │  Cancel  │         │ │
│ │    └─────────┘   └──────────┘   └─────────┘   └──────────┘         │ │
│ └────────────────────────────────────────────────────────────────────┘│
│  Summarize system memory usage                  | System Information    │
│                                                                        │
└──────────────────────────────────────────────────────────────────────┘
```

Figure 22.9: Memory Summary screen for an 80386 computer with 2MB of active memory

Finally, any ROM BIOS extensions that System Information finds are listed separately. The ROM chips that contain these extensions do not have to be on the motherboard; they also can be on expansion boards plugged into the bus. The ROM BIOS extensions needed to run these accessories are loaded automatically when you boot up the computer. The only constraint is that no two extensions can occupy the same memory area. That is why most add-on boards include jumpers or switches that let you alter their configurations—so you can reassign the addresses used by their BIOS extensions.

TSR PROGRAMS

One of the main limitations of DOS is that it cannot support more than one program running at one time. DOS is a single-user, single-tasking operating system. The terminate-and-stay-resident program is an ingenious method that partially overcomes this limitation.

After you load a TSR program into memory, it returns control to DOS, but waits in the background. When you press a certain key combination (the *hotkey*), the TSR interrupts the application program you were running and executes its own services. When you finish using the TSR program and exit, control returns to your application program again.

Other memory resident programs work in a slightly different way: they attach themselves to the operating system and remain in memory, working constantly in the background. The DOS PRINT utility is an example of this; indeed, PRINT is often called the first real memory-resident program. The Norton Disk Monitor program also falls into this category.

Because DOS interrupts are always channeled through the same interrupt vector table, it is relatively easy for a TSR program to alter these vectors to change the way the interrupts work. For example, virtually all programs read the keyboard through interrupt 16H, which normally points to a service routine in the BIOS. It is a simple matter for a program to change the response of the system to keyboard-read requests by rerouting this vector through an alternative procedure. These replaced vectors are called *hooked* vectors. If you choose TSR Programs from the Memory pull-down menu, you can list all of the TSR programs installed in your computer. You can see several of these hooked vectors listed in Figure 22.10.

See Chapter 14 for a complete description of the Disk Monitor program.

In Figure 22.10, note that the Disk Monitor program is using several interrupt vectors. Interrupt 25H is the DOS absolute disk read; it reads data from a logical sector into a specific memory location. Interrupt 26H is the DOS absolute disk write, which writes data from a specified memory buffer to a logical disk sector. With these services available, it is easy to see why Disk Monitor is such a powerful and useful program.

As you move the highlight up and down the list of TSR programs, System Information displays additional information if it is available, including the path, the command line arguments used to load the program, and the number of memory allocation blocks the program uses.

You can switch between the Memory Summary display and the TSR Programs display to evaluate the effects of loading additional

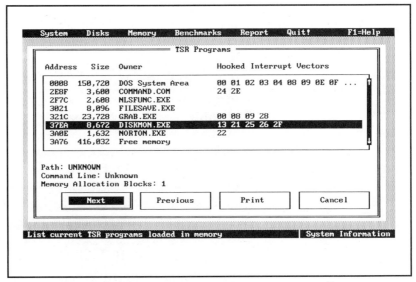

Figure 22.10: System Information's TSR Programs screen lists program names and hooked vectors

TSR programs. The amount of memory in your computer is fixed, so as you add TSR programs, the amount of memory space available for your applications programs decreases. At some point you may find that you cannot open a large database or use a large applications program because there is no longer sufficient room. You must then decide if the utility of your TSRs is worth the memory space that they occupy; try to strike the right balance for the way you work.

DOS MEMORY BLOCKS

Select Memory Block List to examine how the memory in your computer is being used. The DOS Memory Blocks screen is shown in Figure 22.11.

At the left of the screen is a list of hex addresses used by your programs. The size in bytes is given next and is followed by the name of the owner, which could be, for example, the DOS system area, COMMAND.COM, Free Memory, or an Unknown

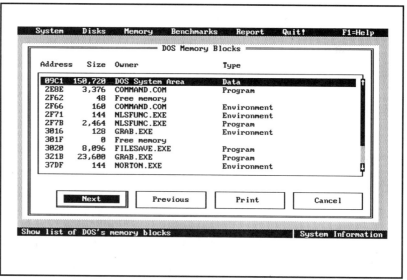

Figure 22.11: Memory Block List shows you how the memory in your computer is being used

Owner. Finally, the right column specifies the type of the memory block, either data, program, or environment. The *environment* is a section of memory used primarily to store the settings of the variables for the DOS PATH, SET and PROMPT commands. When DOS loads a program, it gives the program a copy of the environment. The program may modify its copy of the environment, but this will not affect the original settings maintained by the command processor. Any program that remains resident in memory retains its copy of the environment; however, this copy is not updated by any subsequent commands that alter DOS's copy of the environment.

DEVICE DRIVERS

A *device driver* is a special program that manipulates one specific piece of hardware. DOS uses device drivers as extensions to the operating system. Some device drivers are actually part of DOS; these are called *built-in device drivers*. Others exist as separate files and are called *loadable device drivers*. These drivers free DOS from having to include code for every single piece of hardware that can be attached to a computer. As long as there is a device driver supplied with hardware, you can use it on your computer. When you want to use a new piece of hardware, merely connect it to your system, copy the device driver into a directory on your boot disk, and add a statement to your CONFIG.SYS or AUTOEXEC.BAT file to load the device driver at boot up time. Loadable device drivers also reduce memory requirements; you only have to load the device drivers that you need for your specific hardware configuration.

For example, if you want to use the Norton Batch Enhancer to full advantage, you must add a line to your CONFIG.SYS file to load the ANSI.SYS device driver. This device driver alters the way that DOS handles the keyboard and screen, often called the *console*. Also, even if you plug a mouse into a serial port, DOS does not know about the device until you add the device driver, often called MOUSE.SYS, into your configuration file.

Select Device Drivers from the Memory pull-down menu to display a list of the device drivers in use on your system. Your screen will look similar to the one shown in Figure 22.12.

In Figure 22.12, you can see the loadable device driver called PC$MOUSE at the top of the screen. Notice also the built-in drivers for the keyboard, screen, and serial and parallel ports.

CPU SPEED

Select CPU Speed from the Benchmarks pull-down menu to display a CPU Speed screen similar to the one in Figure 22.13.

The Computing Index is a measure of your computer's CPU or disk-independent computing power. A basic IBM PC/XT running an 8088 at 4.77 megahertz has a computing index equal to 1, an IBM PC/AT running an 80286 at 8 MHz has a computing index of 4.4, and a Compaq 386 running an 80386 at 33 MHz has a computing index of 34.7. In other words, the Compaq 386 runs the System Information computing index

The benchmarks calculated by version 5.0 of System Information give lower speed values than earlier versions of the program. This does not mean that your computer has slowed down; it just means that different benchmark calculations are being performed in this version of the program.

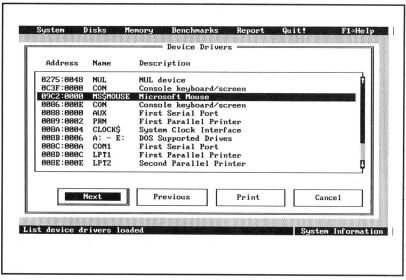

Figure 22.12: Loadable device drivers, such as that needed for the mouse, are shown in this display

tests 34.7 times faster than the original IBM PC/XT.

The computing index is calculated constantly, so you can immediately see the effect that something as simple as moving the mouse has on the computing index. The type of processor in your computer and its speed in MHz is shown directly under the graph. If your computer has a "turbo" button, press it to see what effect changing the speed has on your computing index.

DISK SPEED

To evaluate the speed of your hard disk against other industry standards, select Hard Disk Speed from the Benchmarks pulldown menu. The Disk Index is the second System Information calculated index, intended this time to let you rate your hard disk's performance against the same three industry standard computers used in the previous test. Figure 22.14 shows the screen that reports the results of the Disk Index tests. Using a

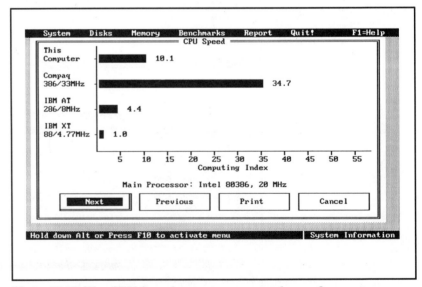

Figure 22.13: The CPU Speed screen compares the performance of your computer with that of three industry standard computers

disk cache program like Norton Cache (described in Chapter 12) will increase your disk's speed. Under the bar graph, the program displays several statistics for your hard disk, including the Average Seek time and the Track-to-Track access time (both in milliseconds), and the Data Transfer Rate (in kilobytes per second).

The *average seek time* is the average length of time the disk takes to access a random piece of data, based on a large number of disk accesses. Actual access times range from less than 15 milliseconds to as long as 150 milliseconds. *Track-to-track access time* is the length of time the disk takes to move from one track to the adjacent track. Both these measurements are determined by hard disk design and construction, specifically in the type of head used and the number of platters in the disk. This is not the complete story of disk speed, however. The disk does not work in isolation; it also must work with the disk controller and the software controlling the drive.

A more complete measurement of system performance is the *data transfer rate*—the rate at which data is read from the disk

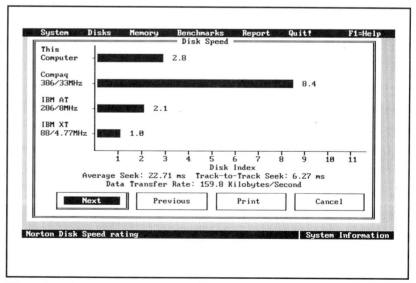

Figure 22.14: The Hard Disk Speed Benchmark calculates the Disk Index

and passes through the disk controller card to the computer it-self. This measurement encompasses raw disk speed, the effec-tiveness of the disk interface, and the computer data bus speed. After all, the performance of a fast disk might be bogged down by a slow controller or data bus.

OVERALL PERFORMANCE INDEX

Choose the Overall Performance Index from the Benchmarks pull-down menu to calculate your computer's final index, as shown in Figure 22.15. The Overall Performance Index is the in-tegration of the Computing Index and Disk Index into a single value. This lets you compare different systems easily.

DISPLAYING YOUR CONFIG.SYS FILE

To display a listing of your CONFIG.SYS file, choose View CONFIG.SYS from the Report pull-down menu. The contents of the file are shown on the screen. Use the cursor control keys to

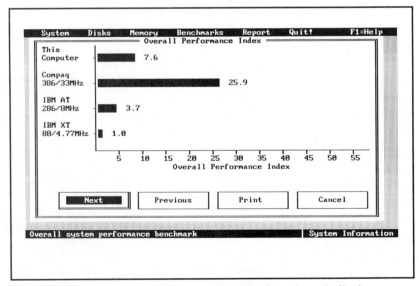

Figure 22.15: The Overall Performance Index benchmark display

scroll through the listing, or click on the scroll bars with the mouse.

DISPLAYING YOUR AUTOEXEC.BAT FILE

To see a listing of your AUTOEXEC.BAT file choose, View AUTOEXEC.BAT from the Report pull-down menu. Again, the contents of the file are displayed on the screen. Use the cursor control keys to scroll the listing, or click on the scroll bars with the mouse.

PRINT REPORT

The last selection in the Report pull-down menu is Print Report. Choosing this selection displays the screen shown in Figure 22.16. This screen lets you configure the System Information report to your requirements. Use the Tab key or the arrow keys to move though the items on the display. To turn an option on or off, press the X key or the spacebar, or click on the

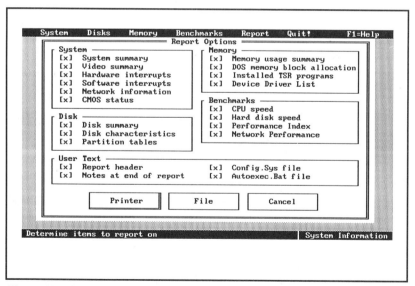

Figure 22.16: The Report Option screen lets you select the System Information elements you want to print in your report

The report made by System Information can be very long if you select all of the print options. The report is not divided into neat pages. Send the output to a disk file first; then use your word processor to edit and arrange the information in the file so that the output is neat and orderly.

option with the mouse. After you have completed your choice of the report options, choose Printer to send the report to your printer, or choose File to send the report to a file. The default file name is SIREPORT.TXT, but the program lets you change this name. You can also enter a line of text into the Report Header screen for inclusion at the top of the report file. If you are working on a customer's computer, you might want to indicate this by adding text into the report file. Similarly, you can enter 10 lines of comments that will be printed at the end of the report. (For example, you could use these notes as the record of a service visit.) After the program saves the report to the disk, a small window opens to let you know that the file was recorded successfully.

USING SYSTEM INFORMATION ON A NETWORK

System Information includes two menu selections—Network Information from the System pull-down menu, and Network Performance Speed from the Benchmarks pull-down menu—that you can use to examine your network. If you are not operating from a Novell network, these two selections will not be available from their respective menus, and they will be displayed in a different color from the other menu selections.

NETWORK INFORMATION

System Information for networks is compatible only with Novell networks.

The Network Information selection from the System pull-down menu summarizes network information, as shown in Figure 22.17. The user name and network identification number are displayed with the login date and time. The file server name and details about the version and date of the Novell network software are also shown.

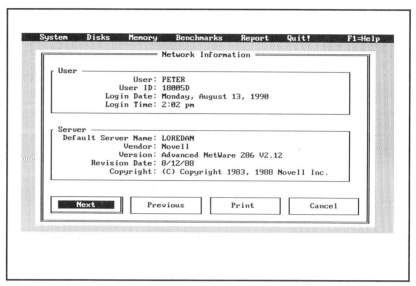

Figure 22.17: The Network Information screen summarizes network
user and file server information

NETWORK PERFORMANCE SPEED

The Network Performance Speed selection from the Benchmarks pull-down menu, tests the speed of the network in terms
of disk reads and disk writes. The Network Drive Benchmark
screen depicts the relative speed of reads and writes for the system as a bar graph that indicates the average throughput in
kilobytes per second.

Part VI contains the two remaining pieces essential to complete the Norton picture.

Chapter 23 is a complete reference guide to all the command line parameters and switches you can use with the Norton Utilities. Chapter 24 details the complex help system contained in the Utilities and describes several useful troubleshooting techniques.

PART

VI

Quick Help

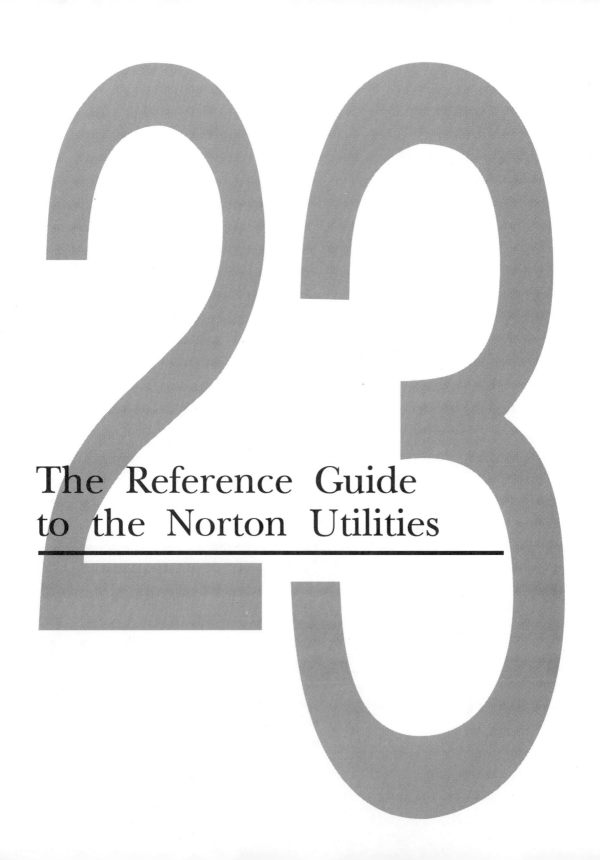

23

The Reference Guide to the Norton Utilities

CHAPTER 23 _____

THIS CHAPTER LISTS ALL OF THE NORTON UTILITIES
programs alphabetically, giving a short description of each program. The syntax and available switches for each utility are also
presented. The descriptions are based on version 5 of the Norton Utilities, which was released in mid-1990. If you have an earlier version of the Norton Utilities, you will be able to follow
most of the program descriptions here, but you will be without
several major new programs, and you should upgrade to
version 5.

To make the syntax easier to read, I have substituted categori-
cal names for the parameters that you can use for a particular
command. The possible choices are then listed and described
individually. The most common parameters are:

- *drive,* which should be replaced by the appropriate
  drive letter, followed by a colon.

- *filename,* which should be replaced by a specific file
  name (and path when necessary). *filename* denotes
  one particular file, so you cannot use the DOS wild
  card characters with this specification.

- *filespec,* which should be replaced by a file name (and
  path when necessary). This is a more general specification, so you can use the DOS wildcard characters to include more than one file.

- *directoryspec,* which should be replaced by a directory
  name (and path when necessary).

- *n,* which should be replaced by a number. The size of
  the number varies according to the utility you are
  using.

Finally, remember that, unless noted otherwise, all parameters are optional.

BATCH ENHANCER

BE (Batch Enhancer) adds several important mechanisms for improved screen handling to the DOS batch-programming language. BE also enables you to create interactive decision-making in a batch file with its ASK subcommand.

Syntax

BE *subcommand*

or

BE *filename*

Description

You can use BE followed by one of the subcommands listed here, or you can use BE with a file that contains all the subcommands and their parameters. When you group the subcommands together in a file and specify the file with BE, the commands will be executed much faster because BE is only invoked once instead of individually for every command. (See the examples in Chapter 17 for more information about improving batch-file screen handling.)

SUBCOMMANDS

Following is a list of the possible subcommands that you can include in a batch file.

BE ASK   This program provides a way to perform conditional branching from a batch file. The prompt you include in the command will be displayed on the screen when the batch file executes the command, and the answer given by the user tells the batch file which commands to execute next.

Syntax

BE ASK "*prompt*" *list* DEFAULT=*key* TIMEOUT=*n* ADJUST=*n color*

Description

The following list explains each parameter:

"*prompt*"   is any text string, usually a question, that offers the user two or more choices. You should also include a list of valid responses, so that the user knows which key to press.

list   specifies the valid keystrokes for BE ASK. If you don't specify anything for *list*, ASK accepts any keystrokes.

DEFAULT=*key*   indicates the response to use if no key is pressed before the allotted time has expired or if Enter is pressed.

TIMEOUT=*n*   specifies the number of seconds BE ASK will wait for a keystroke after the *prompt* test has been displayed. If TIMEOUT equals zero or if you do not include TIMEOUT in the command statement, BE ASK waits forever for a keystroke.

ADJUST=*n*   adjusts the return value by the amount *n*.

color   specifies the color of the prompt text. See BE SA for a description of the available colors.

BE BEEP This program plays a tone on the computer's speaker. A single tone can be specified at the DOS prompt, or a series of tones can be played by loading a file.

Syntax

BE BEEP *switches*

plays a single tone.

BE BEEP *filename*

plays all the tones specified by the switches in the file. You can include a path name to specify a file in another directory, but you cannot use wildcard characters.

Description

To create a single tone, you need to include the $/Dn$ and $/Fn$ switches in the command statement. You can also repeat the tone by adding the $/Rn$ and $/Wn$ switches to the same statement. Here is what each switch does:

$/Dn$ gives the duration of the tone in 18ths of a second.

$/E$ echoes the text in the file specified by *filename*.

$/Fn$ specifies the frequency of the tone in Hertz (cycles per second). Setting /F equal to 1 sounds a moderately low note; setting it to 10,000 sounds a high-pitched squeak.

$/Rn$ tells BE BEEP how many times to repeat the tone.

$/Wn$ specifies the duration of the wait period between tones, in 18ths of a second.

BE BOX   This program draws a box on the screen, according to your specifications.

Syntax

To run BE BOX, use:

BOX *top left bottom right outline color*

in your batch file.

Use BE BOX when you want to create a framed box. (Specifying two colors produces a two-toned frame.) Use BE WINDOW when you want to fill in the outline with color.

Description

To draw a box, you must include the *top, left, bottom,* and *right* parameters. The two remaining parameters are optional. Here is what all of these parameters represent:

top	specifies the row of the top-left corner of the box.
left	specifies the column of the top-left corner of the box.
bottom	specifies the row of the bottom-right corner of the box.
right	specifies the column of the bottom-right corner of the box.
outline	specifying SINGLE draws a single-line outline for the box; specifying DOUBLE draws a double-line outline for the box.
color	specifies the color of the box. (See BE SA for a description of the color selections.)

BE CLS   This program clears the screen and positions the cursor at the home position, which is the top-left corner of the screen.

Syntax

BE CLS

BE CLS does not take any parameters.

BE DELAY This program sets a specified time delay before executing the next command in the batch file.

Syntax

BE DELAY *counts*

Description

You must specify the *counts* parameter when you invoke BE DELAY. You can use this program to display text for a set period of time, such as in a message in a window or in a prompt that gives instructions.

The *counts* parameter determines how long (in 18ths of a second) the batch-file processor will wait before continuing to execute the batch file.

BE GOTO This program causes a batch file to branch to a label line somewhere else in the batch file.

Syntax

BE GOTO *label*

Description

BE GOTO requires a destination label to which execution branches in the batch file.

BE PRINTCHAR This program displays the specified character at the current cursor location.

Syntax

BE PRINTCHAR *character repetitions color*

Description

The definitions for PRINTCHAR's parameters are as follows:

character   specifies the character to be displayed.

repetitions   specifies the number of times the character will be displayed, to a maximum of 80 repetitions.

color   determines the color to be used for the character.

BE ROWCOL   This program moves the cursor to the specified location on the screen and can display text.

Syntax

BE ROWCOL *row column text color*

Description

You don't have to specify *text* or *color* when you invoke BE ROWCOL. The program accepts the following parameters:

row   specifies a new row for the cursor.

column   specifies a new column for the cursor.

text   provides optional text to be displayed at the new cursor location. If the text contains space characters, enclose the entire string in quotation marks.

color   specifies the color to be used for the text. (See the description of BE SA for the colors available.)

BE SA   This program enables you to set the screen foreground and background colors, and vary the intensity of the characters. BE SA works only if the ANSI.SYS driver is installed in your installed in your CONFIG.SYS file. If ANSI.SYS is not installed, BE displays an error message telling you that ANSI.SYS is required.

BE SA can be used in two ways.

Syntax 1

The first syntax:

BE SA *main-setting switches*

lets you set up your screen's display of text.

Description 1

The *main-setting* parameter can be one of the following:

NORMAL

REVERSE

UNDERLINE

The *switches* you can include are:

/N   does not set the border color. The EGA is a borderless display so using this switch with an EGA will have no effect; however, you can set the border for a VGA by omitting this switch.

/CLS   clears the screen after setting the color and screen attributes.

Syntax 2

The second syntax:

BE SA *intensity foreground* ON *background switches*

lets you set the screen colors' attributes.

Description 2

The *switches* are the same ones you can use with BE SA's first syntax. The remaining parameters are:

Bright and Bold refer to the same attribute.

intensity	BRIGHT
	BLINKING
	BOLD
foreground	WHITE
	BLACK
	RED
	MAGENTA
	BLUE
	GREEN
	CYAN
	YELLOW
background	same color as *foreground*

You can abbreviate the color in the command statement by listing only the first three letters of their name. Therefore,

BE SA BRIGHT WHITE ON BLUE

can be specified as:

BE SA BRI WHI ON BLU

BE WINDOW   This program creates a window on the screen, according to your specifications.

Syntax

BE WINDOW *top left bottom right color switches*

Description

top	specifies the row of the top-left corner of the window.
left	specifies the column of the top-left corner of the window.
bottom	specifies the row of the bottom-right corner of the window.
right	specifies the column of the bottom-right corner of the window.
SHADOW	adds an optional drop shadow to the window.
EXPLODE	makes the window zoom, or expand as it opens.

CALIBRATE

The Calibrate utility optimizes the speed of your hard disk by calculating the current interleave factor and then (if necessary) performing a nondestructive low-level format of your hard disk using a more efficient interleave factor.

Syntax

To run Calibrate, type:

CALIBRAT *drive switches*

Description

Calibrate's parameters are as follows:

/BATCH	skips all prompts and exits to DOS when done.
/BLANK	clears the screen while performing the pattern testing.

/NOCOPY	prevents copying of the current track being tested.
/NOSEEK	cancels the seek tests.
/NOFORMAT	performs only the pattern testing; cancels the nondestructive low-level format.
/PATTERN:*n*	performs pattern testing at level *n*; *n* can be set to 5, 40, or 80 different patterns.
/R:*filename*	generates a Calibrate report and writes it to the file name specified by *filename*.
/RA:*filename*	generates a Calibrate report and appends it to the file specified by *filename*.
/X:*drive*	excludes drive or drives from the testing (for example, to exclude drives D and E, use /X:DE).

DISK EDITOR

The Disk Editor lets you examine and edit any part of a disk, including the boot record, partition table, or file allocation tables. You can also use the advanced search capabilities to help you manually recover erased files.

Syntax

To run the Disk Editor in full-screen mode, type:

DISKEDIT

To run Disk Editor using switches from the DOS command line, type:

DISKEDIT *drive filename switches*

Description

With the Disk Editor, you can use the following parameters:

/M runs the Disk Editor in maintenance mode to bypass the initial scan of the directory structure. Use this mode if your disk is badly damaged.

/X:*drives* excludes the specified drives from absolute sector-processing. If you are having trouble running the Disk Editor in absolute-sector mode, use this switch to exclude allocated but nonexistent drives from the processing.

DISK MONITOR

Disk Monitor prevents unauthorized writes to your hard disk, displays the drive letter of the drive being accessed, and parks your hard disk heads.

Syntax

To run Disk Monitor from the DOS command line, type:

DISKMON *switches*

Description

/STATUS displays Disk Monitor status; Disk Light will be on or off; Disk Protect will also be on or off.

/PROTECT+ or − enables or disables Disk Protect.

/LIGHT+ or − enables or disables Disk Light.

/PARK parks the hard disk heads on all drives.

/UNINSTALL removes or uninstalls Disk Monitor protection.

DISKREET

The Diskreet utility provides a high degree of data security for your files. Diskreet encrypts and decrypts files, and creates password-protected disk drives called Ndisks.

Syntax

To run Diskreet from the DOS prompt, type:

DISKREET *switches*

Description

The Diskreet switches are as follows:

/ENCRYPT:*filespec*	encrypts the file or files specified by the file specification.
/DECRYPT:*filename*	decrypts the specified file.
/PASSWORD:*xxxxxx*	specifies the password for file encryption or decryption.
/SHOW:*drive*	opens the Ndisk defined by *drive* so that it is visible.
/HIDE:*drive*	hides the Ndisk defined by *drive*.
/CLOSE	closes all open Ndisks.
/ON	enables the Diskreet device driver.
/OFF	disables the Diskreet device driver.

DISK TOOLS

The Disk Tools utility comprises six smaller utilities that let you make a disk into a bootable disk, recover from the DOS RECOVER command, revive a hard-to-read diskette, mark specific bad clusters, and make or restore a rescue disk containing a copy of the system area of your hard disk.

Syntax

To run Disk Tools from the DOS command line, type:

DISKTOOL

Description

There are no command line switches for Disk Tools.

FILEFIND

FileFind locates lost or misplaced files by searching all available drives for the file name or for data contained in the file. You can also use FileFind to change file attributes and the creation date or time on a file.

Syntax

To run FileFind from the DOS command line, type:

FILEFIND *filename search-text switches*

Description

The FileFind parameters fall into two main categories: the parameters that complete the file specification and the optional switches that tell FileFind how to operate.

The file specification can include:

.	searches the entire current drive.
.*.*	searches the current directory.
:.*	extends the search to all drives.

The *search-text* specifies the text that you want FileFind to search for; if it contains any spaces, you must enclose the entire search string in quotes.

The following switches are optional:

/S includes all files in subdirectories in the search.

/C searches the current directory.

/CS makes the search case sensitive.

To set a file attribute, use one of the following switches with a plus sign. To turn off a file attribute, use the same switches but add a minus sign.

/+ or –A	sets or resets the file's archive bit.
/+ or –R	sets or resets the file's read-only bit.
/+ or –HID	sets or resets the file's hidden bit.
/+ or –SYS	sets or resets the file's system bit.
/CLEAR	clears all the attributes from the file.
/D*date*	sets the date of the file to *date.* If you don't include a date, the date is cleared.
/T*time*	sets the time of the file to *time.* If you don't include a time, the time is cleared.
/NOW	sets the file date and time to the current date and time.
/TARGET:*drive*	tests to see if the specified files will fit on the target *drive.*
/O:*filename*	saves the list to the file specified in *filename.*
/BATCH	automatically exits the program when the search is complete.

FILE FIX

File Fix repairs damaged Lotus 1-2-3, Symphony, or dBASE files. File Fix can also repair zapped dBASE files.

Syntax

To run File Fix from the DOS prompt, type:

FILEFIX *filename*

Description

The only optional parameter you can use with File Fix is a file name. If you use a file name, File Fix automatically identifies the kind of file you are repairing and skips the first two File Fix windows.

FILESAVE

FileSave is a small terminate-and-stay-resident program that moves deleted or erased files to another part of your disk to protect them from being overwritten. These protected files are automatically removed from your disk after a specified period of time.

Syntax

To use FileSave from the DOS prompt, type:

FILESAVE *switches*

Description

You can use the following switches with FileSave:

/STATUS	displays the current FileSave status.
/ON	enables FileSave if FileSave was turned off.

| /OFF | turns off FileSave but keeps the program in memory. |
| /UNINSTALL | uninstalls FileSave as long as it was the last TSR program loaded into memory. |

IMAGE

Image takes an instant picture of the system area (boot record, file allocation tables, and root directory information) and stores the information in a file in the root directory of your hard disk. UnFormat and UnErase will both use the Image file if it is present.

Syntax

To use Image from the DOS prompt, type:

IMAGE *drive switch*

If you have several logical drives, you can protect all of them if you include a separate Image statement for each drive in your AUTOEXEC.BAT file. For example, to protect drives C, D, and E, add:

IMAGE C:
IMAGE D:
IMAGE E:

to your AUTOEXEC.BAT file.

Description

There is only one switch you can use with Image:

/NOBACKUP prevents the creation of a backup copy of the Image data file.

NORTON

The NORTON program is a shell that you can use to run all the other utilities. You can also add references to your own applications programs into the NORTON program.

Syntax

To run the NORTON program, type:

NORTON *switches*

Description

The switches you can use with the NORTON program control the mouse cursor, the radio boxes, and the checkboxes.

/BW	forces the color display to monochrome.
/LCD	forces the NORTON program to use the LCD color set.
/G0	changes the mouse cursor from an arrow to a square character, and changes the radio buttons and check boxes from graphics characters to to parentheses.
/G1	changes the mouse cursor only; leaves the radio buttons and the checkboxes as graphics characters.
/NOZOOM	turns off the zoom for dialog boxes.

NORTON CACHE PROGRAMS

There are two hard disk caching programs provided with the Norton Utilities; NCACHE-F emphasizes speed, and NCACHE-S conserves memory.

Syntax

Use only one of the cache programs on your system at a time. You can load them from the DOS prompt by typing:

NCACHE-F *switches*

or

NCACHE-S *switches*

but including them in your CONFIG.SYS or AUTOEXEC.BAT file is a much more convenient way of loading them.

Description

There are many different options that you can use to configure the cache programs to your own individual working environment. Because there are potentially hundreds of different combinations of computer hardware and applications software, it is very difficult to suggest values for the following parameters. You should follow the general guidelines given here, and then experiment with different settings until you find the combination that works best for you.

The following parameters apply to both NCACHE-F and NCACHE-S:

/BLOCK=*nnn*	sets the size of the cache blocks (in kilobytes). Larger blocks allow the cache table to be smaller, and smaller blocks make the cache buffer more efficient.
/EXT=*nnn*	uses this amount of extended memory (in kilobytes).

/EXT=−*nnn*   leaves this amount of extended memory (in kilobytes) free for other application programs. If you do not make an extended memory specification, the cache program will use all the extended memory it can find.

/EXP=*nnn*   uses this amount of expanded memory for the cache (specified in kilobytes).

/EXP=−*nnn*   leaves this amount of expanded memory (specified in kilobytes) free. If you do not make an expanded memory specification, the cache program will use as much expanded memory as it can find.

/DOS=*nnn*   uses this much conventional DOS memory (specified in kilobytes).

/DOS=−*nnn*   leaves this much conventional DOS memory free (specified in kilobytes). If you don't make a DOS memory specification, the cache program will create a cache of 128K in size. If you have extended or expanded memory, do not use this option because it reduces the amount of DOS memory space available to your applications programs.

/INI=*path*   specifies the path of the parameter file containing the installation options.

/RESET   resets the cache statistics shown on the status screen.

/HELP or ?   displays a help screen.

/STATUS	displays the status screen detailing cache statistics.
/UNINSTALL	removes the cache if it was loaded from AUTOEXEC.BAT or the DOS prompt. You cannot remove the cache if you loaded it using CONFIG.SYS.
/USEHIDOS YES or NO	uses high memory provided by memory managers such as QEMM or 386-to-the-Max, which can reduce the requirement for main DOS memory to as little as 12K. The usual default is NO.
/USEHMA YES or NO	uses XMS high memory made available by extended memory managers such as HIMEM.SYS or EME.EXE. The default is YES.
/SAVE	saves the current cache configuration as the default setting.
/PRINT	copies the display to the printer.
/PAUSE	pauses display scrolling.

The following parameters apply only to NCACHE-F:

/DELAY=*ss.hh*	specifies a time delay in seconds and hundredths of seconds to delay disk writes. If you cache a floppy disk, do not remove the disk from the drive until the write buffer has been cleared; otherwise, you will lose data. If this data includes an update to the FAT, the results could be devastating. The default is no delay.

/QUICK ON or OFF	if QUICK is set to ON, and the Intelli-Writes switch is also on, DOS prompts are shown on the screen even though the current disk operation may not be complete. If you use this setting and cache a floppy disk drive, be sure that all write operations are complete before you remove the floppy disk; otherwise, you may lose data. The default is QUICK OFF which completes all write operations before returning the DOS prompt.

The following options apply to both cache programs. For those options with a + or − designation, the + sign enables the option and the − sign disables the option.

/+ or −A	enables or disables disk caching.
/+ or −C	enables or disables the caching of additional data.
/F	flushes or empties the cache. All remaining writes are written to disk before the buffer is reinitialized.
/G=*nnn*	specifies the Group Sector Size, which limits the amount of data loaded into the buffer from each read. The default value is 128, equivalent to 64K.
/+ or −W	enables or disables write-through caching. If you enable this setting, the cache copies writes to the disk and to the cache. If you turn it off, writes are not copied to the cache. This option has no effect if Intelli-Writes are on.

These final options only apply to NCACHE-F:

/+ or −I   enables or disables IntelliWrites. If you turn on this setting, you accelerate disk writes and return control to the application program before the write is complete.

/R=*nnn*   specifies how many sectors ahead the cache should read. R=*nnn* always allows read ahead, and R=D*nnn* allows read ahead only if the sectors are sequential and not random. R can be set to a value between 0 and 15. R=0 or R=D0 disable the read ahead setting.

/+ or −S   enables or disables SmartReads. Enabling SmartReads allows the cache to read additional data before writing data. This will almost always improve the performance of your computer, because programs usually make more reads than writes. If you turn SmartReads off, all data must be written to the disk before any new data can be read.

NORTON CHANGE DIRECTORY

Run from the DOS prompt, NCD lets you change to another directory without having to type the complete path for the directory. NCD also has a full-screen mode that enables you to create, change, delete, or rename directories.

Syntax

To run NCD in full-screen mode, enter

NCD *switches*

Description

You can use the following as the *switches* parameter:

/R   rereads the directory structure on the disk.

/N   tells NCD to ignore the changes made—to not write them to the TREEINFO.NCD file.

/V:*label*   writes an 11-character volume label on the disk.

Syntax for Command-Line Mode

To create a directory directly from the DOS prompt, enter:

NCD MD *directoryspec*

To remove a directory without running NCD in full-screen mode, type:

NCD RD *directoryspec*

You can also enter:

NCD *directoryspec switches*

to make *directoryspec* the current directory.

Description

directoryspec specifies which directory NCD should create, remove, or change to. You do not need to enter the complete path, only enough of the directory name to make it unique so that NCD can identify it. You can also use the /R, /N, and /V switches in this mode.

NORTON CONTROL CENTER

NCC controls the computer's hardware, including the display, keyboard, mouse, serial ports, battery powered clock, and the country information. You can run it in full-screen mode to use the organized menu and graphical display window, or you can run it from the DOS prompt if you saved your settings in a file, or if you know exactly which switch you want to use. If you need to adjust several items, you will find it quicker and easier to run NCC in full-screen mode.

Syntax

To run NCC with a previously saved file, you can type:

NCC *filename* /SET

or if you want to work with the stopwatches, type:

NCC *stopwatch-switches*

or if you want to use the quick switches, type:

NCC *quick-switches*

Description

You can choose from the following stopwatch switches:

/START:*n*	starts stopwatch number *n* (*n* can be one through four). The default is stopwatch number one.
/STOP:*n*	stops stopwatch number *n* (*n* can be one through four). The default is stopwatch number one.
/N	suppresses the display of the current time and date.
/L	displays the current time and date at the left side of the monitor screen instead of at the right.
/C:*comment*	displays any text as a comment.

You can also use these quick switches:

/FAST   sets the keyboard type rate to the fastest speed possible. Be careful because this alters the key-repeat timing, and may cause you to make typing errors.

/BW80   sets the monitor display mode to monochrome, 25 rows by 80 columns.

/CO80   sets the monitor display mode to color, 25 rows by 80 columns.

/*nn*   sets the number of lines for EGA or VGA adapters (for EGA, *nn* can be 25, 35, or 43; for VGA, *nn* can be 25, 40, or 50).

NORTON DISK DOCTOR II

NDD automatically finds and corrects logical and physical errors on hard and floppy disks. You can run NDD in either full-screen mode or in command-line mode. Each mode enables you to test the disk completely or partially.

Syntax for Full-Screen Mode

To run NDD in full-screen mode, enter:

NDD *switches*

Syntax for Command-Line Mode

To run NDD directly from the DOS prompt, type:

NDD *drive drive switches*

Description

The following switches modify the NDD command:

drive	selects the drive to be tested. You can select more than one drive for testing at the same time if you separate each drive letter from the next with a space.
/QUICK	tests the system area, but not the data area.
/COMPLETE	tests both the system area and the data area.
/R:*filename*	sends the NDD report to the file specified by *filename*.
/RA:*filename*	appends the NDD report to the file specified by *filename*.
/X:*drive*	excludes the drives specified by *drive* from physical testing.
/FORMAT	formats a physically bad track.

SAFE FORMAT

Safe Format is a fast and safe alternative to the DOS FORMAT command; it lets you easily recover from an accidentally reformatted disk because it does not overwrite the existing data when you format a disk.

Syntax

To run Safe Format in full-screen mode, type:

SFORMAT

To run it from the command line, type:

SFORMAT *drive switches*

Description

You can use any of the following switches to specify a particular format for a disk:

/A	puts Safe Format into automatic mode which is useful in batch files.
/S	copies the DOS system files to the disk.
/B	leaves space on the disk for the DOS system files so you can add them later.
/V:*label*	adds a volume name, specified by *label*, of 11 characters or less.
/1	selects single-sided formatting.
/4	formats a 360K floppy disk in a 1.2MB drive.
/8	formats 8 sectors per track.
/N:*n*	selects the number of sectors per track (*n* can be 8, 9, 15, or 18 sectors per track).
/T:*n*	selects the number of tracks (*n* can be either 40 or 80 tracks).
/*size*	selects the size of the floppy disk. For example, use /720 for a 720K floppy disk.
/Q	selects the quick format. This places a new system area on the disk, leaving everything else intact.
/D	selects the DOS format in which everything on the disk is erased.

SPEED DISK

Speed Disk optimizes your hard disk performance by eliminating file fragmentation and by reorganizing the layout of files and directories on your disk.

Syntax

To run Speed Disk, type:

SPEEDISK *drive switches*

Description

You can use the following switches with Speed Disk:

drive	instructs Speed Disk to use this drive.
/C	selects complete disk optimization.
/D	selects optimize directories only.
/U	selects unfragment files only.
/Q	selects unfragment free space.
/V	turns on read-after-write verify.
/B	reboots your computer when the optimization is complete.

If you are sorting files, you can reverse the sort order (making it descending) by adding a minus sign after the sort-key letter:

/SN[-]	sorts files by name.
/SE[-]	sorts files by extension.
/SD[-]	sorts files by date.
/SS[-]	sorts files by size.

SYSTEM INFO

System Info displays information about your computer's configuration and calculates three performance indicators.

Syntax

To run System Info, enter:

SYSINFO *switches*

Description

You can use the following switches with System Info:

/AUTO:*n* selects the automatic mode. System Info cycles through all information screens, displaying each one for *n* seconds before moving on to the next screen.

/DEMO cycles through the benchmark tests.

/TSR prints a list of all your terminate-and-stay-resident (TSR) programs to the screen or to a file (if you use DOS's redirection capabilities).

/N skips the live memory test, which will require you to reboot your computer should it fail.

/SOUND beeps between the CPU tests.

/SUMMARY prints the System Info summary screen. This screen is identical to the output from the old SI program released with version 4.5 of the Norton Utilities.

UNERASE

UnErase finds and recovers accidentally erased files in automatic or in manual mode.

Syntax

To run UnErase, type:

UNERASE *filespec*

Description

You can use a file specification with UnErase. If you know the original file name, including the first letter, you can use UnErase from the DOS prompt. For example, typing:

UNERASE MYFILE.TXT

recovers the file without UnErase going into full-screen mode.

If you have forgotten the first letter, specify the ? DOS wildcard character instead, and UnErase opens into full-screen mode. For example, type:

UNERASE ?YFILE.TXT

and use the normal UnErase techniques to recover the file.

UNFORMAT

UnFormat recovers data and program files from a hard disk after it has been reformatted by the DOS FORMAT command.

Syntax

To run UnFormat, type:

UNFORMAT

Description

The only parameter you can use with UnFormat is the drive you want to unformat:

UNFORMAT *drive*

WIPEINFO

WipeInfo completely obliterates deleted files so that they can never be recovered, not even by the Norton Utilities.

Syntax

You can use WipeInfo in several different ways:

WIPEINFO *drive disk-switch common-switches*

or

WIPEINFO *filespec file-switches common-switches*

Description

You can use one disk switch with WipeInfo:

/E   specifies that only the erased or unused data space should be overwritten.

Choose from the following file switches:

/N   puts WipeInfo into delete mode. WipeInfo deletes the files, but does not wipe them. This has the same effect as the DOS ERASE or DELETE commands.

/K   wipes the unused slack space at the end of a file.

/S   extends the operation to subdirectories.

Choose from these common switches:

/G*n*   selects a government-specified algorithm for wiping, in which *n* determines the number of times the wipe operation is performed (the default is 3; the maximum is 999).

/R*n*   sets the repeat factor for the number of times the data will be overwritten (the default is 1; the maximum is 999).

/V*n*   sets the value to be used for overwriting and can be any number from 0 to 255. The default is 0 unless you have used the /G switch, in which case /V*n* equals 245 decimal or F6 hex.

Troubleshooting

CHAPTER **24** _____

MOST OF THE CHAPTERS IN THIS BOOK HAVE DEALT
with a specific utility, describing how to use it in detail. This final
chapter describes how you can use the remarkable troubleshooting facilities available in the NORTON program to help understand and solve your disk related problems.

USING THE ADVISE PULL-DOWN MENU IN THE NORTON PROGRAM

The selections in the Advise pull-down menu work in much
the same way as the context-sensitive help that is available
throughout the rest of the Norton Utilities. You select one topic
from the list using the up and down arrow keys or the mouse,
and then choose the Expand box to see a more detailed explana-
tion. This second level window often includes specific suggestions about which of the Norton Utilities you can use to help
solve your problem. If DOS reports an error that you are unfamiliar with, you can learn more about the error message from
the selections in the Advise pull-down menu, and then you can
run the appropriate Norton Utility to fix the problem. The
selections in the Advise menu are divided into three categories,
with each category defining a different group of problems. In
the next three sections, I will describe how to use each of these
menu selections.

COMMON DISK PROBLEMS

Let's assume you are having disk problems, and you run the
NORTON program to access the Advise menu. First you choose

the Advise pull-down menu, and then you select Common Disk Problems. This opens the window shown in Figure 24.1. You think the problem has something to do with cross-linked files. Move the highlight in the **Problem** box until it is on the second selection, Cross-Linked Files, and then choose the **Expand** box. Another window opens to display a more complete description of the proposed solution, as shown in Figure 24.2. If you choose the **Run Disk Doctor** box, you can actually run NDD from within the help window to diagnose the problem disk and fix the cross-linked files. Choose the **Done** box to return to the list of errors, and choose it again to return to the main NORTON program menu.

DOS ERROR MESSAGES

The second selection from the Advise pull-down menu displays a list of the common DOS errors you might see from time to time. The list includes many disk related error messages, but it is by no means a complete list of all the DOS errors. Some of

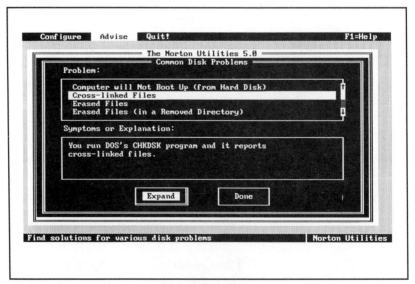

Figure 24.1: The first Common Disk Problems window

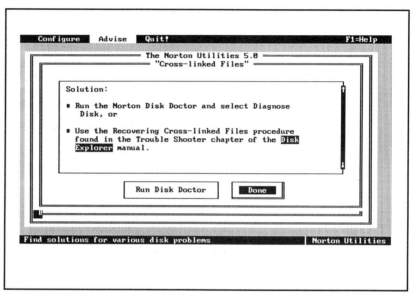

Figure 24.2: You can run NDD from the help window if you want

the error messages are relatively insignificant, such as:

Abort, Retry, Ignore, Fail?

which often results if you try to read a drive before you have inserted a floppy disk. However, some of the other errors can panic even the most seasoned computer user. Error messages such as:

Invalid drive specification

which can mean that your partition table has been corrupted or that the boot track has been destroyed, should not be ignored because they can indicate a deteriorating hard disk.

If you do see the error message "Invalid drive specification," and you know that you used to be able to access that drive, load the NORTON program, select the Advise pull-down menu, and choose the Invalid drive specification error message from the list of DOS Error Messages. This displays the window shown in Figure 24.3. When you select the Expand box, another window

Figure 24.3: Choose the appropriate error message from the list on the
screen

opens, as Figure 24.4 shows. The window in Figure 24.4 displays
more detailed information about the error message and offers
two sets of reasons why the error occurred: the disk has a bad
partition table or boot track, or the disk was formatted with one
version of DOS, and you are trying to read it with a different
version.

The next step is to run the Norton Disk Doctor directly from
this window so that you can check the partition table and the
boot track. You can also select the **Done** box to return to the previous window.

CHKDSK ERROR MESSAGES

You can use the DOS command CHKDSK to check the formatted size and the amount of free space on a disk. CHKDSK
also reports the amount of space used by hidden files, directories, user files, and bad sectors, as well as detailing the
memory size and the amount of free memory available in your
computer. CHKDSK tests for logical errors in the file allocation

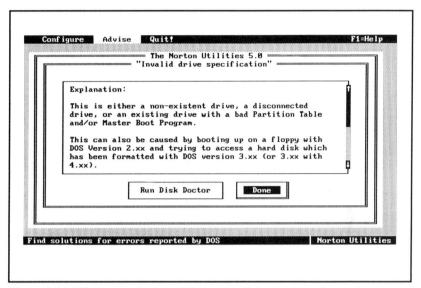

Figure 24.4: The next window offers more information about the error you selected in the previous screen

tables and the directories, and can output a series of error messages depending on what it finds.

You can also use the CHKDSK command to give you a report on the fragmentation of a file. CHKDSK reports that the file contains a number of non-contiguous blocks if the file is split up into pieces.

If you see this error, load the Norton program and select CHKDSK Error Messages from the Advise pull-down menu. Move the highlight to the Contains xxx non-contiguous blocks message as Figure 24.5 shows, and select the Expand box.

The next window contains a description of the CHKDSK error message telling you that the file is fragmented, or broken into several pieces. Because the file is in several different areas of the disk, it will take longer to load all the pieces than it would take to load the file if it were in only one piece. To fix this file fragmentation, the window recommends that you run the disk optimizer Speed Disk, as shown in Figure 24.6.

After you start Speed Disk, you can generate a detailed report about the fragmentation of all your files and then choose an

Figure 24.5: Choose the appropriate CHKDSK error message

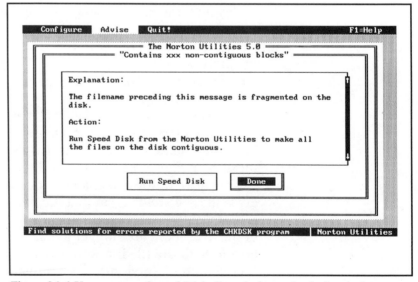

Figure 24.6: You can run Speed Disk directly from the help window to fix file fragmentation

appropriate optimization method. If you don't want to run Speed Disk, select the Done box to return to the list of CHKDSK errors, and then select Done again to return to the main NORTON menu.

APPENDIX

Using Binary and ASCII Files

APPENDIX

THROUGHOUT THIS BOOK I HAVE REFERRED TO ASCII and program files. As you can work with both types of files when you run the Norton Utilities, acquiring a better understanding of what these file types are and the numbering systems they rely on will enable you to enhance your productivity. As you may know, ASCII files are often called text or nondocument (this last term comes from word processors) files. Program files are actually binary files.

BINARY FILES

Binary files contain instructions and data (encoded as numbers) that your system's processor can decode and act on. Such files will execute only on a specific microprocessor or microprocessor family. For example, a binary file prepared for an Intel microprocessor will not run on a Motorola microprocessor, and vice versa, without special software.

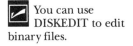 You can use DISKEDIT to edit binary files.

You cannot read or edit binary files with a word processor. Programmers initially write programs in human-readable computer languages, which are then *compiled, interpreted,* or *assembled* by the computer into binary files.

ASCII FILES

ASCII files are text files. ASCII (pronounced "as-key") stands for the American Standard Code for Information Interchange. ASCII codes represent letters, punctuation symbols, numbers, mathematical symbols, and so on. When you type a character, what the computer actually "reads" is the ASCII code for that

APP.

The standard ASCII codes use seven of the eight bits in a byte.

character. You can also employ ASCII codes to control devices (such as monitors and printers).

Each ASCII character is represented by a unique integer value, which is commonly referred to as a *decimal value*. The values 0 through 31 are used as control codes, and the values 32 through 127 are used to represent numbers, the letters of the alphabet, and common punctuation symbols. The entire set (0 through 127) is called *standard* ASCII. All computers that use ASCII characters can understand the standard ASCII set, although not all can work with the *extended character set*, which are the values 128 through 255. These values encode line-drawing characters and less common symbols and punctuation marks, for example, Greek letters. (We'll examine this set shortly.)

ASCII CONTROL CHARACTERS

The *control code* characters (0 to 31) are reserved for special purposes that usually have to do with controlling devices or communications.

Codes 1–4 are generally not used in modern microcomputer communications.

Codes 1 through 4, which stand for SOH, STX, ETX, and EOT, are used in communications to indicate the start and end of the transmission (codes 1 and 4) and its text (codes 2 and 3). Other codes are used to control the flow of transmitted data: for example, ACK (acknowledge) and NAK (negative acknowledge) indicate whether the data was received successfully; and ENQ (enquire), SYN (synchronize), ETB (end-of-transmission block), and CAN (cancel) are also used to control the flow. Additional codes punctuate the flow of information; FS (file separator), GS (group separator), RS (record separator), and US (unit separator) all fall into this category.

The VT sequence is rarely used to control devices.

Several codes are used to control peripheral devices, particularly printers. The CR (carriage return), LF (line feed), FF (form feed, which is sometimes referred to as *new page*), HT (horizontal tab), BS (backspace), and VT (vertical tab) sequences are important codes in device control. For a complete listing of the control codes, see Table A.1.

Table A.1: The ASCII Control Codes

DECIMAL VALUE	HEX VALUE	KEYS TO PRESS	NAME
000	00	Crtl-@	NUL (nul character)
001	01	Ctrl-A	SOH (start of header)
002	02	Crtl-B	STX (start of text)
003	03	Ctrl-C	ETX (end of text)
004	04	Ctrl-D	EOT (end of transmission)
005	05	Ctrl-E	ENQ (enquire)
006	06	Ctrl-F	ACK (acknowledge)
007	07	Ctrl-G	BEL (bell)
008	08	Ctrl-H	BS (backspace)
009	09	Ctrl-I	HT (horizonal tab)
010	0A	Ctrl-J	LF (line feed)
011	0B	Ctrl-K	VT (vertical tab)
012	0C	Ctrl-L	FF (form feed or new page)
013	0D	Ctrl-M	CR (carriage return)
014	0E	Ctrl-N	SO (shift out)
015	0F	Ctrl-O	SI (shift in)
016	10	Ctrl-P	DLE (data link escape)
017	11	Ctrl-Q	DC1 (X-ON)
018	12	Ctrl-R	DC2 (tape)
019	13	Ctrl-S	DC3 (X-OFF)
020	14	Ctrl-T	DC4 (no tape)
021	15	Ctrl-U	NAK (negative acknowledge)

Table A.1: The ASCII Control Codes (continued)

DECIMAL VALUE	HEX VALUE	KEYS TO PRESS	NAME
022	16	Ctrl-V	SYN (synchronize)
023	17	Crtl-W	ETB (end of transmission block)
024	18	Ctrl-X	CAN (cancel)
025	19	Ctrl-Y	EM (end of medium)
026	1A	Ctrl-Z	SUB (substitute)
027	1B	Ctrl-[	ESC (escape)
028	1C	Ctrl-/	FS (file separator)
029	1D	Ctrl-]	GS (group separator)
030	1E	Ctrl-^	RS (record separator)
031	1F	Ctrl-_	US (unit separator)

Ctrl-S and Ctrl-Q are often used as pause and restart commands, and Ctrl-[produces the Esc character. An escape sequence—consisting of the Esc character, followed by one or more other characters in a specific order—is a common way of controlling complex devices such as terminals and printers, which have more capabilities than can be controlled by the individual ASCII control characters alone. (See your modem or printer manual for more details.)

Ctrl-S is often called X-OFF, and Ctrl-Q is often referred to as X-ON.

THE EXTENDED CHARACTER SET

The IBM extended character set starts where the standard ASCII set leaves off. The next available decimal code is 128, and the extended set runs from 128 to 255. Its characters, which include the PC line-drawing set, mathematical symbols, and graphics characters, are not standard on computers that are not compatible with IBM's microcomputers. Word processing

255 is the largest decimal value that can be represented by using all eight of the bits in one byte.

programs have different ways of allowing you to use the characters in the extended ASCII set. In WordStar, for example, you can display these characters by simultaneously pressing the Alt key and typing the decimal value of the appropriate character on the numeric keypad (you cannot use the regular number keys for this purpose). Printers vary in their ability to print these characters.

Because different languages (for example, Norwegian and Portuguese) use different characters and keyboard layouts, there are several language-specific ASCII tables. These tables use decimal codes 128–255 for necessary characters that are not provided by the standard ASCII set. Each of these tables is called a *code page*. See *Encyclopedia DOS* by Judd Robbins for information about code pages.

Table A.2 lists the standard and IBM extended ASCII characters and their decimal and hexadecimal values.

Table A.2:   The Standard and Extended ASCII Sets

CHARACTER	DECIMAL VALUE	HEX VALUE	CHARACTER	DECIMAL VALUE	HEX VALUE
	000	00	◘	008	08
☺	001	01	○	009	09
☻	002	02	◙	010	0A
♥	003	03	♂	011	0B
♦	004	04	♀	012	0C
♣	005	05	♪	013	0D
♠	006	06	♫	014	0E
•	007	07	☼	015	0F

Table A.2: The Standard and Extended ASCII Sets (continued)

CHARACTER	DECIMAL VALUE	HEX VALUE	CHARACTER	DECIMAL VALUE	HEX VALUE
▶	016	10	"	034	22
◀	017	11	#	035	23
↕	018	12	$	036	24
‼	019	13	%	037	25
¶	020	14	&	038	26
§	021	15	'	039	27
▬	022	16	(	040	28
↨	023	17	)	041	29
↑	024	18	✳	042	2A
↓	025	19	+	043	2B
→	026	1A	,	044	2C
←	027	1B	–	045	2D
∟	028	1C	.	046	2E
↔	029	1D	/	047	2F
▲	030	1E	0	048	30
▼	031	1F	1	049	31
	032	20	2	050	32
!	033	21	3	051	33

Table A.2: The Standard and Extended ASCII Sets (continued)

CHARACTER	DECIMAL VALUE	HEX VALUE	CHARACTER	DECIMAL VALUE	HEX VALUE
4	052	34	F	070	46
5	053	35	G	071	47
6	054	36	H	072	48
7	055	37	I	073	49
8	056	38	J	074	4A
9	057	39	K	075	4B
:	058	3A	L	076	4C
;	059	3B	M	077	4D
<	060	3C	N	078	4E
=	061	3D	O	079	4F
>	062	3E	P	080	50
?	063	3F	Q	081	51
@	064	40	R	082	52
A	065	41	S	083	53
B	066	42	T	084	54
C	067	43	U	085	55
D	068	44	V	086	56
E	069	45	W	087	57

Table A.2: The Standard and Extended ASCII Sets (continued)

CHARACTER	DECIMAL VALUE	HEX VALUE	CHARACTER	DECIMAL VALUE	HEX VALUE
X	088	58	j	106	6A
Y	089	59	k	107	6B
Z	090	5A	l	108	6C
[	091	5B	m	109	6D
\	092	5C	n	110	6E
]	093	5D	o	111	6F
^	094	5E	p	112	70
_	095	5F	q	113	71
`	096	60	r	114	72
a	097	61	s	115	73
b	098	62	t	116	74
c	099	63	u	117	75
d	100	64	v	118	76
e	101	65	w	119	77
f	102	66	x	120	78
g	103	67	y	121	79
h	104	68	z	122	7A
i	105	69	{	123	7B

Table A.2: The Standard and Extended ASCII Sets (continued)

Character	Decimal Value	Hex Value	Character	Decimal Value	Hex Value
¦	124	7C	Ä	142	8E
}	125	7D	Å	143	8F
~	126	7E	É	144	90
∧	127	7F	æ	145	91
Ç	128	80	Æ	146	92
ü	129	81	ô	147	93
é	130	82	ö	148	94
â	131	83	ò	149	95
ä	132	84	û	150	96
à	133	85	ù	151	97
å	134	86	ÿ	152	98
ç	135	87	ö	153	99
ê	136	88	Ü	154	9A
ë	137	89	¢	155	9B
è	138	8A	£	156	9C
ï	139	8B	¥	157	9D
î	140	8C	₧	158	9E
ì	141	8D	ƒ	159	9F

Table A.2: The Standard and Extended ASCII Sets (continued)

CHARACTER	DECIMAL VALUE	HEX VALUE	CHARACTER	DECIMAL VALUE	HEX VALUE
á	160	A0	▓	178	B2
í	161	A1	│	179	B3
ó	162	A2	┤	180	B4
ú	163	A3	╡	181	B5
ñ	164	A4	╢	182	B6
Ñ	165	A5	╖	183	B7
ª	166	A6	╕	184	B8
º	167	A7	╣	185	B9
¿	168	A8	║	186	BA
⌐	169	A9	╗	187	BB
¬	170	AA	╝	188	BC
½	171	AB	╜	189	BD
¼	172	AC	╛	190	BE
¡	173	AD	┐	191	BF
«	174	AE	└	192	C0
»	175	AF	┴	193	C1
░	176	B0	┬	194	C2
▒	177	B1	├	195	C3

Table A.2: The Standard and Extended ASCII Sets (continued)

CHARACTER	DECIMAL VALUE	HEX VALUE	CHARACTER	DECIMAL VALUE	HEX VALUE
─	196	C4	π	214	D6
┼	197	C5	╫	215	D7
╞	198	C6	╪	216	D8
╟	199	C7	┘	217	D9
╚	200	C8	┌	218	DA
╔	201	C9	█	219	DB
╩	202	CA	▄	220	DC
╦	203	CB	▌	221	DD
╠	204	CC	▐	222	DE
═	205	CD	▀	223	DF
╬	206	CE	α	224	E0
╧	207	CF	β	225	E1
╨	208	D0	Γ	226	E2
╤	209	D1	π	227	E3
╥	210	D2	Σ	228	E4
╙	211	D3	σ	229	E5
╘	212	D4	μ	230	E6
╒	213	D5	τ	231	E7

Table A.2: The Standard and Extended ASCII Sets (continued)

CHARACTER	DECIMAL VALUE	HEX VALUE	CHARACTER	DECIMAL VALUE	HEX VALUE
Φ	232	E8	Γ	244	F4
θ	233	E9	J	245	F5
Ω	234	EA	÷	246	F6
δ	235	EB	≈	247	F7
∞	236	EC	°	248	F8
ø	237	ED	•	249	F9
∈	238	EE	·	250	FA
∩	239	EF	√	251	FB
≡	240	F0	n	252	FC
±	241	F1	z	253	FD
≥	242	F2	■	254	FE
≤	243	F3		255	FF

A NOTE ON DIFFERENT NUMBERING SCHEMES

As you have seen in the previous section, a computer responds to various numbering systems. Understanding these systems will make it easier for you to work with your computer—you'll have a better grasp of what is happening and why. The main thing to remember about these numbering systems is that they are different methods of representing the same thing.

DECIMAL

The *decimal* system is the system people are most familiar with, as it is the first numbering system taught in school. It counts in base 10 using ten digits—0, 1, 2, 3, 4, 5, 6, 7, 8, and 9—to represent numbers.

The position of each digit is important and contributes to the value of the number. The right-hand digit is the *ones* place, the second position (moving to the left) is the *tens* place, the third is the *hundreds* place, and so on. To determine a decimal number's value, you can multiply each digit by its position and then add the individual sums together. For example, the decimal number 1234 equals:

$$(1 \times 4) + (10 \times 3) + (100 \times 2) + (1000 \times 1)$$
$$= 4 \quad + \quad 30 \quad + \quad 200 \quad + \quad 1000$$

BINARY

The *binary* system uses only two digits, 0 and 1, which represent the only possible states of a bit—off or on. Counting in binary is relatively straightforward, although it is rather different from the traditional decimal-numbering scheme.

In the binary system, the weight of each position doubles each time you move a position to the left, instead of increasing by a factor of ten as in the decimal system. To convert the binary number 1011 into decimal, for example, you would perform the following calculation:

$$(1 \times 2^0) + (1 \times 2^1) + (0 \times 2^2) + (1 \times 2^3)$$
$$= 1 \quad + \quad 2 \quad + \quad 0 \quad + \quad 8$$
$$= 11$$

The top row of Figure A.1 shows the place values of the first eight places in the binary system. The bottom row shows the binary equivalent of decimal 11.

The binary system represents the exact state of the bits in a byte, but it is inconvenient when all you want to know is the value of the byte and don't care about the status of its individual bits. In these cases, it is often easier to work with the hexadecimal system.

HEXADECIMAL

The third major numbering scheme used when working with computers is the *hexadecimal* system. This is often abbreviated to hex, or even to the single letter H. Sometimes even the H is omitted, and you have to guess from the context that the number is expressed in hexadecimal.

The hexadecimal system counts in base 16, using the digits 0 through 9 and A through F in the sequence: 0, 1, 2, 3, 4, 5, 6, 7, 8, 9, A, B, C, D, E, and F. The decimal and binary equivalents for this sequence are shown in Table A.3. In a hexadecimal number, each digit's value is 16 times greater than the digit immediately to its right.

For example, to convert the hex number FF to decimal, remembering that F in hex is equivalent to 15 in the decimal system, perform the following calculation:

$$(15 \times 16^0) + (15 \times 16^1)$$
$$= \quad 15 \quad + \quad 240$$
$$= \quad 255$$

Hexadecimal notation is a convenient way to express byte values because a single hexadecimal digit is equivalent to four binary digits. Because there are eight binary digits in a byte, the value of any byte can be expressed as only two hex digits.

The hexadecimal digits A–F are almost always uppercase.

PLACE VALUES	128	64	32	16	8	4	2	1
BINARY DIGITS	0	0	0	0	1	0	1	1

Figure A.1: Decimal 11 in the binary system

Table A.3: A Comparison of Decimal, Binary, and Hexadecimal Numbers

DECIMAL	BINARY	HEX	DECIMAL	BINARY	HEX
0	0	0	8	1000	8
1	1	1	9	1001	9
2	10	2	10	1010	A
3	11	3	11	1011	B
4	100	4	12	1100	C
5	101	5	13	1101	D
6	110	6	14	1110	E
7	111	7	15	1111	F

Index

SYBEX ®

TO JOIN THE SYBEX MAILING LIST OR ORDER BOOKS
PLEASE COMPLETE THIS FORM

NAME _____ COMPANY _____

STREET _____ CITY _____

STATE _____ ZIP _____

☐ PLEASE MAIL ME MORE INFORMATION ABOUT **SYBEX** TITLES

ORDER FORM (There is no obligation to order)

PLEASE SEND ME THE FOLLOWING:

TITLE	QTY	PRICE
_____	___	___
_____	___	___
_____	___	___
_____	___	___

TOTAL BOOK ORDER   ___ $___

CUSTOMER SIGNATURE _____

SHIPPING AND HANDLING PLEASE ADD $2.00 PER BOOK VIA UPS   _____

FOR OVERSEAS SURFACE ADD $5.25 PER BOOK PLUS $4.40 REGISTRATION FEE   _____

FOR OVERSEAS AIRMAIL ADD $18.25 PER BOOK PLUS $4.40 REGISTRATION FEE   _____

CALIFORNIA RESIDENTS PLEASE ADD APPLICABLE SALES TAX   _____

TOTAL AMOUNT PAYABLE   _____

☐ CHECK ENCLOSED   ☐ VISA
☐ MASTERCARD   ☐ AMERICAN EXPRESS

ACCOUNT NUMBER _____

EXPIR. DATE _____ DAYTIME PHONE _____

CHECK AREA OF COMPUTER INTEREST:

☐ BUSINESS SOFTWARE

☐ TECHNICAL PROGRAMMING

☐ OTHER: _____

THE FACTOR THAT WAS MOST IMPORTANT IN YOUR SELECTION:

☐ THE SYBEX NAME

☐ QUALITY

☐ PRICE

☐ EXTRA FEATURES

☐ COMPREHENSIVENESS

☐ CLEAR WRITING

☐ OTHER _____

OTHER COMPUTER TITLES YOU WOULD LIKE TO SEE IN PRINT:

_____

_____

OCCUPATION

☐ PROGRAMMER   ☐ TEACHER

☐ SENIOR EXECUTIVE   ☐ HOMEMAKER

☐ COMPUTER CONSULTANT   ☐ RETIRED

☐ SUPERVISOR   ☐ STUDENT

☐ MIDDLE MANAGEMENT   ☐ OTHER:

☐ ENGINEER/TECHNICAL   _____

☐ CLERICAL/SERVICE

☐ BUSINESS OWNER/SELF EMPLOYED

CHECK YOUR LEVEL OF COMPUTER USE

☐ NEW TO COMPUTERS

☐ INFREQUENT COMPUTER USER

☐ FREQUENT USER OF ONE SOFTWARE

   PACKAGE:

   NAME _____

☐ FREQUENT USER OF MANY SOFTWARE

   PACKAGES

☐ PROFESSIONAL PROGRAMMER

OTHER COMMENTS:

_____

_____

_____

_____

_____

_____

_____

PLEASE FOLD, SEAL, AND MAIL TO SYBEX

SYBEX, INC.
2021 CHALLENGER DR. #100
ALAMEDA, CALIFORNIA USA
              94501

SYBEX ®

SEAL

SYBEX Computer Books are different.

Here is why . . .

At SYBEX, each book is designed with you in mind. Every manuscript is carefully selected and supervised by our editors, who are themselves computer experts. We publish the best authors, whose technical expertise is matched by an ability to write clearly and to communicate effectively. Programs are thoroughly tested for accuracy by our technical staff. Our computerized production department goes to great lengths to make sure that each book is well-designed.

In the pursuit of timeliness, SYBEX has achieved many publishing firsts. SYBEX was among the first to integrate personal computers used by authors and staff into the publishing process. SYBEX was the first to publish books on the CP/M operating system, microprocessor interfacing techniques, word processing, and many more topics.

Expertise in computers and dedication to the highest quality product have made SYBEX a world leader in computer book publishing. Translated into fourteen languages, SYBEX books have helped millions of people around the world to get the most from their computers. We hope we have helped you, too.

For a complete catalog of our publications:

SYBEX, Inc. 2021 Challenger Drive, #100, Alameda, CA 94501
Tel: (415) 523-8233/(800) 227-2346   Telex: 336311
Fax: (415) 523-2373

Task	Utility	Chapter
Eliminate file fragmentation	Speed Disk	13
Encrypt a file	Diskreet	15
Find a lost file	FileFind	19
Find and fix disk problems	NDD	3
Find text in a file	Disk Editor, FileFind	4, 19
Fix a bad boot track	NDD, Disk Editor	3, 4
Fix a bad File Allocation Table	NDD, Disk Editor	3, 4
Fix a bad partition table	NDD, Disk Editor	3, 4
Format a floppy disk	Safe Format	21
Go to a label in a batch file	BE GOTO	17
List disk information	Speed Disk, System Info	13, 22
List memory usage	System Info	22
List TSR programs	System Info	22
Lock the keyboard	Diskreet	15
Look at file attributes	Disk Editor, FileFind	4, 19
Make a disk bootable	Disk Tools	5
Make a new directory	NCD	20
Mark a bad cluster	Disk Tools	5
Move to a specific screen location	BE ROWCOL	17
Obliterate files	WipeInfo	16
Open a window from a batch file	BE WINDOW	17
Optimize hard disk file organization	Speed Disk	13
Optimize interleave factor	Calibrate	11
Park your hard disk heads	Disk Monitor	14
Password-protect a drive	Diskreet	15
Pause your batch file	BE DELAY	17